THE AUTUMN MAN

A Memoir

by
Albert Slugocki

authorHOUSE®

AuthorHouse™ LLC
1663 Liberty Drive
Bloomington, IN 47403
www.authorhouse.com
Phone: 1-800-839-8640

© 2013 Albert Slugocki. All rights reserved.

No part of this book may be reproduced, stored in a retrieval system, or transmitted by any means without the written permission of the author.

Published by AuthorHouse   07/03/2013

ISBN: 978-1-4817-5943-4 (sc)
ISBN: 978-1-4817-5941-0 (hc)
ISBN: 978-1-4817-5942-7 (e)

Library of Congress Control Number: 2013909889

Editor: Roger A. Zona

Any people depicted in stock imagery provided by Thinkstock are models, and such images are being used for illustrative purposes only. Certain stock imagery © Thinkstock.

This book is printed on acid-free paper.

Because of the dynamic nature of the Internet, any web addresses or links contained in this book may have changed since publication and may no longer be valid. The views expressed in this work are solely those of the author and do not necessarily reflect the views of the publisher, and the publisher hereby disclaims any responsibility for them.

A PERCENTAGE OF THE PROCEEDS FROM THE SALE
OF THIS BOOK IS ALLOCATED TO THE CONTINUED
BENEFICIAL WORK OF PROJECT AMAZONAS.

PROJECT AMAZONAS, INC. is a not-for-profit organization dedicated to the protection of the Peruvian rain forest and its people, through conservation, research, education, medical assistance and sustainable development in the Amazon.

Dedication

This book is dedicated to all the children of the world who in their earliest years were confronted with the stark terrors of war, who suffered the loss of parents and loved ones and who, abandoned to their own devices and fate, were left alone in the world to survive or perish. Many among them however, were forced to witness the horrible brutality of man against man long before they could understand the hatred within the adult world. Those who perished were perhaps fortunate for they did not suffer after death. Those who survived bore lingering memories of falling bombs, the stench of death, burning homes, and cities, and the cries of fallen adults from whom they helplessly expected comfort and safety to no avail. Many were forcibly removed from their mothers loving arms and became inconsolable in their expression of grief. They cried until they ran out of tears. The strong ones went on with their shattered lives, forcing themselves to overcome their terrifying memories in order to continue. The truly lucky ones were those who, after the war ended, were able to surmount their tragic lives and somehow manage to make a living, raise a family and escape the madness of their past.

Acknowledgements

Throughout my tumultuous life I have had the good fortune to meet and befriend many people who deserve my acknowledgement. All these Poles and Americans gave me help and encouragement when I needed it the most. Though I have only memories of them, they have remained with me for life. While in the military many fellow soldiers and officers were there when I needed them the most:

Devon Graham, PhD, President and Scientific Director of Project Amazonas, Inc.

Fernando Gabino Rios Tulumba. Chief of In-country Operations for Project Amazonas, Inc. Iquitos, Peru, S.A.

Dr. Ernesto Salazar-Sanchez, MD, Chief Medical Officer for Project Amazonas, Inc. Iquitos, Peru, S.A.

Sr. Manuel Ramirez Lopez, Presidente Comunal de Tribu Yaguas Rio Orosa and Apayacu—Peru, Amazonas.

Sr. Juan Perez-Kaiapa—Peru-Native member Achual tribe, upper Napo River.

Joseph (Joe) Vaccaro, Ret. Special Forces & CIA and brother of my wife Margaret.

Gerry & Christian Miller. Friends. Shaman, survivors of brutal attack on their lives in the jungle of Peru.

Richard Jagusztyn, MST, CPA. Loyal friend. Secretary and treasurer of Project Amazonas, Inc.

Claus Fessler, Benefactor of Project Amazonas, Inc.

Capt. Robert Firth. Pilot for Air America in Vietnam.

Major R. John (Jack) Thurgar of the Australian army. Served in Vietnam.

Col. Andrew L. (Andy) Irzyk (Ret) U.S. Army Special Forces. Lifelong friend.

In Memory of: Capt. Larkin W. "Rocky" Nesom. U.S. Special Forces. Pilot with Air America and Continental Air. Laos and Vietnam. Rest in peace "Gunga Din".

In Memory of: Master Sgt Special Forces Mike (Doc) Hollingsworth. Exemplary S.F. Medic and volunteer for Project Amazonas, Inc., Iquitos, Peru, S.A.

In Memory of: Master Sgt Special Forces Lionel (ChuChu) Pinn, American native Indian of the Osage Tribe. Encouraged me to write my memoirs.

In Memory of: Capt. Paul Hittscher of Iquitos, Peru. German Navy U-boat crewmember in WWII. River boat captain in Peru.

In Memory of: Terrence Young. Personal friend. Met in Berlin, 1965. British film maker and director.

In Memory of: Ut Soul. Very reverent Abbott of the Buddhist monastery of Chua Tot Pagoda, Chi Lang, Seven Mountains area, upper Delta Region of Vietnam border with Cambodia. Presumed murdered by Khmer Rouge communist troops around 1977.

Prologue

It isn't every day that someone walks into your office and over the space of a few minutes turns the course of your life head over heels. It was the summer of 1994 when I first met Albert Slugocki. I had recently completed field work for my doctorate degree in biology in Costa Rica and was deep into the writing stage of my dissertation—spending long hours in my cubicle at the University of Miami. Albert had been given my name and contact information by a mutual friend and after a couple of phone calls he drove from Ft. Lauderdale to Miami to visit me.

I distinctly remember that first visit. Albert is an imposing man, well over 6' and very solidly built. Snow-white hair, a charming smile and a restrained, yet potentially bone-crushing handshake added to a first impression of a person to whom there was no obstacle that couldn't be overcome. He had me at "hello".

We talked at length: about my research in Costa Rica, about our mutual friend, and especially about the Amazon. As a boy, I had devoured stories about exploring the Amazon, and was enthralled with tales of deadly bushmaster snakes, giant anacondas, army ants and native tribes. As a biologist, the Amazon was my Holy Grail—a hotbed of biodiversity waiting to be discovered. So when Albert casually mentioned that he was traveling to Peru in a couple months to build a field station for a new non-profit organization that had recently been formed, and "would I like to come along and write an evaluation of the site?" there was no hesitation. "Forget about Costa Rica. I can give you the Amazon", was what he said.

So it was that in September 1994 I traveled with Albert to Iquitos, Peru, in the heart of the Western Amazon region. We traveled by local pamacari boat to the site of the new biological station. I was enthralled by the journey—the vastness of the Amazon River, even at 2,300 miles from the mouth of the river—the expanse of sky with its billowing every-changing clouds, flocks of parrots, oropendolas, terns and other birds winging across the river or foraging along the shoreline.

Day turned into night as we traveled, and the Milky Way glittered far above. With no lights for miles around, each star was a hard pinprick of light. I was amazed that the pilot could find his way, since the silhouette of the rainforest along the banks was barely visible and nearly featureless. It was about that time that the boat ran aground on a concealed sandbar. We shuddered to a halt. The boatmen tried unsuccessfully to maneuver off of the sandbar, but to no avail. There was a short consultation, and then Albert called for everyone to jump into the river to lighten the boat and push.

My first trip to the Amazon, it is pitch black, I'm on a grounded boat of dubious integrity with people I just met, for the most part, and I'm supposed to jump into water teeming with who-knows-what and push . . . I should have been alarmed, I suppose, but Albert's calm, assured air conveyed the impression that this was just a routine part of travel on the river, and so in I went—though thoughts of stepping on a sting-ray or encountering an electric eel were certainly at the forefront of my mind. We successfully pushed off of the sandbar, and continued into the night, arriving at our destination in the wee hours of the morning.

In the following days, I learned a bit more about Albert, mostly through observation of his interactions with the work crew and with the local Yagua Indians, to whom he was universally known as "Don Alberto". The mutual love and respect that they had for each other was clear, though I had no knowledge of how that relationship had developed. Meanwhile I was exploring the rainforest, making the most of this once-in-a-lifetime trip. I still had no inkling where Albert would end up leading me in life.

I returned the following summer, again at Albert's invitation, spending several weeks at the new field station and learning the flora and fauna of the Amazon, as well as picking up a bit of Spanish here and there. The caretaker at the site, Adriano Arevalo, was a wealth of knowledge about the Amazon, and even though my poor Spanish made for difficult conversation, I owe him a debt of gratitude for all that he taught me. He was as keen an observer of nature as I have ever met.

As time passed, Albert brought me along on eco-tour trips as a naturalist, patiently teaching me the ropes, and it was on these trips that I started to learn more about his past. Albert never spoke much about his history, or about what brought him to the Amazon, but in after-dinner conversations with passengers, tidbits would slip out. Many of them were so incredible that I dismissed them out of hand, thinking that they were tall tales to amuse the guests aboard. I came to realize, however, that these were but snippets of information about an amazing life experience—they fit together in a comprehensive story and were corroborated by independent sources. Gradually a fuller picture emerged, of a man deeply wounded by war, both as a child and as an adult, but who found redemption and peace on the rivers of the Amazon.

In time, I started leading Amazon trips myself, and in 2004 accepted the position of president and scientific director of Project Amazonas, the non-profit organization that Albert formed to repay the people and the rainforest of the Amazon for the healing power that they had brought to his life. To me, Albert has been a source of inspiration, a wealth of knowledge, and someone I can always rely on. I trust him with my life. Despite his almost unbelievable life-story and rough edges, I have also found him to be one of the most gentle, accepting and generous individuals I have met—no doubt due to the strong influence of Theravada Buddhism with which he became acquainted during the many years he spent in South-East Asia. Project Amazonas would never have survived as an organization without his energy and dedication, and it is my hope that it will continue to serve the wonderful people of the Amazon and to conserve the rainforest's natural treasures for decades to come.

It was only through considerable pressure over many years from friends and acquaintances that Albert agreed to put his life story on paper. I am pleased that he did so—it is a story that deserves to be shared, and I am only one of many people whose lives have been touched by this man. Albert Slugocki did "give" me the Amazon, just as he promised during that first meeting. My life has been forever changed though his influence and I have no regrets. His passion for the people and nature of the Amazon has become my passion, and as a result I have been honored to introduce others to this special corner of the globe.

Friend, teacher, inspiration—this is dedicated to you, Albert.

Devon Graham, PhD
Miami, Florida, USA

Table of Contents

Dedication		v
Acknowledgements		vii
Prologue		ix
A Gypsy Poem	The Autumn Man	xv
A Poem by Albert Slugocki	The Angel of Death	xvii

Early Life

Chapter 1	My Childhood	1
Chapter 2	Helping the Cause	21
Chapter 3	Introduction to USA	35
Chapter 4	Surviving in America	51

Korea

Chapter 5	Journey to a Far Away War	61
Chapter 6	Land of the Morning Calm	71
Chapter 7	Korean War, 1951 – Code of Honor	75

Special Forces

Chapter 8	Two Brothers – Worlds Apart	89
Chapter 9	Funerals of Special Americans	97
Chapter 10	Berlin – The Good Life & Movies	105

Vietnam

Chapter 11	The Ghosts of Duc Lap – 1966	115
Chapter 12	A Family Affair	129
Chapter 13	The Story of the Beehive Buddha	135

Civilian Life

Chapter 14	A U.S. Marshal – The Wrong Choice	155

Brazil

Chapter 15	The Amazon River – My Life's Choice	163
Chapter 16	Brazil to Peru – The Long Voyage – Manaus Nights	165
Chapter 17	Brazil – Port of Educandos, Manaus	169
Chapter 18	Brazil to Peru – A Voyage to Remember	179

Peru

Chapter 19	See No Evil – Hear No Evil	203
Chapter 20	Juan Perez Kaiapa	211
Chapter 21	Mayorunas – The Jaguar People	223
Chapter 22	Vision of Tragedy – Night of Shenango	231
Chapter 23	Mystery Jungle Flight	239
Chapter 24	El Encuentro con Comendante Tiberio	247
Chapter 25	Shamans, Curanderos & Ayahuasca	259
Chapter 26	Conversations with the River Dolphins	267
Chapter 27	The Legend of the Dolphin Bride	271

Project Amazonas

Chapter 28	The Good Work	277
Chapter 29	A Farewell to the River	287

An Ode to My Mother	Regrets	291
About the Author		293

A GYPSY POEM
The Autumn Man

A man born in late autumn time
Is like the last leaves of summer that fall
And are seized by the winds of the coming
Wintertime, blown away and driven
To the four corners of the world,
Forever to wander without
Peace in one's heart

A POEM BY ALBERT SLUGOCKI

The Angel of Death

You know me well. You held me in your arms in my tender years when buildings were falling all around me and people screamed in fear.

You would always be near and I thought you would come and take me. You would kiss my forehead and softly sigh—"it's not your time" you whisper.

Later as the years went by I always felt your presence. I did not have to see you for when I closed my eyes you stood there before me. Your face so still and your frozen smile.

After the years have gone by you still walked beside me. Was it Korea or Vietnam?

By then we were old friends and more like lovers. Through all the passing years and wars I fought, you walked by my side.

Do you remember me asking—"take me". You would brush me aside and tell me "it's not your time".

I have faced your might without fear and cry. You smile and take men all around me. You spared me.

Many would cry and fight your embrace. You would gather them one by one and carry them into the sky—to somewhere—to one of your special places.

Early Life

CHAPTER 1

My Childhood

I was born in Warsaw, Poland on the 29th of October 1931, the second son of Helena Eugenia (nee Hodder) Slugocki and Marian Slepowron-Slugocki. Christened Wojciech after the first Polish Roman Catholic Martyr, Saint Wojciech, (circa 965AD). Later, after leaving Poland, and for the sake of convenience, I was renamed Albert, but kept my family name when I was issued a Hansen Passport, given, at that time, to stateless persons.

My father was a hereditary member of the Polish nobility whose ancestors had served Polish Kings as knights, *Kasztelans* (castle keepers), and *Ziemian* (landowners). Our family traces a continuous history back to the fifteenth century and possesses a Knight's Coat of Arms bearing a *Slepowron*, signifying the Blind Black Raven Clan.

My Father, Marian Slugocki
—Artist & Sculptor. Pre-WWII

A noted artist and sculptor, my father was born in 1883 and educated at the Académie des Beaux Arts in Geneva. He pursued advanced studies at the Université de Lausanne, Switzerland, and later at the Université de Paris, where he came under the patronage of a famous French teacher, Professor Mercier.

After ten years of working in Switzerland and France, he returned to Poland in 1917 or 1918 to fight for his country's freedom. He refused an officer's commission and instead fought in the army as a simple soldier. For his service in World War I and the Polish War of Independence (1916-1920), he was awarded the highest military decoration for valor, the Virtuti Militari (Latin for Military Valor) and Poland's highest military decoration for courage in the face of the enemy. Created in 1792 and the oldest military decoration in the world still in use, it is very much the equivalent of the United States Medal of Honor.

My mother was the daughter of Benjamin Hodder, a British citizen from Winham in Somerset, England, who was working in Poland as an industrial engineer. He was forced to leave Poland at the outbreak of the First World War in 1914. His Polish wife and my maternal grandmother, Alexandra Eugenia Astrid Merska, stayed in Poland. My English grandfather, upon returning to his native country, was called upon to serve Her Majesty as a as a reserve Royal Naval Engineer Officer, aboard HMS Invincible, and in 1915, he perished at sea in the battle of Jutland.

**My Mother, Helena Eugenia Slugocki
—Opera Diva. Pre-WWII**

Mother was an opera singer educated at the Conservatory of Music in Warsaw, followed by operatic voice studies at the Stadt Opera in Vienna. Later, in the early 1920's, she studied at the *Conservatorio di Bel Canto della Scala di Milano,* and later sang at the Warsaw, Poznan and Katowice operas. From the time of my birth through my early childhood, we resided either at our ancestral home in Hilnicze, in eastern Poland, or in Warsaw. I was privately tutored at home until the Germans invaded Poland on September 1, 1939.

On that fateful day my entire life and the future of my family took a dramatic course. The good life with my family, all the happiness and protection that comes with loving parents came to a sudden end as Hitler launched the war against my country with all his military might. At this time, Poland had existed as a free nation for less than twenty years, and it was really no match for Nazi Germany's monumental military strength. Still it fought on, especially in Warsaw, where we as a family found ourselves on that terrible day of the Nazi invasion.

Against all odds, the city of Warsaw continued fighting long after the rest of Poland lay already conquered. I do not remember where my brother Richard or our father was at this time, but I vividly recall that my mother and I spent a great deal of time in the cellar of our apartment building. Every day the German airplanes would come and lay destruction and death. The cellar served us as an underground air raid shelter while the war raged on all around us. I still remember the horribly frightening sounds the Stuka dive-bombers made before they dropped their bombs. We were constantly underground, living with dripping ceilings and the stench of human excrement, suffering from a lack of food and water and the constant fear of being killed or buried alive in the rubble.

One night while we were in the shelter, an explosion went off very nearby. In a single instant, we heard a large boom, all the candles, and oil lamps were extinguished, and there was complete darkness. The overhead water pipes broke, and sheets of water drenched us all as parts of the cellar ceiling fell down on us. My mother hugged me close and began praying. Some people went crazy and screamed that we had been buried. It was a night of real terror that I will never forget. Somehow, we survived until early morning, when some of the men managed to clear the debris blocking the only entrance to our shelter, and a ray of daylight assured us that we were still alive.

A mad dash for the staircase ensued with people actually fighting to get out. As we spilled out of our shelter, we saw that several top floors of the building were missing. Here and there, we could see half a room hanging in the air, furniture dangling at the edges, and part of the stairway leading up to nonexistent floors above. We were extremely lucky, as those who did not go to the cellar perished. Our apartment building had two parts, one, facing the street, was where our basement air raid shelter was located, and it was here the upper floors had received the bomb. Our apartment, luckily, had been spared serious damage, for although we lived on the third floor, the apartment was located in the other part of the building, behind an inner courtyard that separated us from the apartments fronting the street.

Sometime later that same day, we went back to our apartment, and discovered it had survived intact, with the exception of broken windows. I was permitted to go outside, and went to play in the courtyard. On the outer sidewalk facing the street, I immediately noticed neat rows of what I perceived to be human-like forms lying completely still and covered with a thick coat of white dust from the ruins of the building. I could barely tell if they were men or women, or unearthly white statues made of plaster. With their tangled white hair, and bald white eyes filled with dust, I could barely tell that they were human. They just lay there quietly, not moving.

With a child's natural curiosity, I could not help but to touch one of the statue-like forms to see if it would move. The body was cold and hard to my touch and did not move. A man wearing a white cloth armband with a red cross on it yelled at me to get away from the dead. I ran straight to my mother and told her what I had seen. When I asked for an explanation, she cried and said they were all people who had died in the air raid.

After a few days, the bombing stopped, and we began to hear the distant staccato of machine gun and rifle fire. Then it went quiet and German soldiers came marching down the street. Shortly thereafter, my family moved to an apartment on another street, where we lived for about a year. My mother was always with me, but I do not remember where my father had gone. He would appear from time to time in the evening and bring us things to eat. He looked ill and very tired. He would hug me sometimes and leave after the German-imposed curfew. I do not remember much about my brother, except that he was not very nice to me. Why, I do not know.

The Germans had occupied us for about a year when we moved to Iwonicz Zdroj, a beautiful, quiet place in southeastern Poland close to the Slovakian border. My father had arranged with his life-long friend, Count Michael Zaluski, with whom he had spent happy times pushing girls around the dance floors in Paris before the outbreak of the First World War.

Our new place in Iwonicz Zdroj, like nearly the entire village, belonged to the Zaluski family. The town had been famous since the end of the eighteenth century for its curative mineral waters, there were many small guesthouses, and hotels catering to sick and weary people looking to recuperate from whatever ailed them. The Count and his family received us like their own their family, letting us stay rent-free in an upstairs apartment in one of their many dwellings.

For a while, it was all fun—until mother's money ran out. Although we had a decent place to live, we had to eat, and this proved to be a great problem. Being of tender age at the time, I remember always feeling hungry. I vaguely remember my mother selling things like her clothes and jewelry in order to survive. My father, who remained in Warsaw, may have helped, but of that, I am not sure. My brother Richard found a job with the local oil drilling outfit and that helped a lot. In 1943, Richard ran away from home at the age of sixteen and joined the *Armia Krajowa* (AK), a Polish National Armed Force fighting as a guerilla partisan unit against the Germans. His unit operated in the surrounding forests, and he would occasionally sneak in to visit us and sometimes even brought us food. I really was proud of my brother. Richard was my hero, and I wished to be older so I could join him in the forest.

One of my starkest boyhood memories took place in the kitchen of a modest hotel at the edge of a forest in Iwonicz Zdroj, a small mountain resort town in southeastern Poland. The Nazi occupation of Poland had been going on for about three years but resistance by clandestine groups still was fierce. My mother and some other women were cooking a pork stew for the *Armia Krajowa* (AK), a Polish National Armed Force fighting as a guerilla partisan unit against the German Army. The local AK partisans operated out of the heavily forested mountain areas surrounding Iwonicz Zdroj. My brother Richard, four years older than I, was one of the freedom fighters. It was the late winter of 1942-43, and I was twelve years old.

**Albert (front) and brother Richard
in toy cars. Pre-WWII**

We suddenly heard loud shouts, issued in German and then Polish ordering all inside to come out with their hands up. Exclamations like "God save us!" burst from the women and some began to cry. We all came out of the kitchen, because the entire building was surrounded by German soldiers. Mother later told me that they were from a regular Wehrmacht Army front line unit, not members of the dreaded SS or *Schutzpolizei* (Protection Police, a branch of the Order Police). Once outside, we were herded up against the wall and guarded at gunpoint while soldiers checked the building. On finding the cooking pots, they came out and asked for whom we were preparing all the food. Some of the women answered, "For the children of the local people." The Germans then relaxed and made us go inside and continue our cooking.

When the meal was ready, the Germans had their fill, eating much of it, and then resumed their search. They shortly came upon a German Army rucksack full of grenades that one of the partisans, who had spent the previous night in the building, had left behind. The Germans immediately began hitting all the women with their rifles, forcing us outside and ordering us all to stand up against the wall. Their officer loudly announced that because our group was giving food and shelter to the enemies of the German Reich, we were all going to be shot. Even as a boy of twelve, I realized that my mom and I had only a few more moments to live. I held tightly to my mom but, strange as it seems, no one cried. We just stood there in silence, waiting to be executed.

Then my mother broke the silence, calling to the German officer in Italian. "*Signore Comendante, prego!*" The officer acted as if he had been struck by lightning. "Are you Italian?" he asked her. "No," my mother answered, still in Italian, "but I lived and studied for four years at the *Conservatorio di Bel Canto della Scala di Milano.*" "Then you are an opera singer!" he exclaimed. "What are you doing in this shithole, helping these criminals?" "I live here with my son, in the hope of surviving this horrible war! I beg of you, at least spare his life." Continuing in Italian, she further told him that the rucksack belonged to a German soldier who had left it while stopping to rest at the house. Since the front lines were nearby, this was entirely plausible. For reasons unknown, the officer believed her or maybe something moved him at the sight of those frightened women, waiting with dignity to be executed. He waived his arm in a gesture of dismissal. The soldiers lowered their rifles and left. We stood there stunned.

By the fall of 1943, we were in a crisis. We had run out of food, and there was just about nothing left to sell or trade. The military situation became very critical and the woods were full of German patrols hunting Polish underground resistance forces, including my brother's unit. There were also Ukrainian Nationalist SS *Galitzien* forces serving as part of the German Nazi army, and varied bandit groups of Soviet Amy deserters crossing into Poland over the Slovakian border. The area surrounding Iwonicz Zdroj became a very dangerous place.

I now came up with the idea of becoming a peddler. It was too dangerous for adults to enter any part of the forest or to go to the surrounding villages, but as a boy of twelve, I could get away with carrying trade goods back and forth, using forest paths with which I was well familiar. I would not get into trouble, since I would carry only small items of primary necessity that the villagers desperately needed: sewing and knitting needles, scissors, thread, buttons, matches, flints, candles, and other small items, all of which I would trade for bread, flour, butter, pork fat, boiled eggs, and anything else that was edible.

Initially, my mother's word was a strong no, but I kept persisting. Our mutual hunger finally convinced her, reluctantly and with the greatest trepidation, to let me go ahead with it. Somehow, she found something to sell. What, I do not remember but she came up with sufficient funds to pay for the items I would trade. With my school rucksack packed to overflowing, I thus embarked on my first business foray.

The first village I visited, Lubatowa, was located some five kilometers away, over a high, forest-covered mountain. Much to my delight, my enterprise met with 100 percent success! I came back loaded with bread, eggs and even a bit of butter. Above all else, of importance the village women asked me to come back. As poor as they were, these women were very kind to a small boy like myself, and always fed me with homemade bread or other goodies.

Therefore, it was that I became a regular to Lubatowa and other nearby villages. At last, we had food sufficient to survive. This lasted throughout the winter and spring of 1943-44. In summer 1944, the German-Soviet front lines came too close to our area to allow me to wander in the local forests. However, by this time, many people had found out about my trading escapades, including local members of the AK. One of them approached me and asked if I could do an errand for them. He wanted me to go on foot to the sister village of Iwonicz, located about four kilometers from Iwonicz Zdroj, and close to a main road connecting the major cities of Krosno and Rymanow. I was to observe German military activities at the ancestral grounds of Count Zaluski. I was only to look from a distance, and return back immediately with information on what I had observed.

Of course, I was proud to be asked and agreed straight away. I left on my assignment early the next morning without telling my mother anything about it, my standard child's backpack strapped to my back.

Upon arrival at my destination, I witnessed strange activity. Armed German soldiers were disarming Ukrainian SS *Galitzien* soldiers, taking the Ukrainians' rifles, removing the bolts, and throwing them into the pond. Many trucks were waiting on the grounds, and the disarmed, black-uniformed soldiers were loaded into them and driven away. Within less than an hour, the place was empty. I should then have left, but did not. Instead, I started rummaging in the interior of the palace gardens where the pond was located, and found a wooden crate full of grenades. I removed twelve grenades, loaded them in the bottom of my rucksack, picked some apples from the orchard, piled them on top, and started back to Iwonicz Zdroj.

Why did I do this foolish thing? I must have been trying to impress the AK people. I was about halfway back, walking along eating one of the apples. When suddenly, four German SS soldiers in camouflage jumped out of nowhere, pointing their weapons at me. "*Kind, wo gehst du?*" they demanded, asking where I was going. "*Bitte, lassen mich gehen. Ich wolle nach hous im Iwonicz Zdroj gehen,*" I responded, asking them please to let me pass so I could return to my home in Iwonicz Zdroj. My answer had surprised them, for they asked me where I had learned my German. I told them I had learned it in school. "*Raus den, Kind mit dein Apfeln, und schnell !*" they hollered: "Go then, kid with the apple, and hurry it up!" I started to run, and doing so, peed in my pants.

Upon reporting to the AK, I fully related my encounter with the SS. I was severely admonished for the grenades in my rucksack and sent home crying. My mother later made an official protest to the local AK commander, threatening him bodily harm should he ever send me on another mission. This episode finished all my adventures on trading trips and all association with the Polish resistance. I was forever grounded and very closely watched by my mother.

It was now the late summer of 1944. The front lines between German and Soviet forces were very close, and we heard artillery fire at night. My father had joined us in a much-depleted state. We were again without food and had nothing for father, who lay in his bed staring at the ceiling, delirious, hardly moving and unable to speak. My brother was permitted to come and visit us. His presence put the entire family in great danger, but we could not manage without his help. He somehow managed to obtain a large piece of meat, which turned out to be part of an unborn calf carved out of a dead cow. As there was absolutely nothing else to eat, my mother cooked a piece of it for father, who had ingested nothing for the last three days. He was unable to eat it, and died.

Father looked peaceful in death. My mother closed his eyelids and we all cried. Two days later, he was still lying in his bed. I went to him and kissed his forehead. My brother searched for some boards to make a coffin but found nothing. The only carpenter in Iwonicz Zdroj wanted money, which we did not have, but finally someone gave my brother a few boards and we made a makeshift coffin. We wrapped his body in an old blanket and assorted rags and, using a child's wagon, loaded him into it. With my mother pulling, my brother holding his legs, and me pushing the wagon, we took him to a small site next to the village church and started digging a hole, with mother and Richard doing most of the work.

When my father's grave was deep enough, my brother went to fetch the parish priest to give my father his last blessing. He found the priest half drunk, and he asked my brother for five zlotys for his service. My brother got very angry and kicked the crap out of the priest, thereby putting an end to any hope of a burial service. These were sad days for us as a family. My brother returned to the forest. The village of Iwonicz became strangely quiet. The Germans left, and the Soviet troops had not yet arrived.

To my recollection, the Soviets arrived one morning in early September, 1944. They were welcomed as our liberators after all the terrible years of German occupation. The Soviets pushed the German Army away from our area into the Dukla Pass, located in the foothills of the Carpathian Mountains, a border area between Poland and Slovakia. One of the most monumental battles of World War II now took place about 20 kilometers away from us and lasted for about a month. Soviet Army casualties amounted to more than 70,000 troops killed and the German Army dead were estimated at 40,000.

During this great battle, Iwonicz Zdroj became a Soviet Army headquarters. The Soviet Army was initially well received and the area quieted down. This, however, was the calm before the storm. Once the Soviets broke through German defenses at the Dukla Pass, pushing the Germans into Slovakia and Hungary, we slowly realized that communism and the Polish communist regime had inexorably descended upon us. Soviet troops, different from those who had fought at the front, appeared in our village. These were the dreaded NKVD, the Internal Security Police, accompanied by Polish communist functionaries representing the Polish government while founded and organized in the Soviet Union. Within just two weeks of their arrival, the Polish communist police arrested the entire Zaluski family and the Polish communist government seized their property. All the members of the family were taken away. To where I do not know.

The arrest of Count Zaluski and his family had a direct impact on my mother and me. We felt very close to them since they had sheltered us during the war, and there were distant family ties to the Zaluskies on the part of my father. While the family members were still held in Iwonicz, my mother made many attempts to see them, hoping to help them in any way she could, but to no avail. Mother, by virtue of her outspoken personality, would not give up and stop talking openly against this injustice, which immediately put us at odds with the Polish communist authorities. Mother felt helpless and very much confused. She and naturally I, too, immediately developed a hatred of the communist regime. As for me, my hatred grew in intensity over time.

Before long, it was my mother's turn to be called to the local Iwonicz tribunal by the communist militia. Some of their members hardly spoke Polish. They were obviously Russian and members of the Soviet NKVD or else belonged to the newly formed *Polski Urzand Bezpieczenstwa* (UB), the Polish communist government's secret police.

My mother was informed that we would have to leave Iwonicz Zdroj, since we did not belong there and were members of a social class unacceptable to the Peoples' Republic of Poland. We were ordered to move to the nearby town of Krosno for temporary residence and to be later "voluntarily" resettled in Pommerania in the town of Slupsk ("Stolp" in German,) not far from the Baltic Sea.

We moved with our meager belongings to Krosno and found a place to live. Mother, being an enterprising person, almost immediately opened a food stall on the main town square, and I attended the local school. At the time of our move, my brother disappeared completely. We heard that he had been detained because, during the German occupation, he had fought with the AK, which was commanded by and loyal to the Polish government in exile in London. The members of the AK were now categorized as enemies of The People's Democratic Government. Further, they were declared traitors and reactionaries and they were arrested and sent to Soviet Siberian labor camps or executed.

One day when I was in school, our teacher informed me that I should go home because my mother was having some serious problems. When I arrived at her food stand, she was all in tears and informed me that Richard was being held in the UB detention station. I was to take him a food package she had prepared. This I did, but was turned away at the entrance by an armed guard. Mother then went herself, and was informed that yes, her son was locked up, but she could not obtain any details.

Strangely enough, shortly after this episode my brother appeared free from detention, and told us that the travel plans had been arranged including a place for us to live in Slupsk. He then disappeared again and we had no idea where he had gone. My mother and I packed up our belongings and headed for Slupsk, where the city gave us a small apartment.

My mother was a natural organizer and very much a leader. Having a background in the Polish theater and opera and knowing the pre-war musical and artistic worlds, she immediately organized a music school. She acquired a building and, being a survivor who knew her way around, she immediately went into business teaching music, voice, and stage acting. The school was a great success.

By now people were disappearing and being taken away to prison. The persecution of the Polish intelligentsia was in full force. Things nevertheless went pretty well for us for a while. Then, out of a clear blue sky, my brother appeared in Slupsk. To my great surprise, he was wearing an Air Force uniform of the Peoples' Army and appeared to be in very good shape. All of this came as a big mystery to me. How could it be that my brother, the hero of our family, a former AK resistance fighter, and prisoner of the UB in Krosno, was now wearing the enemy's uniform? The whole thing was very confusing.

I immediately sought an explanation from my mother, but her words were even more confusing yet. She told me that Richard was not actually a member of the communist Air Force, but of the recently formed Civil Aviation Corps. She also warned me not to ask my brother too many questions. My suspicions remained. Richard became a member of the elite diplomatic corps of communist Poland, serving as Consul General to the government of Algeria, Ambassador (Chargé d'affairs) to the government of Syria, and finally as Ambassador Plenipotentiary to Qaddafi's government in Libya.

At this point, Richard became very helpful to us, and life went on quietly for a few months. Enrolled in the local high school, I was attending regular classes for the first time in my life. There I met and became friends with several other children, including one boy in particular named Bronek. After class, we would go to a small park adjacent to the school to talk about our country, World War II and, naturally, political events occurring in the so-called New Peoples' Poland. We agreed that we did not like communism, and firmly believed that the Polish Army and its western Allies, the Americans and English, were coming to liberate our country from oppression. The hated Russians were going to be pushed out of Poland and the Polish government in exile in London would become our country's government.

In hindsight, it seems easy to wonder why boys of our age held such a deeply felt faith in their country. In those days, however, things were different. We had grown up in a time of war, and lived under the brutal oppression of both the Nazi and Soviet occupation. We thus matured much earlier—you might even say we had never been children. Seeing what was happening in our country, the persecutions, arrests, exiles to Soviet labor camps, forced relocations and general lack of freedom of speech, had made us into enemies of communism.

Bronek now told me in very great confidence that I could help in a small way to bring about a new Poland. Being so young, I was very much impressed by such things and asked what I could do. He told me I could become a Polish Youth Auxiliary member of the *Narodowe Sily Zbrojne* (NSZ), a secret military organization that became active immediately after the arrival of the Russians and the establishment of the communist regime. Although many members of the former and now persecuted AK had been arrested and imprisoned, some of them had survived, and they had begun the new freedom movement under the auspices of the NSZ. I really did not understand the whole thing, but I was all for it.

This is how, in 1946, at the age of fourteen I started working in the first of a series of clandestine organizations that would shape the course of my life as an adult. Bronek informed me that he had already told his superiors that he had recruited me. He also said other boys were involved but, for the sake of security, he was not informed of their identity. We were to behave ourselves and be ready to act How, I did not really know.

We soon got tired of waiting around, and in the zeal of youth decided to begin something on our own. We came up with the dumbest thing that boys like us could do. We got some paint and brushes, and began painting slogans, starting with the main railroad station. *Precz z Komunizmem! Down with Communism!* Suddenly all over Slupsk, the walls, buildings, and newspaper kiosks were covered with anti-communist graffiti. This activity kept us busy until Bronek came to me at school one day and said, "We have to quit everything. The man in charge of us said to "stop immediately." However, we were not about to listen.

Soon thereafter, we obtained a pistol that somehow fell into Bronek's hands. Every day we would meet at a certain hour and play with it. Then we would put it away for a better day. Finally, the NSZ agent called upon us to actually do something useful. I had to become familiar with security and intelligence procedures. Bronek and I formed an "operational cell" and Bronek was a "cutout man"—the one person in the cell who knew the NSZ member in charge of us. Thus, it was I became part of the "criminal reactionary movement," as communist Polish authorities called it.

I also now learned that our *raison d'être* was to be couriers. Bronek took his first trip from Slupsk to Gdynia, the major Baltic Seaport, delivered a package to someone at the railroad station, and then came back to Slupsk with another package. Then it was my turn. At the time, no one ever asked kids or students for any identification. Bronek gave me a train ticket and I delivered my package, and returned with another.

Devoted to my duties with Bronek, painting slogans, and getting ready to do bigger and better things, I was now failing in school. Our courier activities had gone on for a couple of months when my brother again mysteriously reappeared. When I told Bronek that my brother was home he said he had to talk to his contact. He came back and told me to have nothing to do with Richard, because he had already crossed over to the communists. Five or six days later, Bronek was caught painting anti-government slogans at the main railroad station in Slupsk and taken into custody by the police, paint and brush in hand. I was informed early in the morning of his arrest by another boy, who called himself Florian. This was in early fall 1946. I immediately knew I had to run.

On the day Bronek was captured, my brother gave me some money to buy light bulbs and other things for my mother's school. I realized that Bronek would be tortured and point the finger at me. I absolutely had to escape. I got in contact with Basia Narutowicz, my good friend and first love, and asked her to buy me a rail ticket to Szczecin (formerly the German town of Stettin), on the new Polish-German border, using the money my brother had given me. I hid in an abandoned factory for the rest of the day and left the same evening, boarding the train after it was already moving slowly through the railroad switch stations. All my life, I have had to live with the fact that I never knew what happened to Bronek and many others. Bronek obviously never revealed my identity. If he had, my mother's life and the career of my brother Richard, who betrayed my concept of a free Poland, would have been completely ruined.

The train arrived in the middle of the night. As I did not know anybody in Szczecin, I asked a couple of railroad workers to help me. They directed to me to the station's travelers' emergency shelter, which was closed. I persisted, beating on the door until it opened and a night's lodging was offered. Once inside, I became fearful of not having gone far enough to escape. Polish railroad stations, just after the war, served many purposes. They were gathering places and information centers for thousands of lost and displaced people, offering a place to go to get a free meal and, if you were lucky, a place to sleep for a few nights. I now started acting like a war orphan looking for his family. The authorities gave me a ticket that was good for a bowl of soup and some bread, and permitted me to shelter at the station for three or four days.

I did not stay. Checking the train schedule, I saw that the next train ran parallel to the German border to Jelenia Góra, located at the far southwestern end of Poland. I got on without a ticket. Sometime during the night or early the next morning, the conductor came by and asked me for my ticket. I told him that I had lost it, and went into my crying orphan act. "Please let me go," I pleaded. "I have to find my mother and my family". Moreover, the conductor agreed. A kind man, he even gave me a piece of bread with marmalade and some hot tea from his thermos.

The station at Jelenia Góra, like others, had an area plastered full of big posters with the names of mothers looking for children, children looking for mothers, wives looking for husbands whom the Germans had taken away and all kinds of other desperate searches. People thronged the platforms waiting for trains arriving from everywhere. They accosted passengers, begging for information. "Where are you coming from? Do you know my husband, my brother, my son, my wife?" It was complete chaos. The attempts of the Polish Militia (Polish police) to control the human sea surging up with each arrival of repatriation trains, failed completely.

A massive exodus was taking place as the borders shifted and millions of people were moved from eastern Poland to the newly acquired western areas. A little person like me could get lost into it very easily and somehow survive. Moreover, I did survive just fine. Of course, I missed my mother, but I knew that if the communist police caught me, that would be the end of her. This was the thought that drove me on.

Soon the railroad station became my home. After a certain number of days, you were authorized to sleep there, but for some reason I was unable to get a ticket to stay in the station, so I lived in the cattle cars at the back of the railroad yard. A bunch of us, both other boys and adults, were in the same situation. We stole coal from the locomotives and all kinds of things were going on. You never knew if you were going to wake up in the morning. Law and order definitely did not reign, which suited me just fine.

Here I met Zigmund, a young man a bit older than myself but who, like me, was very eager to make his way out of Poland. He suggested we should try to escape the country and join the Polish Army. Of course we did not know that in 1946 the Polish Army in the west no longer existed. Many of the demobilized members of the Polish Army, Navy, and Air Force had been resettled to Australia, New Zealand, England, and the United States.

Those who had returned to Poland with the rank of sergeant or above had been imprisoned. Zigmund told me he knew how to cross into Czechoslovakia, which did not have a communist government. From there, he proposed to go to Austria, which he swore was under American occupation. In this we were wrong again. It was occupied by the Russians. The idea was to make our way to the border town of Zgorzelec and there cross the River Nysa, which would put us in the Czechoslovakian Republic. Wrong again. We would then be in a Soviet-occupied area in what would later become part of East Germany.

So off we went. The train ride was short and without incident. By then, we knew how to jump on and off, and do all sorts of things to survive. I had quickly adapted to the dangerous post-war world, becoming part of the chaos and honing my survival instincts. Passing through Zgorzelec, we saw Polish army patrols. Very few Poles had yet been resettled there. The area authorities were still throwing the Germans out; lock, stock and barrel, creating more chaos and making it all the easier for us.

Zigmund picked an area on the outskirts of town where there were no houses. It was now early winter, and the river, covered with light snow, looked frozen. About 200 yards wide, it was actually more of a large stream, with a forest on either side. "This is the place," he declared. "We're going to cross the ice tonight." Neither my friend nor I was warmly dressed and we knew we would freeze to death unless we could find warmer clothes. So before scouting out our crossing point, we had stolen a couple of coats from the railroad workers' cloakroom. Mine hung all way down to my ankles and nearly dragged on the ground.

Ziggy went first. We came to the forest and looked for border guards. We then approached the river and, seeing no one, crept onto the ice. With its thin layer of snow, the surface looked safe. As my friend proceeded well ahead of me, the ice suddenly broke and he fell into the river. "Help me! Help me!" he screamed. Scared and now very much confused, I yelled back that I was coming. I got my big heavy coat off and threw it to him, holding onto the near end of a sleeve. He took hold of it and started pulling, but in his panic he was pulling me into the river. Icy water splashed up and over me and I was dangerously near the broken edge. Alerted by Zigmund's cries, guards on the other side of river were shouting and firing their rifles blindly in our direction. *"Zigmund, nie moge wiencej, boje sie utopic!"* I said. "Zigmund, I can't get you out! I'm afraid I'm going to drown!" I let go, and Zigmund and my overcoat disappeared under the ice.

CHAPTER 2

Helping the Cause

As I high-tailed it into the forest, the guards on the other side of the river fired a couple of flares, illuminating the area where Zigmund had just gone under. Freezing and soaking wet, I continued to run. I did not go back into town, but to the railroad station, remembering the cloakroom with its warm stove. I must have looked in quite bad shape when I somehow managed to arrive, for the people there looked at me in horror. They undressed me, and out from somewhere came a bottle of vodka with which they commenced to massage my body. I became delirious and do not remember much after that. I woke up early in the morning lying on a cot, with my clothes hanging next to a red-hot stove. The men were gone. I felt sick and went to vomit, then slowly dressed in my now dry clothes and left to catch a train to Jelenia Gorá. I did not even know Zigmund's last name, who he was, or where he came from.

Shocked, and with my plans for escape thwarted, I arrived back at Jelenia Gorá. Different people were in charge of the shelter, and since they did not know me, I was able to get another ticket for a three or four day stay. Now, I really wanted to leave Poland. I was very upset about Zigmund's drowning, and his cries for help kept me awake for many a night.

I soon ran into a woman and a man who would play significant roles in my immediate future. I do not remember their names: I shall name her Claudine and him Jan, Polish for "John". She had lived in France during the war, and afterwards had volunteered to be repatriated to Poland. The young man who accompanied her was from the extreme eastern part of Poland. It was clear to me that Claudine was really in charge. Of course, I initially told them the standard lie that I was looking for my mother. They replied immediately that they wanted to escape from Poland, and so I made a very bad mistake that I would later regret, and told them about my misadventure with Zigmund. They informed me that we had gone about it all wrong, and that the border with Czechoslovakia was at the top of a mountain not far from Jelenia Góra. The three of us could cross there. We would collect food, heavy coats, winter boots and various other equipment, and together walk across the mountain to our freedom. The mountain they were referring to was Snieżka, part of the Karkonosze Mountain Chain astride the Polish-Czechoslovakian border. At an elevation of 4,809 feet (1,624 meters), it was a wild, uninhabited area. It would be quite an undertaking to traverse it in the middle of winter.

To me it sounded like a well-organized effort, and so I joined them. They told me not to worry we would walk across Czechoslovakia to the German, not Austrian, border, and there cross into Western Europe, where I could join the Polish Army and fight the communists. I got all enthused about the whole idea, as everything sounded very logical at my age. Crossing a high mountainous area did not faze me, as I was accustomed to walking in the mountains from my peddler days in Iwonicz Zdroj.

And so we started collecting food. The three of us now became fast friends, and through our many conversations it came out that Claudine had worked at the oldest profession in the world in France and her real goal was to get back to the streets of Paris. All this did not bother me in the least, as I was too young to have been exposed to such realities of life. Plying her trade, Claudine came up with sufficient funds in the next few days. Her "john" scrounged a rucksack and we loaded it up and got ready to go. We traveled from Jelenia Góra to the little mountain village of Karpacz, very close to the border, where we were lucky to obtain lodgings with a recently resettled Polish family who had been forcefully repatriated from the extreme eastern area of Poland, which was now part of Russia. It did not take too long for this family of friendly people to find out our plans about crossing the border, and of course Claudine's monetary generosity helped.

We were soon informed by our newfound friends that a lot of smuggling was going on, and that in the middle of winter, especially in the higher elevations, the border was not closely watched. I spent a lot of time with the family's grandfather, who briefed me in detail about trails, the terrain features of our proposed crossing and the location of the Polish Border Police control points. These latter, according to the old man, were not manned at this time of winter. The only danger to our undertaking would be the weather—snowstorms or getting lost and freezing to death. I briefed Claudine and Ján on all the details, and it was decided I would be the guide for the crossing.

After a short period of bad weather, we left our warm lodgings and began our journey, traveling southwest to the abandoned village of Wilcza Poremba. Our arrival gave me a lot of confidence in myself and credence in the route our contacts' grandfather had outlined. At this point we walked directly south, towards the summit of Śnieżka. After a few hours of steadily walking uphill through lightly snow-covered terrain, we encountered some bad weather. I suggested we stop and let it pass, as I was afraid to lose my bearings. We were able to travel again around noon, and were very near the top of the mountain when, once more, fog and wind closed in on us. We had to stop in an abandoned hut, which was nothing more than a slanted roof open on three sides. This time I was able to start a small fire on the lee side of the hut. Jan did not volunteer to help with collecting firewood. We warmed up, waiting for the wind to die down a little and for better visibility.

As we started our ascent, Jan became increasingly unhappy with the situation, questioning my judgment and wanting to give up. I just kept my mouth shut. Soon the winds died down a little, the fog lifted, and we were able to continue. I decided that instead of going for the summit that we should go around, putting it to our back, and head downhill. It took us some time, but we did it. Looking back north, we could clearly see the summit directly behind us. We had crossed over the border, and were in Czechoslovakia!

Now we had to watch for the Czech Border Police. Shortly we found a well-marked trail bearing a sign in German with an arrow pointing down the slope. Jan complained of being tired and wanted to go down the open trail. I wanted to go through a wooded area, parallel to the trail but at some distance from it, to avoid running into the Border Police. Thank God, I had this foresight! As we were walking downhill to the right of the trail, we heard voices coming from the trail speaking in Czech. We went to the ground and stayed quiet and the voices drifted off.

We began to move again, but it was now getting dark and very cold. We stopped for the night in a mountain meadow where there were several haystacks. Claudine and I dug into a haystack all the way to the center. Jan did not help but he was the first one to get inside the lair. Huddled together, we spent the night. We awoke with the first light and it was cold, miserable, and hungry. We walked downhill in a southerly direction through the open fields and apple orchards, staying away from the distant houses. At about noon, we stopped and ate some of our rations. We saw no people at this point, although we were at a road junction. My companions stayed in the fields as I snuck up to the road, where a sign indicated Jablonec to the west and Turnov and Mlada Boleslav to the south. It was late afternoon and getting dark, so we decided to find a place to spend the night. We entered an orchard in a sort of ravine and found a shed or half-ruined small barn, perfect for a night's lodging. I built a fire and made it nice and cozy inside and then we slept.

By the late afternoon of the third day we had reached the outskirts of the large town of Mlada Boleslav. There was no way to go around the city. We encountered factories and a river, and on the other side it looked like there was a railroad station. The town lay straight in front of us, and so we took a chance and decided to walk right through it. I stopped a young man on the sidewalk and asked him for directions to Prague. We had a short conversation, not knowing each other's native tongue but understanding each other since our languages both had Slavic roots. He said we should go to the railroad station and try to get on a train to Prague. I was not to worry, he said, because Czechoslovakia was free and under the rule of Jan Massaryk, who had come back from England to assume the presidency. He pointed the way to the railroad station and left, wishing us good luck.

Walking to the railroad station, we came upon a long brick wall with a sidewalk running alongside of it. Behind the wall was some kind of factory. As we were walking beside it, along came a Czech police officer on a bicycle. Seeing him, Jan, like the idiot he was, started to run. The police officer hollered for him to stop, but Jan continued running. The police officer pulled his pistol on us, and marched all three of us off to jail.

After a thorough search, we were asked who we were, where we had come from, and where we were going. We were required to produce personal documents, which we did not have. We were then separated: Jan and I were put in one cell and Claudine in another. The jail was like a circus. It was a very large area under a common roof, with a series of cage-like cells separated from each other by bars from floor to ceiling. We got fed every day, but no one asked us anything or cared that we were there. Finally, about four or five days later, Jan and Claudine were taken away. That was the end of our relationship as far as I was concerned. I blamed Jan and his damned stupidity for all of our misfortunes.

I was now left on my own. A couple of days later during a short interrogation session, some sort of civilian official asked me to confirm my nationality. I answered that I had been born in Poland and then tried to explain why I was attempting to escape. He left and then came back with some bad news. Since I was a minor, he had no choice but to turn me back to Poland. They were going put me on a train to Moravská Ostrava, where I would be temporarily incarcerated pending an escorted transport under guard to the border and where I would be turned over to the Polish authorities.

When the day came for me to be transported by rail and under guard to the Moravska Ostrava prison, I was not very smart. I told my armed guard, "Before you get me to Moravská Ostrava, I'll escape. "Will you, now?" he said, and clapped me in shackles. We went on a local train, a big police officer, and a kid in cuffs. The Czechs kept looking at me in surprise and talking to me. Czech is close to Polish, so I could understand about half of what they were saying. "What's going on, little boy, what have you done, why are you in handcuffs?" they kept asking. My guard became very embarrassed by all this attention, especially when one of the women in our train compartment demanded he take my shackles off.

After a long train ride, my guard delivered me to the prison, where I was processed, given gray prison clothes much too big for me, and took a shower. It was nearly nightfall before I was finally placed in a large cell with twelve to eighteen other inmates, all adult males. There were no pillows or blankets, just a hard, wooden, shelf-like sleeping bench. But it was warm, which was a blessing in winter. The next day I had the pleasure of meeting my cellmates.

There were all kinds of folks and nationalities, both civilian and military, including deserters from the Soviet Army. Having deserted during time of war, hidden and married local Czechoslovakian girls, they had had their marriages annulled, and were now waiting to be handed over to their government for execution by the NKVD. There was also a man who had thrown a grenade into the wedding reception of his former girlfriend, killing several people. There were former Czech Nazi sympathizers awaiting execution by hanging, and plenty of smugglers who worked the borders between Poland and Czechoslovakia or Austria. A number of incarcerated Croat Nazi party members, awaiting extradition to Tito's Yugoslavia, were also facing death.

As I was the only minor, some of these lovely folks protected me from being raped. I did not quite understand what it was all about. A couple of men in particular were extra friendly towards me, coming up and offering me their ration of bread. The next thing I knew, both were severely beaten by my self-appointed protectors. Beaten so badly, as a matter of fact, that they were carried unconscious out of our cell. After this incident, I had no problems. We were fed twice a day, and once a week we were taken to shower. The Russians always shared their bread with me, and in the evening before lights out they sang beautiful Russian songs.

Before too long, all the Poles were taken out of the cellblock. This was maybe a quarter of the prisoners. We were placed on a train destined for the Polish border, with guards armed with submachine guns. There we were turned over to the Polish Political Police, the uniformed UB. We were then chained, marched across the border, and put on a prison train bound for Katowice, a large town in Silesia, Poland, where we were placed in a regular prison.

This time I was locked up with the women. The cell was full of female smugglers who carried cigarettes and other things back and forth across the Polish-Czech border. They had all been caught four, five, or six times, and all of them laughed about their adventures. There was nothing political involved. These women washed my clothes and in general took care of me. At last, things were beginning to look a little better.

After about a week, I was summoned to appear before a court and taken by armed guard to a courthouse where a woman judge presided. The whole thing took about half an hour. The charges against me, read by this middle-aged kindly female judge, were very minor. To the best of my recollection, they consisted of "illegally crossing of the border and smuggling prohibited merchandise." Due to my age, I was to be released as soon as the administrative procedures required by court were prepared. On the way back to prison, I was not even shackled. I reported the good news and everybody in our cell was very happy for me.

All would have come to good end, except for Jan and Claudine who, unbeknownst to me, were in another prison in Katowice. When the time came for their court appearance, or maybe during their interrogations, the UB police had beaten Jan, who had immediately ratted on me, stating that I was a dangerous reactionary escaping

Poland to join the Polish Army in exile. He further attested that I was involved in an unsuccessful escape at the Polish-East German border in Zgorzelec that had created an international incident between East Germany and Poland, and that I was directly responsible for the death by drowning of my companion.

Now my offense was more than just a border crossing. I was accused of being involved in a seriously criminal act. Instead of hitting the street, I passed into the custody of the UB, and the next thing I knew, they put me in shackles and marched me to court through the streets. The sight of an adolescent being marched between two members of the dreaded UB police, armed with submachine guns, caused quite a public spectacle. My buddies Jan and Claudine were standing there in the court. Jan, with a swollen, bruised face, was asked by the judge if I were the person accused of these crimes. He answered "yes," and then was asked to point at me and repeat what he had said. Again he said "yes," and I was immediately whisked away to a different kind of prison, located in the cellar under the UB offices.

This place was something out of the movies—a dark cellar corridor with iron cell doors featuring a Judas window. It was very dank and cold inside the cells, which measured about 12 by 12 feet, and featured a barred window high on the wall near the ceiling. There was no bed, only straw piled up in a corner. A shit bucket completed the décor.

Every day, early in the morning, I was called out to empty my bucket. Upon returning to my cell, I was given two slices of bread and warm water for breakfast, after which it was time for interrogation. Every day I was made to write my life story, and every day I wrote something different. As I was not cooperative, I received a beating every day before I returned to my cell. Late in the afternoon I was fed, usually some sort of red beet and potato soup. Finally, I got very weak and could hardly walk. My face, swollen from daily beatings, must have looked very bad.

The down-stair guards in the cellar began to feel sorry for me and told me to say something when my interrogator confronted me, even if it were a lie, to save myself from daily beatings. They also started feeding me better, so I now received daily bread and hot tea, and they gave me two blankets. I am sure that the officials upstairs were not aware of their kindness. After a couple of weeks, I was given a shower and some clothes, because those I possessed were now nothing but rags. I was then marched through the streets of Katowice, again creating the spectacle of a skinny, fourteen-year-old boy flanked by two burly, communist guards armed with submachine guns.

In court, the presiding judge was yet another woman—a nasty, hateful bitch. This time, it took only about ten minutes for her to read the verdict. I was sentenced to four years of juvenile prison; when I reached eighteen, my status would be legally determined. Again I was marched away, this time not to my hole in the basement of the UB, but to a juvenile detention house, where I was locked up awaiting transfer to my permanent place of detention. Where that would be, I was not informed. In the juvenile prison, I became a sort of celebrity among my contemporaries. Having served hard time and being held by the UB gave me a certain respect and status. I was challenged only once by a pimply-faced, much older boy, who could not stand to see my rising popularity. He told me he was going to kick the shit out of me. I quickly took care of him, beating him severely on his head with a metal bunk end. Extra charges of "assault with the intent to kill" were placed against me.

After waiting some time for transport to an unknown location for my incarceration, I was informed the day had come for me to leave Katowice. Early one winter afternoon, I was ordered to pick up my personal belongings and was escorted outside, where I was given a blanket and told to get aboard the rear of a small truck. The rear of the truck bed was thickly covered with straw, with folding wooden benches on both sides. The whole thing was covered with tarpaulins, with an open curtain in the rear. Once inside, I was ordered to sit close to the truck cab. My guard sat opposite me, more to the back of the truck. He was completely bundled up in some sort of heavy fleece coat and a Russian fur hat with the earflaps pulled down so far that I could hardly see his face. On his lap was a PPSH Russian submachine gun, the shoulder strap hanging around his neck. Amazingly I was not shackled but firmly warned that I would be shot should I attempt to flee.

I sat there thinking that since it was already afternoon we could not be going very far, especially as in winter darkness fell around 3:00 o'clock. Still not knowing where they were taking me, I thought I had better move soon and make my escape, for I was determined not be locked up for four years. Even if they killed me trying, I was willing to take my chances. I was wrong about the length of the voyage. As darkness came, we were still on the road. Staying on the main route, we passed the city of Sosnowiec, then a series of factories on both sides of the road. After traveling for some time, it looked as if we were in the country, with forest to my left. On the right, although I could not see anything on that side, I heard a train.

At this point, my guard came forward toward the cab and yelled for the driver to stop so he could take a piss. The driver either did not hear him, or paid no attention. Now it is going to happen, I told myself. I can feel it. The guard was on his feet, walking to the open rear curtain, hands over his head, holding onto the metal support ribs that secured the tarpaulins, while the truck bounced up and down. Walking like this, hand over hand, he steadied himself all the way to the open curtain, then with one hand holding on, he attempted to piss from the rear of the truck.

I lunged from behind and with all my strength hit him at mid back, pushing him out of the truck. As he fell screaming to the ground, I jumped right after him, hit the road, rolled over, got up, and ran for my life across the railroad tracks into the open fields toward the far-off forest. Taking a quick look back, out of breath, I could see the guard still laying where he had fallen, and the truck disappearing down the road. I watched all this as if in a trance, as the truck lights receded in the distance.

I then checked myself over. I was sore but not hurt. There was one thought in my head: to get away as far as I could. Ahead of me was a lightly wooded area. I must have run for a long time. I was very tired and upset, for if the man died from the fall, should I get caught now it would be the end of me. "Keep on going, keep on going," I told myself. Clearing the woods, I could see bunches of dim lights and discovered another set of railroad tracks as I approached. Not far to my right front was a tall building several stories high with many rail tracks running in front of it. Dim lights glowed in the windows high in the building and across the front was a sign indicating the Polskie Koleje Panstwowe (PKP; Polish National Railroads). Next to the building was a water tower where the steam locomotives replenished their water tanks. At ground level, the area was also full of flickering colored lights.

Obviously at some sort of rail yard, I knew I had to hide quickly before I was seen. It must have been past midnight, and I was exhausted and sore from my fall. By that time it was very dark and had begun to snow. As I scoured the area for shelter, I spied several boxcars and wagons on the far side of the yard, and headed over to them. Close-up, they looked decrepit and abandoned, and since I could not walk any further, I spent the rest of the night inside a boxcar. I woke in the morning with winter fog and wet, falling snow all around me. Peering about, I saw a long train with its locomotive taking on water that looked like it would shortly depart east. The train was composed of many open cars loaded with coal, a few regular boxcars toward the rear, and a crew car at the very end. Each boxcar had a set of narrow stairs running up the end to a small, elevated, cabin-like enclosure. I immediately headed for the train and climbed into it. The train lurched, we began to move, and I fell asleep.

When I woke up much later, we had stopped in the middle of nowhere with open fields on both sides. I again fell asleep, only to be awakened by voices. I had been discovered by the train crew, two elderly men dressed in PKP uniforms. I played poor-kid-looking-for-his-family, and begged them not to turn me over to the police. Instead of throwing me off the train, they asked where I was going. Without even thinking, I said "Warsaw." They then asked me if I were hurt. I was not aware that the left side of my face was all black and blue and swollen. I said "yes," and they told me to come with them to warm up in the crew car.

The crew told me that the train was destined for the Port of Gdynia, but that the crew change would be at Radom, a short distance from Warsaw. They gave me breakfast, hot tea, and bread with slonina (pork fat), the train was moving, and everything looked good for me, all due to human kindness. Warm and full, I fell asleep. Sometime early in the evening, the train arrived at Radom. Before entering the rail yard, it slowed down at one of the track signals. Feeling rested, with two pieces of bread in my pocket, I jumped off and headed for town. I was able to reach Warsaw the next day.

Although 80 percent of the city had been destroyed in the war, Warsaw had somehow managed to survive. Amazingly, the city's electric trams were functioning, and it was now full of all sorts of domestic, religious, and international relief organizations offering shelter for homeless and displaced people. Soup kitchens abounded and clothes could be had through the UNRA, the United Nations Relief, and Rehabilitation Administration. However, to obtain a night's lodging in any shelter, it was necessary to register in your full name. This initially was not a problem because I would use a phony name, but over time the Militia (Polish Police) began to interrogate everyone using the shelters about their identity. Life became increasingly more difficult for me as identity checks increased in the city. People began to ask why I was not in school and wanted to see my official documents. As a criminal on the run, it was time for me to go elsewhere.

I began to frequent the underground of Warsaw's bombed-out Central Train Station. Although the immense building was in complete ruins above ground, the underground area with its maze of tunnels and rail tracks now offered illegal shelter to refuges like me. Even the Polish Militia was afraid to enter its warren of dark corridors, crevices, and tunnels leading nowhere.

This, then, became my new home, and here I found many people in situations similar to mine. Little known to me, it had also become a place for the Narodowe Sily Zbrojne, the Polish anti-communist armed resistance movement known as the NSZ, for which I had worked as a courier with my friend Bronek. When other subterranean denizens told me about the presence of this movement, I began to make moves to find out where in the vast, underground labyrinth it was located. Doing so, I somehow alerted their people, and soon found myself confronted by a couple of men. They clearly showed me they were armed and told me to come with them.

I was made to sit down in a small, well-lit room and my interrogation began. Not knowing the identity of my captors, I was very uneasy and afraid, but after a while, I found out who they were and out came a full confession of my involvement as a courier for the NSZ, my escape, and all that had happened to me thereafter. By doing so I was taking one of the biggest chances of my life! They made no comments one way or the other. They just listened, then handcuffed me to a wall support stanchion and locked the room.

Finally, after a full day and night, the door opened and in came a woman who informed me that they were sorry about the treatment I had received, but that all was now well and I would be helped. She also informed me that by escaping from the UB, I had put myself in mortal danger and had to leave Poland. She said I was to leave Warsaw for Gdynia as soon they could make my travel arrangements. They would provide some clean clothes, railroad tickets and a student ID card for me in the name of Adam Hodder, Hodder being my English grandfather's last name.

A couple days later I was happily ensconced aboard a morning passenger train on my way to Gdynia. Not being accustomed to legal travel, I had a quite a laugh about it. Following my instructions, I went directly to the address provided: 26 Weglowa Ulica (Coal Street), the home and headquarters of the Polska Unia Marynarzy (the Polish Seamen's Union). I do not wish to reveal the name of my contact there. Because I arrived late in the afternoon, I was informed that I would have to sleep in the reception hall. This was certainly no problem to me. The next day I was briefed in detail on how to conduct myself and given a temporary ID card as a "Polish Merchant Marine Crew-Boy Candidate." This, the lowest crew rating aboard any ocean-going ship, gave me the privilege of temporary shelter at the Polish Seamen's Home.

In a few days, my contact informed me I was to start attending a daily shipping muster at the union hiring hall. This was a large community room equipped with chairs where daily announcements like the following were advertised on a big poster board: Gdynia America Line S/S Atlantic trip #324—Date of sailing. Crew of two Steam Firemen needed in the Engine Department. Deck department—3 AB's (Able Seamen). Report to window #2 for muster. I didn't take me long to understand the system as I daily mingled with the people in the hiring hall, picking up on all things marine.

I had been going to the hiring hall for some time when a stranger approached me one day. He explained that he was my "uncle" and would personally take me to the office of the Port Captain to receive my Polish Merchant Seaman's Identification Document. Upon hearing this I got very nervous and upset. My "uncle" smiled and told me not to worry, that everything had been arranged and all was well. He then filled out all the official-looking forms, and I had my picture taken for the first time in my life.

With the greatest trepidation, I crossed into the strictly controlled "Restricted International Zone of Gdynia Seaport." The entire procedure took less than half an hour. I noticed at the time we entered the port area that my "uncle" presented his identification as an official of the Seamen's Union, but to my great horror, he also produced his red-colored PPR credentials as a member of the Polska Partia Robotnicza, or Polish Communist Party. Back out on the streets of Gdynia, my "uncle" departed for parts unknown, wishing me good luck.

CHAPTER 3

Introduction to USA

Despite my trepidation, the words of my "uncle" proved true. A few days after he presented me to the Port Captain's office, I was called to the muster window in the hiring hall, asked for my documents, and mustered out as Engine Department Mess Boy aboard the SS General Pulaski bound with a cargo of coal for Stavanger, Norway and the port of New York in the United States. I gathered my personal belongings and boarded an intercity train for Gdansk, where SS Pulaski was being outfitted for its long sea voyage. The trip to Gdansk was brief, about half an hour east, and by late afternoon I was aboard my ship.

My duties included serving all the meals for the engine room crew, washing all the dishes, and cleaning and scrubbing the bulkheads and interior decks of the mess hall. In a few days we began to receive our cargo and coal for the ship's bunkers. The captain and ship's officers then came aboard and SS Pulaski sailed. Sometime during the night we cleared the Bay of Hel and were on our way to Norway. Twenty hours later, in early evening we passed, on our starboard side, the city lights of Malmo, Sweden, and entered the Straits of Kattegat and Skagerrack, Denmark. Four days later, we arrived at Stavanger, Norway.

Life on ship became routine, but we encountered rough seas in the North Sea, and carrying hot tea and plates of food back and forth while puking my guts out from seasickness was no fun at all. While we were in port at Stavanger, we were not permitted ashore. After a full day of discharging our cargo of coal, we received provisions aboard and sailed for the United States. The provisions from Stavanger were wonderful. There were unbelievable goodies like bananas, oranges, meat, chicken, sugar, tea, coffee, and fresh vegetables. The sort of food we could only dream about in Poland.

I forget how many days we were at sea, but one sunny morning we came to land: the United States of America. We stopped our engines well outside the harbor, awaiting the arrival of a harbor pilot who now took command of our ship and brought it to berth. The first American I saw was a nattily dressed gentleman who boarded our ship via a small, over-the-side gangway ladder and proceeded directly to the bridge. We entered New York Harbor with its famous Statue of Liberty to our portside and, sailing without cargo and under ballast, went up the Hudson River to our berth at East Asia Pier in Hoboken, New Jersey. The crew got its cargo hatches ready and there was a flurry of activity. All dressed up, the captain went ashore, and then the GAL (Gdynia America Lines) folks came aboard.

Finally we were also permitted to go ashore. The chief steward first paid us according to our rank. I, the lowest on the rung, received six dollars. Four of us went ashore together, led by an older seaman who knew his way around. We went to a used clothing store owned by a Polish Jew and I bought a pair of decent shoes, a nice sweater and a jacket, all for five dollars. Not knowing English or where to go, I was very much afraid to jump ship, although I knew I had to do it. Standing in a strange country, looking across the river at the immense buildings, I knew my moment had arrived, but I did not know what to do. Numb with fear, I stayed aboard.

Three days later, we departed New York and were underway to Boston Harbor, where we had been diverted to pick up our cargo of Marshal Plan relief goods for Poland. Our seamen's documents were, as usual, locked up in the chief purser's cabin, although I did not know why. A few days later we docked at Chelsea, the main cargo port serving Boston. Here, as seamen serving aboard foreign flag vessels, we were required by the U.S. authorities to carry on our persons our seaman identification books, which the Americans diligently checked both when we came ashore and returned aboard.

This I secretly welcomed, for I had decided come hell or high water to jump ship in Boston.

While taking on our cargo, we had shore leave almost every day, usually in the afternoon or evening. This gave us ample opportunity to visit the Polish section of town, which had a church and, above all else, the Polish American National Club, a social club catering to Polish Americans in the Boston area. We there met all sorts of nice people who were very anxious to find out what was really happening in the home country, and were often invited to dinner at their homes.

Here I meet Mike, the owner of a small, workingman's luncheonette, and confided in him my plans to jump ship. After hearing my life story, he was ready and willing to help. We discussed how and when I could make my escape. Our cargo was now almost completely loaded, and so two days before our scheduled departure, I left my meager personal possessions behind and walked off the ship with nothing except the clothes on my back. I headed for Mike's apartment, located above his restaurant, and stayed low for the next few days. SS Pulaski sailed for Poland. I was now 15 years old.

After a few days of hiding, I found out from Mike that U.S. Immigration was looking for the missing seaman from the SS Pulaski. Mike got nervous and told me I had to leave Boston. He suggested I go to his mother's farm, which was located not too far away but well into the countryside, and off we went. When he delivered me to my new home, I was greeted by a very old Polish widow, a village woman who after many years in America spoke only Polish and knew very few words in English. We got along just fine, and I learned to perform the chores required of me, like collecting eggs every morning, feeding the many caged rabbits and, much less unsuccessfully, milking the farm's two cows. It was now late autumn.

The next time Mike made his weekly run to pick up eggs, he suggested that I should be paid for my work, but of course his mother could not afford to pay me. He mentioned that he knew a very affluent Polish-American farmer, who was already aware of my defection from the ship, and was willing to give me a job on his pig farm near the small Massachusetts town of North Abbington. Naturally I jumped at this offer of work. Mike moved me to Gawronski's Pig Emporium, an immense operation with over two hundred pigs. Mr. Gawronski spoke good Polish and seemed like a decent man, offering me a monthly salary and a place to sleep in a small bunkhouse with his three other workers.

The next day at about 4:00 a.m., I woke with others and the four of us loaded into the back of a truck carrying many empty 55-gallon drums headed for Boston. We made our rounds in the back alleys of the city, passing behind several restaurants to pick up full 55-gallon drums of restaurant garbage as swill for our pigs. On the first stop, at the rear of Schraft's Restaurant and on top of the daily swill, our breakfast awaited. An assortment of day-old pastries in a brown paper bag. A container of hot coffee was produced from the truck cab, and presto—breakfast was served. We ate outside in the cold, early morning air, standing next to the truck. Upon returning to the farm, we shoveled the shit from the pigpens and fed the pig's fresh swill. Welcome to America, Albert!

A week later, Gawronski stopped by and gave me five one-dollar bills. I figured it was a tip, but shortly found out it was my weekly pay. It also did not take me too long to realize that my bunkhouse mates were not all there, mentally. After long, protracted questioning, I discovered that all three were former patients at a state mental institution who had been permitted to leave the nuthouse to work for Gawronski's Pig Emporium during World War II because of a severe shortage in farm laborers.

After I had been employed at the Pig Emporium for about two months, Mr. Gawronski traveled to Florida, leaving the farm in the capable hands of his much younger wife. After he had left, I went to the house and had a long conversation with the Mrs., who was a good and honest person. After hearing me out, she became very sympathetic to my situation. She suggested I leave for New York, where no one was looking for me, and contact the large Polish Community Center in lower Manhattan. Where it was exactly located she did not know, but she was sure I would find it. She further offered to take me to the Boston bus station and asked if I had any money. I told her yes, I had twenty dollars, and she gave me an additional twenty.

The next morning we left North Abbington for Boston, where I bought a ticket at the Greyhound Bus Station and was on my way. I arrived in New York in the middle of winter with no place to go. I managed to find a cheap place in the Bowery, which was full of drunks and down-and-outs, with many poor people sleeping on the sidewalk next to heat exhaust grilles. The price of lodgings was seventy-five cents a night. After wandering about some four or five days, I decided this was not for me and went looking for the nearest police station, in the hope the police would help me find an International Seamen's House. This was a worldwide organization found in all major seaports. I still had my Polish Seaman's Book, which would allow me to muster out of the United States on any flag merchant ship.

I walked as far downtown as City Hall, where there was a police information kiosk. Yet unable to speak comprehensible English, I tried my best to make the middle-aged policeman understand what I was looking for. He was a kind man who did his best to understand me. Finally figuring out that I was Polish and in need of help, he closed the booth and walked me over to the 3rd Avenue Elevated Train station, paid the five-cent fare, and told me to get off at the 10th Street Station. He took some paper and drew me a map, wrote down the address of the Polish National Home at St Mark's Place, and said goodbye.

With the greatest of luck I got off at the right station. I soon found the place, a very impressive building located in the middle of the block. There were a bar and restaurant at street level and offices and a large ballroom upstairs. On the first floor was the Polish Immigration Committee, where the people who received me were very willing and helpful. That is, until they found out that I was underage and an illegal alien. Nevertheless, they offered me help, giving me a gift of

$10.00 and a hotel voucher for five nights at the Chelsea Hotel on 23rd street. Immediately, things began to look better.

I stopped at a small restaurant just around the corner on 3rd Avenue, indulged in a great meal of beef stew and a piece of all-American apple pie. Then I walked a long ways to the Chelsea Hotel. The next few days I spent in and out of the Polish Immigration Office at St Mark's Place, where the people simply did not know what to do with me. Jumping a Polish flagship created great problems, since immediately after the Second World War, the United States recognized the so-called People's Republic of Poland as the de facto government. Technically the U.S. authorities were obligated to take me into custody, place me in detention at Ellis Island, and deport me back to communist Poland. Of course the people I spoke to were all against it, but as a humanitarian organization sanctioned by the U.S. government to help legal immigrants arriving in the States, they did not have a lot of leeway in the matter. They had no authority to classify me as a Displaced Person, which would have provided legal status.

The only way out was to hide and live the life of an illegal alien. This meant no Social Security card giving me the right to study or work in the States. The immigration laws at the time were different from those of today and very strict. The people at the Polish Immigration Office really tried to help me, offering to find me farm work, but remembering my Gawronski's Pig Emporium experience, I declined. I next decided to seek help from the International Seamen's Union in Battery Park. They offered me temporary shelter, not to exceed thirty days, and put me in touch with some crew employment agencies. For a fee, collected from the shipping agents, they were willing to help me find a junior steward berth on a ship registered in Panama or Liberia.

Little could I have known that in just a few more months, events on the world stage would transpire to make me and any other citizen of the so-called Eastern Block eligible for entry to the United Sates as political refugees? The validity of the Polish communist government the Soviets had placed in power in late 1944 had been challenged by the de facto Polish government in exile, led by Stanislaw Mikolajczyk and supported by the western powers. An agreement between the West and the Soviet Union emerged to resolve this situation, whereby free elections would take place in Poland. When elections were held in 1947, early returns showed Mikolajczyk's victory. The Polish communists, seeing their defeat in the making, unsuccessfully tried to assassinate him. And so the Cold War began, and Poland and all of Eastern Europe found itself behind the Iron Curtain.

Meanwhile, still an illegal alien, I shuttled back and forth between St Mark's and the agency offices for several weeks before an offering of berth was finally posted. As I had become a regular at the agency, I was greeted upon arrival, "Hey, today's your luck day! You're on!" The owner told me that he had personally found me a berth because he was sick and tired of looking at my sorry face every day. One day in January 1948, I mustered as junior steward aboard MV Maria Maersk, a Danish flagship sailing, from all the places in the world, from Hoboken, New Jersey. We were bound for the port of Santos, Brazil, with a call of port at Port of Spain, Trinidad. I said my goodbyes at the Polish Immigration Office and bright and early the next morning took the Manhattan ferry to MV Maria Maersk.

Once aboard, I was assigned to bunk with a young Danish mess boy named Lars in a double cabin located mid-ship. The bunk was nice and clean and even had a porthole on the bulkhead. We left our mooring on a cold, gray afternoon and headed out to sea without a glimpse of the Statue of Liberty, which was completely hidden in fog. Some four days later we arrived at Port of Spain, Trinidad, where we refueled and sailed on to Santos, Brazil. The crew was mostly Danish, with a sprinkling of Portuguese and Croatians from Monte Negro. At Santos, we took on a cargo of coffee for Marseille, France, a long voyage of some twelve days. Santos was a major port for the inland city of Sao Paulo. We went ashore just about every about day, and the crew, including myself, hit all the waterfront bars and bordellos, engaging in the typical conduct expected of seamen in the dark, dirty corners of every waterfront city in the world, including fist and knife fights.

We left port on Sunday, a quiet day, and began our ocean crossing for Marseille. The weather was rough all the way. Crossing the Strait of Gibraltar, we arrived in two days at Marseille, where problems with our main engine required the ship to be serviced in dry dock. The Danish crewmembers were given railroad tickets to Copenhagen, their mother port, but the rest of us were paid off and dumped ashore after receiving Danish Merchant Marine certificates of service. This gave us the right of muster on Danish merchant vessels. I was permitted a limited stay aboard the dry-docked ship. I now gradually began to explore the port of Marseille. The stay-aboard crew was fed ashore at one of the many waterfront restaurants. The food was decent—so far, so good. However, as all good things must come to an end, I was finally asked to leave the ship. But I first had to fill out a declaration of temporary stay in France, awaiting muster on another ship.

My stay was issued by the port captain at Marseille. This accomplished, I was lost in the beautiful, but very dangerous, mean streets of the city. I headed for the old city district of Pannier, a legendary area well known to sailors and whores: the entire Vieux Port was one great brothel. I signed the register for a cheap hotel room and began to scout out the local bistros. The streets were full of bars packed with sailors, stevedores, and other shady characters of every description from all around the world.

In the Bar Violette I met a group of Polish seamen from a Dutch ship who were celebrating their last night in Marseille before sailing for the Dutch East India port of Surabaya, in what is now Indonesia. My compatriots gave me good advice. First, I was to apply immediately at the Marseille Prefecture for an international Hansen Passport, the so-called "white passport" issued to all stateless persons. This document would give me the right of temporary refuge in France. Second, I was to stay off the streets in the Vieux Port at night. Third, I should muster on any flagship as soon as possible. Fourth, to avoid theft, I was not to carry my personal documents on my person, but leave them with the hotel concierge for safekeeping.

Following their advice, I applied for a Hansen Passport and continued to lodge at the hotel. Meanwhile, I slowly widened my exploration of the city, extending my walks from the lower parts of the Rue Canabière all the way to the Saint Charles railroad station. Walking all the way back to the Vieux Port section and down the Quai du Port, I found a very decent, cheap place to eat at the Bar de la Marine in a safer area of the city. There I meet a waiter, a middle-aged man and long-time resident of France originally from the Czarist Russia. Finally, I was able to communicate with someone, since Russian is very close to Polish. We became friends and quickly found we shared a passion: we both hated communism with a vengeance.

Of course I told him my life story and my dream of returning to Poland to fight the communists. He set me straight on that accord, informing me that my efforts would be futile: the war was over and for now, things would remain as they were. But he also told me the fascinating news that a war was going on at that very moment against communist Vietminh forces in French Indochina. Moreover, I further learned that the majority of people doing the fighting were not French, but foreigners like me who had joined the French Foreign Legion.

My vivid interest was trumped in the immediate by my extreme concern with daily survival, as the money I had been paid from the Maria Maersk was just about gone. There was absolutely no chance of finding work in Marseille, and so every day I went to the Seamen's Union hiring hall. And every day found nothing.

To make matters worse, my girlfriend Véronique disappeared. A woman of the street, Véronique was born in Madagascar of a Madagascarene mother and a French father. She was a few years older than I, and very beautiful. I had had a fight with her Corsican pimp, which I won, but I lost Véronique and never did find her. I enquired at all the bars and places where she worked the streets, but the street girls just shrugged their shoulders and walked away. I missed her greatly, for she was my first love.

Everything was possible in the violent, crime-infested Vieux Port. It was as if I didn't have enough troubles in my life, but since my affair with Veronique my Russian friend, the waiter at "Bar de La Marine" advised me to watch my back as a word from the streets told him that Veronique's Corsican pimp, with whom I had a fight, is looking to avenge the beating I gave him. Anatoly advised me to carry a knife to defend myself so we went shopping the street vendors and I purchased a second hand Italian switchblade stiletto. It was quite fancy with an imitation pearl handle. From that date on, from Marseille to Algeria, the knife was at my side.

I now desperately wanted to return to Poland, but as that was no longer possible, I started thinking more and more about joining the French Foreign Legion. The one thing that scared me was the required five-year enlistment. Five years to a sixteen-year-old is a lifetime. On the other hand, I thought all that training would make a good soldier out of me. Although my dream of fighting the communists was deferred, maybe I could later return to Poland as a well-trained soldier and help to liberate my country. It is extremely difficult now, writing about my early days in the winter of my life, to tell you exactly why I decided to join the Legion, but join I did. The main recruitment office in Marseille, a forbidding-looking fortress called Fort Saint Jean, was located very close to the port. As I left my hotel early in the morning to go sign up, I confided my plan to the concierge, a kind old lady named Honorine. She served me a hunk of baguette and coffee, hugged me, and said she would keep my belongings safe. She sent me off with a heart-felt bonne chance!

The recruitment hall at Fort Saint Jean was an immense room lined with wooden benches facing a row of desks manned by uniformed officials. Upon entry, I received a small metal token with a number stamped on it and was told to sit down. By noon the entire hall was jammed with applicants, and I was still waiting. Filled with conversations in many strange-sounding languages, the place was a veritable Babble. I soon picked out the sounds of Polish, and shifted my seat to sit with my countrymen. My fellow hopefuls informed me that, since I was only sixteen, I could not join unless I claimed to be eighteen but stated I was without documents. I would need two "of-age witnesses" to swear that I was eighteen or older; several of my new comrades immediately volunteered to do so.

As I was tall and well-built for my age, it looked like I would have no difficulty passing for eighteen. Finally in late afternoon my number was called. A uniformed men man asked me my nationality then sent me to another desk where a military man spoke to me in Polish, asking me my age and some other personal questions. Noting my real birthday, he looked at me and smiled. He then took my Hansen Passport and seaman's papers.

I was then required to sign a document, written in French, stating I would serve for five years in the Legion. It was that simple. Those selected were moved to another room where we were made to strip naked, form a single line, and wait for a medical examination. The medical officer asked us to cough while probing our testicles among other personal indignities that followed. The point was to pass the test for venereal disease, including the Wasserman test for syphilis.

The whole evaluation process took a few days, during which we were bunked in an open hall equipped with beds, and feed twice daily. As people from all over the world were bunked down closely together, many fights broke out in the hall. There was no enforced discipline. Very little was asked about recruit's life: if you looked healthy and were willing to fight for France, that is all that mattered. In a couple days, about half the group was dismissed and ejected like garbage back onto the streets of Marseille. The rest of us were transported by sea to Oran, French Algeria, from which we journeyed to Fort Mascara to receive four months of basic training. This was a tough thing to survive. Even in French language class, given after a hard day's training, we were beaten over the head with a swagger stick if we fell asleep or simply failed to repeat a sentence correctly.

As recruits we were referred to as bleus, and all given a serial number, or numéro matricule. Should we be unable to remember it, we got more beating with the swagger stick. The training and discipline were tough, but being young and physically strong, I had no real difficulty passing. At the end of our training, the cadre—corporals, adjutants and other noncoms, or sous officers—became friendlier and more humane in the treatment of their charges. We now learned songs and the history of legion. In my training platoon of some forty men less than twenty survived.

It was now the end of summer, 1948. Before graduation we faced one last major training obstacle: to march alone, wearing no socks, carrying a full pack including an MAS-36 rifle with two clips of five rounds each and just two canteens of water. The trek was 100 kilometers of through mountainous desert countryside (the blistering Algerian Bled) in 100-degree plus heat. Only half of the trainees made it. The bloody feet of all who completed the course would take them no farther. The day we ended our training we hobbled around and had a great celebration. Our former cadres were now calling us their brothers, and we donned our newly issued kepi blancs, the white caps of the French Foreign Legion, as full-fledged soldiers with the rank of Legionnaire, 2ème Classe. I passed the course and immediately volunteered for parachute training and assignment with the Foreign Legion Parachute Battalion Etranger Parachutiste (BEP), which was already fighting in the Tonkin area of North Vietnam. I felt that life was becoming beautiful, and looked forward to my future deployment to the war in Indochina and the sweet revenge of killing communists.

Those of us waiting to take the parachute course were temporarily assigned to the Sidi Bel Abbes garrison (commonly called Bel Abbes by us) and where on most weekends we were permitted an overnight pass in Sidi Bel Abbes. As long as we still had a few franks to spend, we made our rounds to all the bistros on Avenue Rollet and its notorious side streets, all the way down to the local souks. One night, accompanied by my friends—a great mixture of nationalities, all members of the volunteer group waiting to take the parachute course—we retired late, stone drunk, to a local hotel.

I do not remember much after that, except that during the night I woke up to discover that someone was groping me. In my muddled state, I thought it was the Algerian girl who had been in the sack with me earlier, but when I heard a man's voice I realized what was happening. A great fight ensued with my attacker, a Polish Chief Corporal, who had earlier joined us in the drinking. I managed to pull my knife and stabbed him several times. The man fell to the ground. My room looked like a butcher shop. The uproar woke up some of my friends and the night concierge, who all came running to my aid.

What happened next is completely befuddled, especially after all the years gone by. But I was taken into custody by the Legion gendarmes, or military police, and locked up at the garrison. The same day, later in the afternoon, I was taken for a formal military disciplinary hearing with an interpreter. More hearings followed, and a few days later I appeared before a military court. Luckily for me my assailant survived, although he was in bad shape. In the meantime, my buddies had left for jump school in Morocco.

I was charged with a very serious criminal offense, assault with a deadly weapon on a sous officer of the French Army, but in personal defense. The Legion severely condemned all homosexuals in its ranks, and the original charge of attempted murder was removed because of the numerous witnesses who testified in my defense. At this juncture, I guess the Legion just did not know what to do with me. After spending so many days locked up, I became seriously ill with pneumonia and was evacuated all the way to the military hospital in Oran. After a while, I was moved to a restricted infectious disease ward and informed that I had been diagnosed with tuberculosis. I was declared medically unfit for military service, given a month's pay and discharged.

God as always watched over me and death would not take me, as my faith or karma would say. Had I completed the parachute training and been assigned to either of the two parachute battalions already fighting in North Vietnam my story would have ended that fateful day on May 7th, 1954 when two Battalions of Legionnaires met their death. Early that morning, from an isolated strong point 2½ miles from Dien Bien Phu, 500 Legionnaires, their rifles with fixed bayonets, and led by their commanders against thousands of the Viet Minh, they marched out to meet the enemy. There were no Legion survivors.

Once again a civilian, I immediately began to miss the Legion and its way of life. Dejected and in a sullen mood, I boarded the Algiers ferry to return to Marseille. The French military authorities had returned all my personal belongings to me, including my white passport and seaman's papers. I now again began living in the human cesspool of the Vieux Port of Marseille. Upon arrival, the customary "International Seaman's Ninety-Day Beach Permit" had been stamped on my Hansen Passport. This precluded any idea of my staying in France. Since I was not allowed to remain, I had to look for a merchant ship.

In early autumn 1949, with only thirty days left on my seaman's visa, I found a berth as an ordinary seaman with a monthly pay of fifty dollars on MV Minerva, a rusty tramp ship sailing under the Panamanian flag bound for Port of Spain, Trinidad, and other unnamed ports of call in the Caribbean. When fully mustered aboard, I discovered that one of the ship's officers was Polish. Adam Zimmer was the second officer; his German name threw me a little, but I found out he came from the Pomeranian region and was a Kashubian, a Polish minority group. He turned out to be a friendly man.

While we were at sea he told me all about the new law in the States, in effect since 1948, pertaining to Polish nationals and their right to political asylum. As the Cold War had inexorably cranked up, nationals of any East Bloc country who wished to apply for political asylum had gained the right to enter the United States without fear of deportation back to their native countries. Those who could prove that political persecution awaited them in their native country and were asking for asylum because they were opposed to communist regimes would be granted asylum.

This was wonderful news to me. As the days at sea went by, my thoughts turned again to the possibility of a war against the communists in Poland. Scuttlebutt had it that after Port of Spain we would sail for Baltimore. And the good news was true: for the second time, I landed in the United States. This time I was legally discharged from my ship. I left the M/V Minerva with seventy dollars in my pocket, and received an International Seaman's landing shore document from U.S. Immigration, valid for a forty-five-day stay in the country. The Baltimore Polish-Americans helped me find temporary lodgings. America, I have arrived!

CHAPTER 4

Surviving in America

For me, Port and the City of Baltimore was nothing more than a place I have landed in the United States. Its Dundalk Avenue area where I was able to find temporary lodgings was well known as a poor immigrant area. I found kindly people of Polish Ancestry who have taken me in, and helped me with my initial contact with the US Immigration people. Who as it turned out had many misgivings and shown a hesitancy in giving me temporary probationary pardon as a Political Refugee. I was very thoroughly interrogated by its agents.

My faith hung in the air, as to being given temporary political status pardon and admitted or not. Finally after some weeks passing, the good news was passed to me, and proper documents of admittance were issued, including a temporary working permit. How I survived all this time without work, quite frankly, was only because of the kindness of the local community of Polish American's. Even as I was being processed by US Immigration they found me a place to stay and a job in a local neighborhood Polish/Jewish bakery as a general flunky washing pots and pans, scrubbing floors, and metal bake molds. All this for a weekly salary of $35.00.

As for food, I gorged myself on all baked goods. Life was good as I lived practically free with an old Polish couple. After some weeks passing and taking my meager savings I decided to leave Baltimore for the bright lights of New York City. Thanking all the folks who helped me, boarded a Greyhound bus, and off I went for several hours on the trip to New York City.

As I looked with a greatest of amazement at the quickly passing American countryside and its never ending car traffic and the hustle and bustle of the cities that we passed through. At the stop we made in Philadelphia, I ventured to leave the safety of the bus. Looking at the great number of similar looking busses parked in great row, all going in very different directions, and the number of people going to and fro, I became deathly afraid I might not find my bus. I quickly returned to the safety of my bus seat, and stayed put at all stops. As we travelled I was overcome by a good feeling about this country and my future. It seemed so much different from Marseille and France where people we not friendly, and one would always be on alert for something threatening to happen. The little that I have learned about Americans, since my arrival was that they were helpful to strangers, friendly, straight forward and good-natured people.

Sitting in my comfortable bus seat, my mind was not troubled about my future. I found truly to be at peace with myself, and my decision to come back and chose this country, not France or any other country, as a place to live. As we were passing through the state of New Jersey and came closer and closer to our arrival in New York City, the mixed feeling of great excitement and apprehension came upon me, and made me somewhat nervous, as my ability to communicate with people in English was rather limited. Still, while we finally arrived at this incredibly colossal bus station, with thousands of people moving to and fro, the great masses of people swallowed me up.

A question came up as where is the exit from this immense place. I joined the people who were moving up a great stairs leading upwards to the next great level of stairs and finally was dumped, with the rest, onto the streets of New York City. It was a late afternoon and I guess most of people were hurrying back home, a bad time to be in "The City." I tried to ask people for directions to closest IRT subway station, but was either ignored or spoken to in the staccato of English which I only half understood. Somehow I found my way, and got on a train that had taken me past the stop at 14th Street, where I was supposed to get off, and travelled all the way to somewhere in Brooklyn, where I finally found my bearings and returned to 14th Street stop. I got off the train and started to walk along the 3rd Avenue south to St Marks Place where I found my overnight lodgings.

Having been granted a temporary Political Refugee Status, I was required to monthly report in person to immigration authorities in the City, at number 1 Columbus Circle. While registering with INS (Immigration Naturalization Service) people, I was assigned to an INS Officer, who was the nicest person you would ever want to meet. His name was Ronald Nolan, he was very helpful and kind, guiding me through mountains of documents, forms, and other official papers required of a political refugee. Almost from the beginning of our formal and official contact, I declared my desires to join, and serve in US Armed forces, and to fight the communist occupiers of my country, Poland. For at that time, as the Iron Curtain fell across Central and Eastern Europe and the Cold War started, I still very much believed that a war between the Soviet Union and the US was unavoidable, and would break out anytime.

The United States, the champion of the free world, would stand up to the Soviet communist oppression and fight. At that particular time my idea of going back to Europe and fight was shared by many reluctant immigrants who thought that the Safe Heaven granted to them was only a temporary arrangement, and that once the communist regimes would fall these folks would go back to the countries of their birth, to get on with their lives. Of course this did not happen for the next 40 years. In the meantime I had to eat, was penniless and was forced to take any job available.

The Polish American Immigration Committee at St Marks Place was doing all they could to help people like myself. Unfortunately for me the person in charge of this humanitarian organization, and a very well-known Polish American Catholic Clergyman by name and title Monsignor Burant, who for some unknown reasons categorically refused to help me. So much for help from my own people. But as they say "One door closes, another opens." And who steps up and offers immediate help in finding me a job, and a place to live? A member of the American Jewish Appeal Committee. Mr. Moshe Herckowicz, who knew my family in Poland, was that person.

And so a few days later I reported to my first legal job in the USA. I was hired as a dishwasher at the "Old Rumanian Restaurant" located on the East Side on Manhattan's Delancey Street. Here I worked all day, every day in the cellar, which was an underground cave like room full of steam from dish washing machines, forever-damp walls, smelled of rotten food, and of other unmentionable things. There was this old worn out pull type of elevator from kitchen upstairs to my underground dungeon from which one would have to extract great piles of soiled plates, dishes and cutlery, and next to washing machine stood always full, great stinking garbage can.

Jokingly, the owner, an elderly Jewish gentleman from Rumania would occasionally visit me and call me his Polish Pearl Diver. But on Saturday there was a check and the pay was good and the food was free. All the waiters and kitchen help were always kind and would give me extra tips. And so the life in the City was kind of good, and I could afford to buy myself some decent clothes; a suit, tie and all those things that made me look presentable. On Saturday nights I would get all dressed up in my new suit and go to dances at the St Marks Polish American Club, or to the Alliance Club on 1st Avenue where the clientele was a mixture of all nationalities, but conversations were mostly in English.

Here I found myself more comfortable, and was given an opportunity to practice my English, the language I desperately wanted to learn. As the time went by I began to plan my escape from my "Pearl diving" job in the underground dungeons of the Old Rumanian Restaurant. On my next visit with a Mr. Nolan of the INS, I was advised that now, as my probationary period was coming to the end, I should think about registering with the US Military Draft Board. Instead of waiting to be called to serve sometime in the future, I would be eligible to volunteer immediately after registration for induction into the US Army. As all these things were happening at one, time I decided to quit The Old Rumanian and look for something to keep me going until I could get into US Armed Forces. In the meantime I began to hang out at a small local neighborhood bar by the name "Ali Baba"

It came to pass that, having nothing else to do I would sometime spend the entire afternoon sucking on a ten-cent draft glass of beer while minding my own business. I became aware of the clientele of this establishment, as they were mostly local people, represented by a great mixture of Italian, Polish and Jewish Americans. As for me, I kind of tried to fit into this ethnic enclave by making myself useful by acting like a proverbial "Steppin Fetchit" and doing some volunteer jobs like cleaning and stocking the bar whenever Beverly the barmaid would ask me to do so.

It came to pass that one of the permanent habitués by the name of Renato befriended me. Sometimes even referring to me as Alberto in Italian, or just as "Kid" he would say to me, "here is a quarter play numbers 10 or 14" on the Ali Baba's centerpiece, a beautifully lighted juke box. Renato obviously did not work for a living and was a small time hustler, having something to do with the so called "Number's Racket." The Ali Baba was Renato's unofficial office. I for one was always very respectful and deferential to his person, by addressing him as Don Renato. Somehow I gained his confidence by not saying too much, spoke only when spoken to, and in this way became a part of the Ali Baba's scene. Having heard from Beverly that I was looking for a job. He come forth and offered to help.

The next day, late in the afternoon, when Ali Baba came to life, with all the "Usual Suspects" present with the juke box playing a Jerry Vale record, "Ti Amo ti Voglio Amor" and all bar stools and in back the rear interior booths filled with local men talking in half tones. Renato called me aside and announced that he got me a real good job. He gave me a small piece of paper, written on it a short message "Pier number 7, United Fruit Lines at 7:00 in morning, signed Renato" and informed me that he had fixed for me a Longshoreman's (Stevedore) job at $2.75 per hour wage. Holly Mackerel! A very good wage at that time with a possibility to earn close to $100.00 dollars a week!

But pulling on my ear, told me, half-jokingly, not to fuck it up, and make sure to be in front of the entrance gates of Pier #7 at the lower part of Manhattan at exactly 7:00 am. For a daily Shape-up, and that there would be a large crowd of men waiting to be hired for this day's work, I was to be standing well in front of the group close to The Shape-up Boss. He would be selecting a number of people for daily work unloading Bananas from a berthed United Fruit Lines freighter. I was to attract this men's attention by moving my hat to right, and then to left. He in turn would call out to me to come forward and give me a numbered brass token. At the same time I was to slip him Renato's note. Then proceed to inside of the Pier's terminal small kiosk's small window where I was to give my name and social security number to a man, and report to Shift Boss man at pier side where I would be given my working instructions, work gloves and a Stevedore's hook.

And this is how I became a so-called "Banana Donkey." For the next three or more months I was carrying great big green Banana bunches from the conveyer belt coming down from the ship's innards and down to where we stood in line. Moving up to the end of the conveyer as our turn came up. Two great black brutes would catch the banana bunch and expertly heave it on your right shoulder. With some of the larger bunches that would make you stagger with its weight. Away you went with your load, onto wide connecting planks from the pier to the cargo barges. You needed to balance your weight properly until you met a man who would grade your bunch and tell you a numbered barge to carry your load to. There, a pair of two other black brutes would relieve you of your load.

Then walk back to the line to pick up another bunch. This would go on continued until three in afternoon. At three o'clock, the whistle would blow indicating the end of workday. Some men would be told to go to Pay Shack to get paid off, for their day's work. Others to take a half/ hour lunch break and come back for cleanup work. I really could not tell you how all this worked, but some of us, from the early morning Shape Up would be the one's told to come back, and given an extra two hours of work until five in afternoon, which meant extra time wages.

For lunch we would go across the street to a greasy spoon luncheonette and bar named Portside Bar & Grill and have a go at the seventy-five cents Blue Plate Special which normally, and to my best recollection, would be greasy lamb shank stew, served with some unrecognizable overcooked vegetables. This place was owned by a Greek family, and the only English-speaking person was an old worn out waitress named Daisy. After finishing our lunch came the most important thing for all of us. We were to go to the rear of restaurant, where a familiar person of the morning, the shape up Man, was comfortably seating in a booth with another well-dressed man. We would approach this man individually, handing him two one dollar bills plus seventy-five cents in change. He in turn would make a note on a small ticket like piece of paper. This daily after work obligatory contribution, to whom I don't' know, was to be our job insurance of the next day's work.

Sometimes we went and worked at the forty fourth street Manhattan pier unloading coffee from Brazil. This was hard and dangerous work in ship's cargo holds picking up with our hooks a 100 pound coffee bag made of hemp, placing four bags on a cargo dolly taking it to a cargo hatch opening to be placed by hand onto a cargo net to be winched out topside. For whatever reasons the offloading could not be stopped until each hold is empty. On a coffee gig we would work without break for some time twelve hours. Such was my life on the New York waterfront. With weekends come good times to be had at Ali Baba, and I would order double shooters of Four Roses whisky from the bar. All things must come to an end. I got my orders from the draft board to report to One Battery Park Street for my volunteer two-year induction into the US Army.

Korea

CHAPTER 5

Journey to a Far Away War

It was Christmas time, late December 1950, the spirit of holidays was in the air, plenty of snow, but it was not so much a merry time as it was the time for me to go to war, a war that was taking place in a very far and distant place called, Korea.

This was my chance to seek vengeance against communist occupation and enslavement of my native Poland. Wearing the United States army uniform, and with recent US Army Basic and Advanced Infantry training behind me, including the Parachute Jump School at Fort Benning, Georgia, I proudly wore a silver paratrooper badge upon my chest. I would also mention that having been an "Honor Graduate" of both Basic & Advanced Infantry training, I had been promoted to the rank of Corporal. Now, I found myself being assigned to the elite 503rd Parachute Infantry Regiment at Camp Campbell, Kentucky, as an Assistant Squad leader of Intelligence and Reconnaissance Platoon. My unit's members were all volunteer regular US Army as the "two year draftees" were not too keen on jumping out of airplanes.

After my promotion, I decided to put in for an immediate overseas assignment with the 187th Airborne RCT (Regimental Combat Team), presently fighting in Korea. It had taken me at least a months' time to receive my orders, as my Unit did not want me to go. Once my orders were received, I traveled by US Army Troop Train, with other volunteers for a long trip to Fort Dix, New Jersey. Fort Dix was the US Army East Coast processing center for all overseas assignments. Ordinarily, combat troops bound for Korean were shipped out of ports located on the west coast of the USA, like Oakland, California or Seattle, Washington. So what are we doing going to the east coast? Why? We found out much later. I might mention at this time there were no such things like mass air transport of troops.

As we arrived at Fort Dix, we found a great number of commercial buses waiting for us and we were quickly ushered on to them and headed for the Staten Island Navy Yard, which was our sea embarkation port.

From what I still can remember, it was one those wintery days with snow falling intermittent with cold rain. Upon arrival on the wharf, we were disgorged from the warmth of our bus, only to find ourselves standing, in awe, next to the Military Sea Transport Service (MSTS). It was a gray monster of a ship, which bore the name, "USS General Black." It was, by far, the most enormous troop ship that I had ever seen.

We stood in a military formation, and then came the order, to board one of the many gangways, already crowded with troops, and their gear. Somehow, order and discipline prevailed. Of course, the ever-indomitable fact, known to all American service members, "hurry up then wait," prevailed for some time.

Eventually, our group of Airborne (Paratroopers), small in size, were berthed together in the ships' great innards. We were in a separate compartment way down below with metal bunks that were hung four high, right next to a common latrine (24 seats) and a shower facility. After settling in, we were briefed in great detail as to feeding time, lifeboat assignments, and other emergency procedures. A selected few of us were assigned special duties for the duration of voyage. I got lucky and was assigned as a member of the Military Police Detail aboard ship.

And so, on that miserable late afternoon, with the help of a couple of Navy tugboats, we pulled away from shore on a very long sea journey to Korea with some "unknowns" to us, in between ports of call. As we left port for this long sea voyage, I started to think back how this present journey, in many ways, mirrored my own life then and now: as someone who is always moving, restless, driven and always on the way to somewhere. This voyage was nothing more than the continuation of events in my life that were always associated with war.

From the time I was a young boy in my native Poland, from 1939, until 1944, I lived through the brutal Nazi occupation. I had witnessed war first hand. The brutality never left me. I became part of war and war became part of me. Then as a career soldier in the United States Army from the late 1950's, intermittently, for the next twenty plus years, until April 1970, when I came back from Viet Nam, war was the essence of my life.

For two years, I fought as a Combat Infantry soldier in Korea, and served five combat tours with US Special Forces in Viet Nam. In total, I was wounded three times in armed combat plus, perhaps unknowingly, I was very mentally scared. Through all that time at war, I never wavered in my faith in God, or my love and loyalty to my adopted country, the United States of America.

At the time of this voyage, back in USA, one could always hear on radio the latest military situation in this far off land of Korea. It was sometimes coined as a "Police Action" by the media. The news was not always good. Printed or broadcast stories were of US military fighting vastly superior forces of Communist North Korea. And, as of just past November 1950, we now faced, in addition to the North Koreans, a half a million strong Chinese Communist Volunteer Army.

America and its allies after all, just five years passing, won the Second World War. And now in some obscure place like Korea, the American Soldiers and Marines found themselves fighting again against an incredibly large communist force. The US troops were locked in a "no quarter given fight." America as a nation was in the beginning of the Cold War and they looked at the Korean conflict as a prelude to the third world war, and considered it essential to defend the Government of South Korea, whatever the costs.

Now that a full realization of the grim military situation facing us had taken place so far away, our regular armed forces, reinforced by its Army Reserves, its National Guard units plus a fully functioning draft of its youth, sprang into action, and began in earnest to immediately train and send troops to fight. We were a part of this effort. We were replacements and reinforcements for the troops holding the line.

As we were sailing along for the last couple days, realization came upon us that we should be sailing westerly towards Panama Canal and we in fact were sailing south. The days became warm with tropical-like weather. Surprise! We were awakened very early in the morning entering the Port of San Juan, Puerto Rico, where we docked at a passenger wharf. Awaiting us was the Puerto Rican National Guard Band playing lively Latin tunes. Shortly after, out of the Passenger Terminal, came smartly marching members of the Puerto Rico National Guard. I would estimate at least three hundred men, all members of the 65th National Guard Regiment, a part of 3rd US Infantry Division already fighting in Korea. The gangways were lowered and they all came aboard.

Ashore were thousands of people saying good-bye, with American and Puerto Rican flags waving, the band playing, adding to the very festive, patriotic mood among all ashore. Nothing like that happened on our departure from Staten Island, to say the least. In late afternoon we departed. As we were steaming away the Military Band marched on the pier alongside with our slowly moving ship. Upon reaching the end of pier, they gave us a loud, Hurrah! A rather moving thing.

Life aboard returned to normal, except for the "bitch box." The frequent announcements from the loud speaker, in both the English and Spanish language, were nonstop. As we sailed now across tranquil and balmy seas, all of us enjoyed the beautiful tropical sun shining weather. Many had now dragged their mattresses top side and slept on the troop deck. In a couple days out from San Juan a new form of entertainment had taken place. The ship's fire hoses were turned on twice daily to cool off the troops. And so with a couple more days of sailing, as the new day came early in the morning, we came upon land. Without any announcements, we were escorted by two tugboats flying a strange unknown flag. They came out to take us into port. And so this is how we entered the large harbor of

Cartagena, Republic of Colombia. As we were towed through the ports' narrow entry channel, on both sides we passed very impressive old Spanish Colonial fortification ramparts. At one time in the 16th and 17th century the ramparts guarded this Spanish Fort from pirates of the Caribbean.

Of course no one of us knew the real reason for making this visit as all military movements of our or allied troops was considered secret. Soon, however, we found out we were here to pick up a part of the Republic of Colombia's all Volunteer Infantry Battalion for Korea. The part of port where we tied up was a Colombian Navy Yard. Here we were meet by a large number of Colombian armed forces, all assembled with great precision, awaiting our arrival. Our Ship's Captain, in white uniform, went ashore to meet with local dignitaries, while we all gawked. Shortly after, a great convoy of trucks arrived shipside, and the Colombian Army soldiers began to board our ship.

The bands were playing the Colombian and American National Anthems. The Colombian Guard of Honor passed by our ship, dipping its colors, the ship's siren blew, and before we knew it all troops were aboard. With the help of couple of Colombian tugboats, we pulled away from Cartagena.

Back at sea we were, for the first time, notified on the ships "bitch box" and in two languages, of our next destination where we would be transiting the Panama Canal to the Pacific Ocean. A couple of days later, we found ourselves outside of the Canal entry and at anchor. The scuttlebutt was that since we were an American Ship, carrying troops in wartime, the Panama Canal would be closed to all other traffic during our time of transit.

Finally, early in the morning before breakfast, the most important person in these parts boarded the ship. He was the Panama Canal Pilot. He would take us thru the many locks, and lakes. We were to transit from the Caribbean Sea to the Pacific Ocean.

Passing through the canal provided us a quite a theater with a verdant jungle on both sides, the sounds of monkeys, birds and smells of land. The ship's water hoses were turned full on, to the great delight of all concerned and this time it was fresh water. Some troops did their laundry while others just got wet and cooled off from the tropical heat as the whole ship of half-naked men watched the scenery passing by.

The whole trip had taken an entire day. And in the early evening, we passed under the famous and very high "Bridge of the Americas," at Panama City, and Balboa. Our Canal Pilot left us, and we entered the Pacific Ocean. By this time, as we sailed into the Pacific Ocean, all that was left of our passage were the last flickering lights of Panama City, rapidly fading away.

The shipboard life again became a routine, the seas were calm and the only sounds heard were the slight rumblings of ship engines coming from somewhere below the decks. The only unwanted sound was coming from the so called "bitch box" with its incessant announcements: "Now hear this!" followed by some imbecilic messages in English or Spanish. The detention cell remained empty, as all the troops turned out to be quite mellow, and a well-behaved bunch.

I quit counting days. It is better just let the days go, until, on the horizon appeared a mountain, rising straight up from the sea. This quickly became identified as Diamond Head, the famous Hawaiian landmark. A couple hours later, again with the help of Navy tugboats, we are taken into Pearl Harbor, just next to Honolulu in the US Territory of Hawaii, Island of Oahu.

This huge Pacific US Naval base was a homeport of the entire US Pacific Navy fleet. While in Pearl Harbor we are allowed to disembark from our ship, and really stretch our sea legs. The part of port where we were docked was designated as an "on limits recreation area" for us. The American Red Cross had set-up a canteen serving free hot dogs, donuts, and other goodies. In the afternoon a small stage was set up, and the Hawaiian musicians were playing beautiful Island music. This was followed, by grass—skirted, young women dancing the traditional island "Hula Dance." Some lucky fellows were invited to dance with the girls, much to the merriment to all. We remained in Pearl Harbor overnight and were ready to sail the next day at about noon. We were sliding out the harbor and went by the great row of US Navy sunken ships, including USS Arizona that is now a WWII National Monument commemorating that faithful day in December 1941, the beginning of the World War II.

Now we started the longest sailing part of our voyage from Hawaii all the way to Tokyo Bay in occupied Japan. Some were saying it was a 10-day journey. A few days later while still at sea, we reached the International Date Line, crossing the Equator at the 18th Meridian. There, in the best of tradition of the worlds' navies, we celebrated the paying of homage to "His Majesty King Neptune" at his domain. The ships' crewmembers were dressed like pirates and a small swimming pool like basin was set up and filled with salt water. Suspended half way and above the pool was a wide wooden plank. Then volunteers from of our contingent were made one by one to walk the plank and were dunked into the water. There were some "other things" that happen to these poor souls. Finally, after being fished out the water, they were received by His majesty King Neptune and given a fancy certificate. Great fun was had by all, especially the Colombians who enjoyed this theater most of all. They wanted to be dunked over and over again.

As the days went by the weather turned cold and waves were bigger than ever. The color of the ocean turned to deep blue, almost an ink blue. When we were some three days, away from Tokyo, the weather got really nasty. The ship was rolling and the ocean was roiling with immense white capped waves. The decks became empty. The troops mostly stayed down below in their compartments and in bed. The down stair decks in the living compartments were full of human puke. The latrines were full of human filth. There were no takers to daily meal calls and our dispensary was full of the sick. As for me and a few others that had spent some time past at sea, it was just another day of bad weather.

Finally the storm subsided some, and on the following day, the 32nd day since New York Harbor, we arrived at Tokyo Bay. Our arrival was good news, but then, for whatever reason, we remained outside the actual harbor and at anchor for the night. It was early next morning when the port Pilot arrived with several small tugs, that we were properly berthed to a wharf at Yokosuka Port, Occupied Japan. Standing on the wharf, facing our ship stood a solid wall of great hordes of Japanese stevedores, patiently waiting for orders to board. This was the first time in my life, that I saw what Japanese people looked like. For sure they were short in height, but a tough looking bunch, wearing some sort of semi-round rain capes around their shoulders, with outlandish canvas footgear where the great toe was separated from the rest of the shoe.

Directly following was the US Army Administrative personnel, who commenced with their processing procedures, separating us into two groups. The first group would disembark and transfer by land to US Army Camp Drake, close to Tokyo. The second group, which was much larger, stayed aboard for further sea transfer to the Port of Pusan, Republic of South Korea.

Those staying aboard were ordered to temporarily disembark the ship and proceed to a gigantic warehouse. Here the US Army Quartermaster people would issue us all sort of goodies. To the best of my recollection, it included all sorts of winter gear: winter underwear, woolen socks, sweaters, and down-filled parkas and field caps, shoepack boots (rubber lower part, leather lace up upper), winter down filled sleeping bags, woolen mittens, wool gloves, a small field pack and steel helmets.

Having finished issuing all this new gear, we were off to an on-shore dispensary, for medical examination which included a "short arm inspection." After completed, we stripped off all out clothes we came aboard with in New York. We were marched buck-naked to the shower unit. We showered in fresh hot water, and got dressed in our new winter clothing, and were declared ready for Korea winter, commonly referred to as "frozen chosen."

While all these things were happening, the weather outside turned nasty with light snow mixed with freezing rain. Although it was still early afternoon, everything turned grey. Outside the port, a proper winter storm was raging, with winds howling about the upper decks, making walking on the troop deck dangerous. The crew was busy with securing, and battening all deck equipment. As we departed from the safety of our harbor, I still remember the two Navy tugboats struggling alongside our ship. They were bobbing and diving in the high seas, at times showing their propellers. Finally, with a "mournful cry" of their horns, the tugs let us go. Off we went into a pitch-black night reaching the Port of Pusan (Busan) South Korea on the following night, thus ending a thirty-five days voyage.

The mood amongst the troops became solemn and everyone was deep into his thoughts. There were no conversations. All became their own private person. The realization of our purpose for being here, finally sunk in. The card games ceased and the horseplay was a thing of the past. We came here to fight and see what we were really made of. As we scanned one another, we knew that some of us would never make it back.

CHAPTER 6

Land of the Morning Calm

For us that served as infantry soldiers this was really a big misnomer. There was in fact nothing 'calm' about Korea. It was a tragic country fighting for its survival from the onslaught of communist forces who were determined to extinguish a flame of newly found independence from its former oppressors, the Japanese Empire. For a very long time Korea was known worldwide, as the Hermit Kingdom. We went there to fight for the freedom of this land. Some of us as volunteers, some because we were drafted by our government into the Armed Forces of our country, and were ordered to fight in this strange and unknown land.

Most of us had not even the slightest idea about Korea, and where you would look for it, on the world's map yet we, the U.S. Army combat soldiers and Marines were being sent there to fight. We were cold in the winter, and hot in summer. It seems we never had enough to eat, and forget about the luxury of sleeping. Initially our sleeping bags (fart sacks) were left over from the "Big One" (WWII) and they were thin blanket like things. We ate C-rations left over rations from WWII. I swear, some boxes had an imprint of the year 1940.

We were served and forced to consume this garbage in winter and summer and mostly unheated. Korea being a very mountainous country, we were to forever walk and fight up or down on "no name" hills. We lived, walked and sometimes slept in mud, rain, and snow. But then, this has been the life of infantrymen since time immemorial. Our predecessors, in previous wars, knew all about the hardship of wars. We were The American Infantrymen. Proud members of the so-called "Queen of The Battle." We carried shoulder-killing packs on our backs, plus our weapons, ammunition, and food with very inviting menus such as spaghetti with meatballs, or Ham and lima beans. We had not the chance, or luxury of changing our smelly and filthy clothes. Well, maybe once a month. In wintertime we were issued the "shoe packs." They have a bottom sole of stiff rubber and leather uppers. Should you forget and take them off in winter, and leave them outside your sleeping bag, the rubber would freeze.

A lot of us received letters from home. "Mail call!" was indeed something good and cheering. Maybe there would not be letter for you, so your Buddy would get one and share it with you. But there were those that did not get any letters at all.

I was in that category, but had a Buddy from Ponce, Puerto Rico. He was my Assistant machine gunner whose name was Pedro Araujo. His 18-year-old sister Naomi wrote letters to me They were nice innocent letters, telling me all about the City of Ponce, where the family lived. Nice home and family information., There was even an invitation that in the future I should visit her family. Then Pedro was killed., His remains were shipped home. I promptly wrote a letter of condolences to his family. I never received a response from his parents or Naomi. I guess with his death there also was the death to any future relationship with Pedro's family. They just had nothing else to say. To death us part. At this time I learned that in war, one must stay away from making friends, as this friendship May only last to the next day.

The GI. on your right or left although, should always be very important to you. Your own life is dependent on their life. Learn and use their nicknames, like as cities, states they came from, Tex, Cowboy, Chicago, Shorty, Bullet Head, and so on. As for people back in USA, we knew they kind of dismissed the whole thing as Truman's Police Action, and many young guys were busy draft dodging. The College Boys attending big name universities would not fight with the exception of our future officers attending West Point, Citadel, VMI, or other military schools. They definitely would be among us, the front line soldiers. For they were our leaders with the rank of Second or First Lieutenant which was the most dangerous rank In combat units fighting in Korea, be it US Army or Marines serving as Infantry Platoon leaders or Company Commanders. The graduates of West Point class of 1950 are a perfect example. More than half of these young men lost their lives in Korea. Folks back home considered the Korean war as an anomaly.

All folks at home only talked about the "Big One," WWII. Then there was always a big question in the back of our mind about the Koreans, on whose behalf we fought. To tell you the truth we did not know what was going on at the next Mountain or Valley, or the right or left perimeter of our rifle company. When we were sandwiched between "our boys on the right and the South Korean Army on the left, we inherently knew, that if the CCF (Chinese Communist Forces) attack, we would immediately be in "deep shit" not knowing if the South Korean troops would hold their position and not *bug-out*.

While in Korea we did not get a chance to see too much of anything. The most of Korea through the eyes of Infantrymen, was a view of utter devastation, with hundreds of Korean people moving from one place to other on foot as the front lines shifted, either to north or south. I feel they suffered the most. With the tide of war ever changing, the displaced Korean population were always on move, clogging the few existing roads, bridges and rail lines. This situation stayed so until early 1952 when the battle lines more or less were stabilized. The most of what I had seen and remembered of Korea, a view of a devastated country side, from a dirty window on a troop train from Pusan to the north and then from the back of a 2 1/2 (deuce and half) truck eating dust in the summer, or freezing numb from cold in the winter.

Then we had a short time in comfort in a squad size US Army tent at the so-called Forward Replacement Depot. Finally These same trucks would transport you to places where it was too dangerous for them go further., Then, on foot and marching in double column spread out. Spread out so one enemy round would not get you all. We marched on both sides of a road or trail or in open terrain until we met with Charlie (CCF) or NKA (North Korea Army) and then all hell would start. Especially with the Chinese and their bugles blaring and drums banging. and loud whistles. You see, they had no radios or field telephones. This was their only means of communication. It has been so since the time of Genghis Khan and it works fine.

Most of the American Infantrymen saw the war from a very short distance of no more than 50 to 100 yards. So close that you could smell Korean Kimchi (Sour Cabbage), or Chinese garlic. At these close quarters, death was always close to you, in a form of a bullet, grenade or mortar shrapnel. Either way it was always there for you.

Who were these American Infantrymen? Well first and foremost "the draftee's" were poor boys from the farms and cities of America. They were sent to Korea to fight this war, simply because they were unfortunate to be drafted, and not sent to Europe or Japan on military occupation duty, a soft, safe assignment, but to Korea. They had no say so, or choice to say, "No I don't want to Go." The remaining were a group of men, who joined the armed forces as volunteers before the outbreak of this war. They were mostly southern boys from the coalmines of Kentucky, West Virginia, or poor farm boys from Georgia and Alabama.

As far as I am concerned these poor boys from 'The Heart Of Dixie' made the best of the Marines and Army as "straight leg" or "[parachute" Infantry soldiers. As for myself, I represented a very small minority within the ranks. As a recent immigrant volunteer, who came and fought for a personal revenge and with a blind hate of everything communist and all that it represented, to whom dangers of war and personal deprivations meant nothing.

For me personally the Korean War was a tough fight. Much more so than the much later Vietnam war where I fought not, as an Infantryman, but as a Special Forces soldier. In Korea sleeping outside in the depths of winter was nothing new. Living first hand as a child for the full five years of WWII in Poland made a man out of me before the age of 13. The harsh training and discipline of the French Foreign Legion at age of 16. Prepared me well for my profession.

CHAPTER 7

Korean War, 1951 – Code of Honor

In combat, never leave behind your comrade in arms, your dead and your wounded. *"Au combat to agis sans passion et sans haine—Tu abandonnes jamais tes morts, ni blesses, ni tes arms. Code d'honneur du Legion Etranger. Par#7"*.

All the men of Company B, 1st Battalion 27th Infantry Regiment were awakened late in the morning of in the fall of 1951. Among our troops there was a feeling of complete euphoria, and a mental relief as we found ourselves in the rear of front lines at a so-called rest area. All of us were looking forward to a late breakfast, with lots of hot coffee and the enjoyment and ultimate pleasure of a hot shower at the field shower unit, which included an issue of clean clothing. Still the weather as found in the late autumn in Korea's hills was miserably cold. With last night's rain, and sleet mixed with snow and having spent the night sleeping on a cold frozen ground, we were stupefied and chilled to the bone. All this misery was due to our late evening arrival from the front lines and our rear rest area was not ready to receive us after spending last three weeks engaged in some tough fighting with CCF Chinks.

Some of us were still in our "fart sacks" as the men stirred and came alive. The entire company was summoned by platoons to the kitchen tents where we were feed. It was almost noon when the last soldier finished eating. We were now standing in formation pending assignment to our squad tent, with its diesel-fueled stove blazing, which was followed by a hot shower, and newly arrived winter sleeping bags. Suddenly all activities came to a full stop. We were left standing in the cold. Next we ordered by platoon and marched away from rest camp to the truck park area. We were lined up in single file and issued winter sleeping bags, moved to another line and issued cold C rations. This unexpected turn of events created a quite a row among all of us. People were swearing and generally raising hell by asking out right of their Platoon leader without much luck as to "what the fuck is happening?" Now we stood in company formation and waited for "what's Next?"

Well for a while nothing happened. Next, orders were given to stand down and wait. In the meantime, with tremendous resourcefulness common to American soldiers, there appeared from nowhere several 55 gal empty fuel barrels with large holes punched in, full of all sorts of things, like non-descriptive fire wood, cardboard rations & ammo boxes went into it, and *presto*, we had a roaring fire going for ourselves. Troops stood, bunched up and huddled, trying to figure out what was going on. As we stood around these wonderful things, and took advantage of being nice and warm facing the fire, while the back of you shivered with cold. Next call came from our Company 1st Sgt. for Platoon Sgt. leaders to report to Company HQ, for an immediate briefing.

Sgt. Stan is our Platoon Sgt. I am not sure what is his last name or if I could spell it correctly. He was called "Sgt. Ski" or "Sgt. Stan" or just "Stan" by other Sergeants. He went to the briefing and returned shortly with some really bad news. "We are going right back from where we just came from". Looking pissed, he hollered, to get ready to move out. Apparently the ROK (Republic of Korea) army unit which relieved us, was attacked in great strength by the CCF (Chinese Communist Forces) taking a great number of casualties, killed and wounded. The ROK were routed by CCF forces, withdrew, leaving a gaping hole in our front lines positions. Before the CCF would exploit this situation further our company was designated to counterattack as soon as possible and push the Chinks out of this position formerly held by us.

Sgt. Ski called me and other Squad Leaders for a briefing. At this time I was Squad Leader of the 1st Squad in Sgt. Ski's Platoon. I might mention also I was his countryman and mentor. It was well known to all concerned that in the absence of Sgt. Ski or upon his death, I was designated to take command temporarily. That is to say, whatever was remaining of a full strength Infantry platoon. I began to take a headcount in my head and quickly realized there were only 23 of us left. Forget about an Infantry Platoon being led by a Lieutenant.

The officers in that grade were always in great shortage and demand, but it seemed like they were always first to get killed or wounded. Therefore mostly Sergeants acted as Platoon Leaders. Our Company Commander was a young Lieutenant and West Point graduate. Young in age but very much respected and an excellent leader. There were only two officers left in our company. Orders are orders, and a soldier must follow them. Next came a hollered order, "By platoons to the ammunition trucks."

The weapons platoon first, 3, 2, and then us. As I said, there are not too many of us left but we, of the First Platoon, are now being reinforced by an LMG (light machine gun) crew of three, machine gunner, assistant and an ammo bearer. Plus, as an extra bonus, we are joined by four KATUSA soldiers (Korean Army soldiers attached to US Army). By my count our platoon is now reinforced with considerable firepower.

One LMG, three BAR's (Browning Automatic Rifles), and the rest of us armed with M-1 rifles. I grab an extra two cases of grenades and distribute it to members of my squad. The whole thing is like a bad dream to me; people move back and forth, commands are yelled out, and then in the late afternoon at, about 3:00 pm, all is quiet and getting dark. Finally after all this bedlam an orderly sequence of events unfolds. We are now moving to recently arrived deuce and half (2.5-ton) trucks. There is a long line of them, grimy dull green trucks, their drivers busily stomping the frozen ground, slapping their arms to keep warm, all anxious to get going. One by one, we mount the waiting trucks. It is not an easy thing to do, being fully loaded with personal gear and ammo. It is now very cold, and in the last light of a short late autumn day an orderly sequence of events unfolds.

We move out. We have been aboard trucks a long time now and have slipped our newly issued sleeping bags over our feet to keep them from freezing. It is completely dark now. There are no conversations, only cigarettes glow in the dark among us. We all are in a sort of freezing stupor, bouncing up and down on a frozen dirt road, the so-called MSR (main Supply Road). As I sit there this new situation is making me nervous. I want to urinate but do not want to pee all over myself. This is my second combat tour in Korea, and just months from the hospital in Osaka, Japan recovering from wounds. And I think, maybe I will get hit again.

Thoughts like this are common among soldiers. I'll bet all the rest of my squad thinks the same. We are now close to the front and truck lights are now turned off. You can hear the far off artillery and on the horizon see occasional flares in the distance. Finally we stop, and people are now ordered to get out of the trucks. Again it was easier said than done. Half of my people can hardly move much less jump out of the back of a truck, some five feet above the frozen ground. We all are tired and stiff from the ride. The great need to pee gets us going. Once off trucks we run back and forth to keep warm.

Then we are ordered to lock and load our weapons and put cigarettes out! We are ordered to pass in a single file, as our cooks serve us with hot coffee and something like toast with warm syrup over it. The whole thing tastes like shit, but who cares. In the meantime our truckers sound off, are pissed off and raising hell as some officer declared the road back was too slick with ice to travel back downhill. All are ordered to stay put until morning. The "lucky fucks". This is the closest they will get to the front, and they are pissed off?

Soon we begin to form into two columns one on each side of the road and we start moving by platoons. You can now hear a distant thumps of outgoing mortar rounds and overhead our artillery. No one talks now. We move silently forward into the night. It is now close to midnight as we arrive at the front lines, and get a short briefing followed by our Platoon Sgts. order to get into our counter attack positions and as close as we can at night. We must now cross the front line perimeter and advance into our predawn attack positions as quietly as we can. Each squad of each platoon advances to a pre-designated line of departure. We move silently and slowly and get down on the ground. All is very deceptively quiet now. In the darkness of the night and on the immediate front and approximate three hundred yards away, stands our objective.

The specific objective of our squad is the left quadrant of a semi-round berm of our former defense perimeter. When the order is given, we will walk up to it, jump in to its foxholes and kick the shit out of its occupants. That is if all goes well. In the meantime we are as close as you can get to this frozen Korean ground. No one moves and after a while the cold seeps through our clothes and your whole body feels like it is frozen. But one must prevail. I really feel I will not be able to get up. Then at 0500 hours sharp, all along our front, our preparatory mortar fire begins I unconsciously count, at least 6 tubes firing. Each accentuated by a loud thump.

Then our artillery jumped in firing high explosive and white phosphorous rounds, all of which creates kind of weird fireworks as all this shit is going right over our heads. The ferocity of all this appears to paralyze the "hill top Chinks" as there is hardly any incoming rounds. I feel somewhat secure, as we are lying there on ground in a well-defined defile in partially covered low scrub thicket with snow. It is still dark. The Chinks have not spotted us or just stayed low due to our mortar and artillery fire. Now one hour has passed since the beginning of indirect fire support. Now it got really damp and lying on the frozen ground becomes unbearable. We are awaiting assault orders. The upward terrain in front of us, now with the coming of first light, is shrouded in freezing fog. At this time terrible thoughts come to my mind.

An expectation of one of us coughing, or just getting up because you are physically unable to lie on ground any longer, or something stupid happening. And so while waiting to go, my mind moved automatically to soldiering, and I take mental inventory of my squad's armament. Each member is armed with their respective weapon with four bandoliers of ammo, a BAR team with two full belts of ammo plus two bandoliers slung across shoulders and each man with four grenades. The LMG (light machine gun) and crew, with two boxes of 500 rounds plus extra loose belts, stays in the rear and only moves forward after we are in enemy trenches with two rolls of common wire, a field phone, carried by an assistant Squad Leader. This grenade thing is really something I noticed while still at the ammo distribution point. My guys were always reluctant to carry more than two grenades, but this time demanding all they could carry.

The counterattack came at 0600 (Oh six hundred) hours sharp, at just about daybreak. Stan calls softly that it is time to go. Leaving our bedrolls and back packs in place, we're now ready to roll! We are up off the frozen ground and are now going up the forward slope, a ragged line of men, tired and cold to the bone, but now ready to take this fucking place from the Chinks. Our platoon is on the left flank of the attacking force while second platoon was on our right and the third platoon as reserve following us. Stanley had given me an unwanted privilege to lead the attack with my squad. We are nine Americans plus two Korean soldiers.

There is a complete silence as we move ahead, cold rain mixed with snow falling and visibility very poor. Most of my Americans are "draftees" straight off the streets of New York, or Tennessee hills. In the entire 1st Platoon there are only about 8 regular army soldiers. The truth is that the "Draftees" are not very keen on fighting this war. Can't say I blame them. My point team consists of 3 men. BAR man in front, with two Koreans deployed forward and advancing in a "V" formation at about 50 yards ahead of us. Suddenly our point is receiving automatic fire burst. The BAR man and Koreans, the most experienced men in my squad, keep their cool and go to the ground and hold their fire. A smart move as we now know exactly where the firing was coming from.

The top of our objective now appeared barely visible and was still shrouded in the morning's winter fog at about three quarters of the way up. The whole trench just above opens fire at us, but they are shooting high over our heads and are on full retreat now. They are just a few yards ahead of us. We all jumped right into their trenches and, in doing so, we took the left side of an inner perimeter trench and began clearing it of the enemy. The second and third platoons in support went to the right. With them went the communications people. In just that short time I found myself without communication with the other two squads.

The BAR team was leading as we enter the trench where the Chinks were caught by surprise. This was due to our fire discipline during our advance and good knowledge of the objective as we were its former occupants, just hours ago. Now inside we went for its three principal bunkers. As we ran into their trench, a "potato masher" grenade exploded right next to me. I heard a scream. It was one of our Koreans named Kim and the explosion lifted his body and blew him at my feet.

The BAR man opened up at Chinese coming up on us from above the trench, and two or three Chinamen came tumbling dead almost on top of us, the other following them ran back along the trench, with us in close pursuit. Around a curve in the trench we came upon a Chink machine gun position, still firing down the slope oblivious of our presence right on top of them. I stopped for a second, pulled a pin on a grenade, let go of the spoon, counted 1, 2, and then threw it into machine gun emplacement. Some immediately went down and the machine gun fell silent. A couple staggered out, although wounded, and managed to fire at us. They were quickly shot dead. However, in this mêlée, I immediately noticed Velasquez the BAR man fell to the ground dead, I shouted to one of our men to grab his BAR and ammo, and let's go!

We then began charging down the trench to reach the entrance to this bunker, built into a high portion of the trench. Noticing human figures standing at its entrance, one of us threw a grenade at them. One of the figures dropped, the rest jumped into the bunker. When we reached its entrance, with its door torn off its hinges, we were met with a hail of automatic fire from inside. We immediately threw several grenades. The explosion was in a confined area close to us and the blast almost lifted me off the ground where I was standing and wounded one of my men. To our surprise, out of this bloody hell hole a Chinaman comes out, his face covered with blood, with a PPSH (Russian submachine gun) in his hands, ready to fight. I shot him at a very close range, knocking him down right where he came from. Peering into the interior we found only bodies. No movement at all.

By now the early fog disappeared and daylight came. For a moment there was a minute of complete silence. Cpl. Brown and Pfc. Ernheim came up to me to see if I was OK. I guess I had blood of the Chink I had just shot, on me. We stood there for a moment. Grenades exploded all around us. All at once Ernheim was hit in both legs and his face. He tried to get up, said something and died. To our right and from the top, above the trench, a group of CCF soldiers came running and throwing grenades and yelling, "GI you die now." The second squad, already in trenches and close behind us, took care of them. We continued running for the main bunker, just ahead of us and reached its entrance without firing a shot. With its entrance door wide open we carefully peeked inside and found a bunch of chinks engaged in sorting out what looked like army rations of rice, evidently captured just twenty-four hours before from South Koreans.

One thing for sure they were either all deaf or completely oblivious of what was happening around them. Private Brown let them have it by sticking his carbine in the room and firing a full magazine, which we followed with a grenade. First screams from inside and then quiet. Next, out of nowhere, a small group of Chinks, (it was difficult to see how many) stood in the trench facing us without weapons that we could see, and with their hands up surrendering. Next I heard Pvt. Cavello screaming "grenades!" A loud bang and that was the last thing I heard and remember.

As I came to, I was laying on my back on a stretcher in a zippered sleeping bag. All around me were many wounded men. I was in a tent where the wounded were American. That was a relief. I hollered loud for somebody to find out what happen to me but then everybody inside was hollering or screaming. No one paid any attention to all of this. Now my attention was turned to my bandaged head.

My head hurt badly and I had continuous pain in both of my ears. I felt with my hands the rest of my body and found that nothing else hurt and there were no holes, I was OK. Slowly I got out of the bag and managed to stand up wobbly on my feet. With my head still bandaged and wearing a casualty tag, which upon reading it, found written, besides my name, serial number, a note saying "severe head concussion, undetermined head injury" and something else that I now don't remember.

And so with a casualty tag still pinned on me I walked out of the Battalion's Medical Casualty Collection & Evacuation Center. I walked up the road and hitched a ride in a supply truck to my company. I exported back to duty to First Sgt. Forrest Smith. He looked at me and immediately told me I belong in a Hospital, and that he is sending me back to Battalion's Aid Station for evacuation.

I convinced him to let me stay at company headquarters for at least overnight. I found out that the company was still deployed at the front, awaiting relief. Also, 1st Sgt. Smith told me that no way would I go back on the hill. Most important was news that we were successful in taking back our former position and thus stabilized the front. The 1st Platoon ceased to exist and the few remnants that survived were now reassigned to 2nd and 3rd Platoon as replacements. Our company had lost 16 KIA's (Killed in Action) and many wounded. Being so under strength and holding the recovered positions lost by Koreans, was sheer luck, and by the grace of God.

The replacements are under way. Sometime by the next night our whole Regiment was replaced by troops from the 40th Infantry. While just making conversation, 1st Sgt. mentioned that he was really sorry about Sgt. Ski, "you know, your Polack buddy, getting himself killed yesterday." Another remark was that his remains are still on the hill and all attempts to recover his body had failed because the Chink sharp shooters had zeroed in and they were determined to deny any further attempts of recovery. All of a sudden it hit me what this man was telling me. The pain in my head become unbearable and my body was numb with sorrow. I cannot describe the grief that fell upon me.

I left the company bunker and wandered around for a while to clear my aching head. It did not take long, however, to accept the horrible fact that Sgt. Ski was dead. I also realized that it would be up to me, no matter what, to get Stan's body back and have him buried. Now to my befuddled mind came the words from the past in French— *"Au combat to agis sans passion et sans haine—Tu abondonnes jamais tes morts, ni blesses, ni tes arms—Code de honneur du Legion Etranger. par#7"* which translates as; "In combat to act without passion or hatred—you never abandon your dead or wounded, or your arms. Code of Honor Legion Etranger par # 7".

I covered my bandaged head with my ear flapped winter hat flaps down, covering the bandages and wearing a poncho to cover the whole shebang, I marched out of company HQ area. Heading a short distance to the front of our company's 2nd Platoon positions. So far there was no one to ask me any questions, until a young 2nd Lt asked me if I was a replacement. I said yes, and kept on going. The second Platoon Sgt. was one of the regulars and hailed from New Mexico. His name was Fernandez but we all called him Cowboy. I went straight to him to tell him of my intentions of getting Sgt. Ski's body. He looked at me strangely and told me to follow him down the trench. He stopped and told me to look at 45 degrees to the right over the parapet. There, at some distance, laid the Sergeant's body, semi exposed in the newly snow covered field.

There was absolutely no cover of any kind between us and the Chinks. Nothing. Next, Cowboy was saying, "How in the fuck will you do it?" I said I don't know but asked him not to tell anybody what I had in mind and what I intended to do. But after a short while, it was he that came up with an idea. He said that the entire company on the front line would have a "Turkey Shoot" tonight at 2000 hrs. The purpose of a "Turkey Shoot", in military lingo, meant to have a massive firing of all weapons against an enemy front, with a dual purpose; one, to test our weapons and two, to draw out the enemy counter-fire in response therefore identifying and marking the location of their individual and crew serviced weapons.

He said that, at that time, if they don't shoot illumination flares and we don't shoot ours, "this, I will promise you, you might stand a chance to crawl out there, and bring him back. How you are going to do it, I just don't know, but I know you're a crazy Polack and you will somehow make it happen." Fernandez further warned me of a possibility that Sgt. Ski's body had been booby trapped. "Make damn sure you, don't get yourself blown up because then we really have a big problem". Armed only with my side arm and a coil of communication wire, I was ready. The Turkey Shoot started at exactly 2000 hours, right on the dot. We waited a few minutes for the Chinks flares and when nothing happened, he tapped me on my shoulder and said, "go get him."

I went over the top at exactly 2015 hours and started rapidly crawling towards the body. I immediately realized that if not for my Mexican buddy's sharp mind, I would have crawled all the way to China. He told me he would be firing his LMG in short bursts with every 6th round a red tracer, directly over my head and in direct line with the body. This led me directly to him. As we parted he wished me luck saying that the "body of an American soldier" in plain sight of his own troops was real tough on their morale, and further, should I became the second body out there in front of his troops that it would really piss him off. So I crawled as low to the ground as I could be guided by the red tracers from my friend's machine gun until I was next to the body. God help me should the Chinks decide to fire illumination flares.

He was frozen solid lying in a sort of fetal position, which made it hard for me to move him. Then, feeling for trip wires connected to his body and finding none, I wrapped doubled communications wires around his body and under his arms and began pulling his body, which would not move. It was frozen to the ground. Finally after "sweating bullets" I began to rock him back and forth and got him loose. I began dragging him slowly, back to our lines. This time simply following my own trail in the snow. In less than 15 minutes the whole thing was over.

As we reached the front of our lines, unseen hands reached out and pulled us over into the trench and that was it. Once inside I kissed the frozen dark blue of Sgt. Ski's forehead. There arose a great roar from American line, followed by a grand fusillade of automatic gunfire, mortars, the 57' and 75' recoilless Rifles, and the entire sky was lit with many flares. It was like the last salute for Sgt. Ski. The time was late December 1951. The place, an unnamed and unnumbered hill north of the 38 parallel, Korea. Staff Sergeant Stan U.S. Army was buried somewhere in Korea. Because he had no next of kin and no address in the USA, Stan did not have the privilege and honor of being an American citizen even though he died for this country.

I have never grieved any man, friend, family member or fellow Soldier's death like this. True, when my Father died, during the 2nd WW, my brother and I had to bury him. I cried, but then I was only a child. My grief for Stan did not happen right away. It kind of crept up on me. A few nights after his death, we were at the rear of the front line, in a rest area and it hit me hard. I went outside, walked away from troop area, sat down in a snow bank and let it all out. Then it was all over. I was promoted to rank of Staff Sergeant and recommended for a decoration of Military Valor. My war service in Korea continued.

I was now the new Platoon Sgt. New replacements were arriving and there was a lot to do. The new men were just off the troopship in Pusan, Korea. These young troops looked at me in strange way. You could hear them talking to others that I was one crazy motherfucker.

Special Forces

CHAPTER 8

Two Brothers – Worlds Apart

It was in the early autumn of 1958 and it was graduation day at Fort Holabird, the US Army Intelligence Center located near the City of Baltimore, MD. After some six months of intensive classroom training, six hours per day, five days a week, plus daily requirements of at least 2 hours reading of selected subjects pertaining to geographical, studies of strategic areas of interest to US military. At that particular time it was the Soviet Union, Communist China and their Communist Satellite States worldwide. For me it was an incredible experience and opportunity to learn about my adopted country's enemies, their military capabilities, and limitations.

The end of my studies marked a point in my military career with US Army Special Forces. I graduated to specialist status as a Combat & Strategic Intelligence Specialist. While awaiting my return to Fort Bragg, NC, I received special orders for immediate overseas assignment to South East Asia. In late autumn of the same year, on a sunny California day at Travis Air Force Base, just outside San Francisco, I was a young US Army Special Forces Sergeant First Class. Wearing civilian attire and carrying an Official red US passport with its appropriate visas, I boarded a US Air force Lockheed Super Constellation aircraft for a very long transpacific trip to southeast Asia with an intermittent stop at Hickam Air Force Base, Oahu, Hawaii.

Then many hours later at Johnson (atoll) Island, a Mid Pacific airstrip for refueling, the flight continued for a multitude of hours before reaching our final destination at Clark Air Force Base in the Philippines. While on the last leg of our flight and a couple hours before Clark, a young US Air force Lieutenant, a passenger in the front row seat, began to complain loudly of shortness of breath and chest pain. He fell out of his seat onto the aircraft's floor and lost consciousness. Then there was a loudspeaker announcement. "Is there a Doctor or a medic aboard to help?" There was no reply. An Air Force crewmember came forward along with yours truly. We took life vital signs, found no heartbeat and immediately both of us began CPR procedures. As I was giving him mouth-to-mouth resuscitation the other guy was pumping his chest. This went on it seemed, like forever. We would swap every few minutes, but never stopping. After some time passing and while we were at a point of exhaustion, and sweating profusely he came to and started breathing. His face color went from blue to normal. Some other crewmember came up with an oxygen bottle to help him breath. He was alive and returned to the world. After about an hour's flight to Clark Field we finally landed and an ambulance took our man away. I and my rescue partner got a loud Thank You from all the passengers and crew.

Off I went on a waiting bus, my ground transportation to NCO transient quarters to get some rest. As we were driving away an Air Force Military Police vehicle, with their blue light flashing and siren wailing stopped us. The Air Force cops took me and my baggage off the bus and ceremoniously took me straight to on-base luxurious quarters. My transient lodging was a suite reserved for VIP's. After a nice long rest of several hours I was summoned to the Flight Operations Center ran by MATS (Military Air Transportation Service) where the person on duty told me of my further air travel plans. I was scheduled to depart the next day aboard a so-called "Embassy Flight" operated and serviced by MATS calling on Than San Nhut airport in Saigon, RVN. Pochentong airport, Phnom Penh, Cambodia, plus other SE Asia capitals.

My destination was Saigon RVN, what appeared on my travel orders, to be my final duty station. I was informed by MATS Duty Officer, that a teletype message had been sent to MAAG Viet Nam notifying them of my arrival. The next day I arrived at Saigon where I was met by a young and amiable civilian man who identified himself as Dave Arsenault, a US Army Captain assigned to the US Embassy in the Republic of Vietnam as an Assistant Military Attaché.

He handed me another set of orders with my assignment not to MAAG Viet Nam, but to MAAG Phnom Penh Cambodia which was a bit confusing to say the least. We had lunch in downtown Saigon, where he shed some light on my assignment. He informed me that unofficially my assignment in Cambodia would be as an Operations Section Noncommissioned Officer with MAAG Cambodia as cover for my real duty assignment as an Intelligence Specialist and member of the US Army Attaché Office Intelligence Section accredited to three countries; Viet Nam, Laos and Cambodia. At that time, the Military Attaché Service personnel were assigned directly to the US Embassy in their respective host countries, and would have diplomatic immunity.

In this instance, the Military Intelligence personnel of the Military Attaché for Intelligence, with responsibilities for three Southeast Asian countries of the former French Indochina (Viet Nam, Cambodia, Laos), operated out of Phnom Penh Cambodia, under cover of US MAAG (Military Aid & Assistance Group). At that time it was only responsible for logistical military materials support for the newly formed Royal Cambodian and Laotian Armed Forces. The actual training of the Cambodian and Laotian Armies was still the responsibility of the French Army Training Group. After lunch Capt. Arsenault had me checked in at Saigon's famous French Colonial Era Hotel Continental for overnight.

The next day an embassy car took me back to Saigon's international airport for a short flight to Phnom Penh. My flight was aboard a US MAAG Cambodia military light aircraft. To the best of my memory it was a DeHavilland DH2 "Beaver" piloted by a US Army Captain whose name I don't remember. Upon arrival I was taken to my in-country quarters, which was the "Sunny Hotel" of Phnom Penh. Early morning, the next day, I reported for duty and met my boss and immediate superior, Col. William Lowe. My one-year tour commenced. While I was in Asia, the times were marked by foreboding uncertainty, danger and intrigue.

Suddenly this part of the world, double quick, became the world's critical strategic area to all concerned. In just a short four years of time and after more than 100 years, French Indochina had ceased to exist. There emerged three free nations. The Republic of Vietnam, two Kingdoms; Cambodia and Laos, and to the north, the Republic of Vietnam. Already under oppressive communist yoke, the so called People's Democratic Republic of Viet Nam. The Viet Nam's one people, with one language, and one history, now stood divided as enemies.

At the same time that I was getting my feet on the ground and beginning my duties assignment, half way around the world, in the country of my birth, Poland, 1959 was having its first days of spring in Warsaw, its capitol. These were dark and oppressive times in the People's Republic of Poland, which was sealed deep behind the Iron Curtain of Eastern Europe. Travel outside its well-guarded borders was strictly limited to only trusted and well-vetted members of the Communist party members and its elite cadre, its diplomats, and news media correspondents. All were carrying their PZPPR (Polish Workers Union Party) little red party membership book.

My brother Ryszard, now a proud member of PZPPR and its Diplomatic Corps, was getting ready to depart Poland for Hanoi to join the United Nations as a member of the newly organized United Nations International Control Commission (ICC). Its members were Composed of official representatives of the Free World (the West) and the so-called neutral countries like India, and the communist socialist countries; China, the Soviet Union and its satellite, Poland.

Sometime before his departure he was summoned by Polish government authorities to attend an extended Intelligence and Intel-craft crash course at the top-secret Unit #2000 in Warsaw. Here he met with two other traveling companions and on a sunny day in early April the trio departs from Okecie International Airport for a very lengthy air voyage to Hanoi aboard a Soviet Aeroflot flight by way of

Moscow. Upon landing in Moscow there was some sort of a briefing to which my brother Ryszard was not privy to.

They had a couple days to go sightseeing in Moscow, which was a pilgrimage to Red Square, and a visit to the Communist Hero's Mausoleum of Stalin and Lenin. After a few days they departed aboard a brand new Tupelov (Tu104) passenger airplane for the long air journey to Bejing, China. After a short stop over at Omsk, Soviet Siberia, they continued to the Siberian City of Irkuck, where they had a three-day delay as their Aeroflot airplane was grounded for mechanical reasons. They had to wait an entire week before leaving aboard a China Airline flight to Bejing. Again delays in Beijing for another week waiting for a weekly three-day long train departure to Hanoi. Upon arrival in Hanoi the three parted company. Ryszard remained in Hanoi for several months before being transferred to Saigon's Republic of Vietnam Polish ICC Delegation Offices, where he worked and lived until his rotation back to Poland.

The specific mission and general purpose of the ICC commission was to monitor the three newly minted countries of the former French Colony of Indochina, South, and North Vietnam, the Kingdom's of Cambodia and Laos. The monitoring mission was to prevent and control importation of equipment, materials of war, protect the integrity of their international borders in accordance with United Nations Charter and to monitor Human Rights abuse within all four countries by their governments.

Three designated UN members of this International Commission would be the country of India as the world's neutral faction, Canada representing the Free World and Poland representing the socialist & communist world. Under the direct auspices of the UN as a three Country Delegation, its members were assured free movement and travel within all countries involved and they manned many control points at borders of all the countries involved. The members of the Polish ICC delegation were all 100% vetted and consisted of the most trusted officers of Its armed forces together with members of the dreaded Internal Security Police (UB) and civilian members of the

Polish Intelligence Service serving under cover overseas as members of the Polish Press (PAP).

Ryszard initially was listed as an English Language Interpreter for the Polish ICC delegation that was assigned to the Hanoi Peoples Democratic Republic of Viet Nam. Sometime later he was transferred to Saigon and the Republic of Viet Nam, as a member of headquarters of the ICC Polish Delegation. While in Saigon his identity was that of a journalist. Later he was officially identified as "Conseiller de Delegation Polonaise ICC". Translating his title to English he was the "Secretary Advisor for Political Affairs, ICC, Saigon". His immediate superior at that time was the Chief of the Polish Delegation in Saigon, who was a high-ranking intelligence agent of the Polish Communist Government.

And so goes this incredible story of two blood brothers who together survived the World War II and who went out into the world in entirely different directions. Both sons of a Polish Hero of the 1st World War who, from 1918 to 1920, who valiantly fought as a volunteer in the Polish National Army Legion against Communists and its Bolshevik Communist Army. Our father was awarded the highest military medal for heroism in the field of battle, the VIRTUTI MARI, an equivalent to the "U.S. Medal of Honor". Our mother was the Daughter of a British Royal Navy (Retired) officer. Both of our parents were born into Polish hereditary nobility. We were a Polish family with deep roots going back to the 16th century and with a past history of honorable service as Knights to Polish Kings. My brother, who at the very young age of sixteen, and during the World War II, fought in the forests with the Polish Partisan Army AK (Armia Krajowa), but was somehow turned the other way and served the same people, who after WWII, enslaved Poland. In this entire time passing I have no answer as to "why?"

While I was serving my adopted country, the United States of America, as a soldier in Vietnam, in that same year (1958/1959) my brother served our enemy, International Communism, and of all improbable circumstances, in the same place and same time. I don't doubt that we walked the same Saigon streets and unknowingly passed each other. We ate at the same restaurants, mostly French owned, like *"Ma Cabane," "La Cigale" and "Guilliame Tell,"* drank at the same bars on *Hai Ba Trung Street and* danced to the music of a Philippine band at *"Tu Do Cabaret."* Was my brother a spy for the Polish Communist regime? I really don't know and never will. But as the saying goes "If you walk like a duck, look and quack like a duck, you must be a duck." I never had any personal contact with my brother since my escape from Poland in 1947 until 1989, some 42 years later. During my first visit to Poland I was looking for my mother's grave site in and around Warsaw. I heard some rumors that, at the same time as my visit, my brother Richard was out of the country and in Tripoli, Libya. Now we are talking about 1988—the same time when American Air Forces bombed Gaddafi, the "bad guy" of Libya." Richard was, in fact, representing the Polish government. Some say he was The Polish Ambassador to Gaddafi's Regime.

Talking about how close we got to one another and without knowing, I must relate to you an incident of long ago. While in Vientiane, Laos, sometime in 1959, and while having a nice dinner at "La Vendome" with and old Indochina acquaintance who was a real personality. He was a famous French pilot, and sort of a legend of that time. Capt. Carty, who flew for Air Laos. mentioned to me half-jokingly about meeting a Polish fellow at Club Cercle Sportif in Saigon (Club Cercle Sportif Saigonnais) who had a name similar to mine, and said something to the affect that maybe this fellow was my relative, ha, ha, ha. Surprisingly, after some 42+ years later my brother mentioned to me and showed me an old membership card to a French Club, "Cercle Sportif—Saigonnais."

CHAPTER 9

Funerals of Special Americans

Two funerals that I attended stand out in my mind as an honor bestowed upon me. long time ago, I was hospitalized at Walter Reed US Army Hospital in Washington, D.C. I was in the convalescent ward pending release from medical care after rather involved neurosurgery on my left arm and elbow resulting from wounds received while serving with a Special Forces unit in Vietnam.

Doing nothing but lying in my bed reading a book, I was approached by the Ward Master, Sergeant Lowell, who was accompanied by a Special Forces Sergeant 1st Class Chester Townsend of the 7th Special Forces Group from Fort Bragg, NC. Chester introduced himself and announced that he was on his way to Vietnam, assigned to detachment A-34 operating in the border area of Vietnam and Cambodia at a place called Chau Lang, the same area where I was wounded some three months ago. He informed me that his duties would be that of Intelligence Sgt. for Operational Detachment A-34. He came all the way from Fort Bragg to talk to me and actually to debrief me regarding the situation existing on the ground since he found out that I was there and assigned in the same position as Intelligence Sgt. some short time ago, before I was wounded and evacuated to the US.

I must mention at this time that Chester's travel to see me was done on his own time and at his own personal expense. I was tremendously impressed by his dedication, professional interest and resourcefulness to come to see me, the person best qualified to brief him on the military situation in this particular area of operations. Needless to say, a long conversation ensued. Actually I had managed to draw a detailed sketch of major terrain features, with its relative location of named villages, distances and all pertinent information pertaining to this area. I included the names of my indigenous intelligence assets working for us in the operation area in our intelligence efforts at that time. That was just some ninety days ago. He had taken copious notes of all information given by me.

I remember specifically briefing him about some areas in the immediate location of our "A-34" detachment camp and considered by me to be sympathetic to communist forces. These were some of the recently established villages, populated by ethnic Vietnamese in an area populated by a majority of Cambodian people, located close to the Vinh Tre Canal, which is the "de-facto" international Vietnamese-Cambodian border. I mentioned specifically, the village of Ba-Chuc where I survived a Viet Cong ambush. Chester thanked me profusely and started his long drive back to Fort Bragg. I would meet with him again under very different and sad circumstances.

I was back on duty in Ft. Bragg upon release from the hospital. It must have been no more than three months time and, while standing in the morning military formation, our company Sgt. Major made the following announcement: "Take note. This is an announcement to let you know that a member of our 7th Special Forces Group deployed in South Vietnam, Sgt. 1st Class Chester Townsend recently was killed in action in the Republic of Vietnam. He will be buried at his hometown in South Carolina. All off duty personnel are invited to attend his funeral. All persons interested in attending his funeral are to check the company bulletin board for details."

I later learned that Chester lost his life in the exact place where I had forewarned him of the dangers in the surrounding areas of the village of Ba Chuc. To the best of my recollection there was some transportation arranged for Chester's funeral but three of us went by car; me, my Green Beret lifetime friend, Andy Irzyk and a little guy that we used to call Pequeno. Just before the burial the funeral director started hassling Chester's widow about extra money for payment of the carpet and chair covers. We offered to pay for it, as we didn't want Mrs. Townsend to be embarrassed or have to spend her money. After the burial had taken place, it was about noon.

Before leaving town for a long drive back to Fort Bragg, we decided to stop by a local luncheonette for some "chow." Still dressed in uniform, the man behind the counter asked me what we were doing here. I said, that we came to bury and honor one of us who fought and died in Vietnam. He then asked for his name. When I told him he answered that he didn't recall anybody by that name living in Saluda. Then he asked where he was buried and I replied he was buried at the local cemetery. He answered, "You mean the Negro Cemetery? We have nothing to do with them. You soldier boys should not mess with our way of life. You just buried another nigger, that's all." He then asked us to leave and find another restaurant! I was so enraged by this that the expletives started to stream out of my mouth, which ended with me calling him "a fucking cracker."

Next thing that happen was the appearance of a uniformed policeman, who stated that "you soldier boys had better leave and get on your way from here or he'd charge us with disturbing the peace." We found ourselves in a "no win" situation. Those were the days that one could witness first hand racial prejudice against black folks. I only wanted to pay my respects to an American Special Forces man who fought for the country of his birth, and paid for it with his life.

After some forty-seven years this incident still bothers me. As for South Carolina, and the city of Saluda, I know times have changed. Things are better and different now but in my mind the past still lingers. Chester, "I apologize for the people who done you wrong." In my mind you are an American Hero!

Recently I learned that the VFW Post in the town of Saluda, South Carolina has been dedicated to Chester. Post 6561, Chester D. Townsend Post, Saluda, S.C.

The second funeral was of international importance and was watched by the whole world.

It all began on a sunny day in late November 22, 1963, when the President of The United States and Commander-in-Chief of the US

Armed Forces, John F. Kennedy left his hotel in Dallas Texas. He was to attend to his official scheduled appointments on this tragic day. While on his way to God knows where, he was felled by an assassin's bullets. The estimated time of this horrid event was at midday. The news spread immediately all around the world. At this moment the world stood shocked to its foundation in fear and disbelief. This horrible happening was not believed by many people in United States and overseas. Yet, hard truth prevailed. Our President was fatally woundedw and in fact was dead.

At just about the same time, some thousand miles away in Fort Bragg, a large military base in North Carolina, I was at my assigned duties in a small office room at the Headquarters of 7th Special Forces Group, Fort Bragg N.C. at the so called "Smoke Bomb Hill."

Sometime in the afternoon, all radios were blaring with the sad news of the death of our Commander—in—Chief and it spread like a wild fire over the entire Fort. All activities came to an abrupt stop. I having been recently released from Walter Reed US Army Hospital in Washington, DC., where I had been treated and recovering from multiple wounds to my left arm and elbow caused by grenade explosion while deployed in the Delta Region of Viet Nam. I remembered that just about one year ago from today's date that I had been privileged and honored to be standing in military formation in the same "Smoke Bomb Hill" parade grounds, listening to President Kennedy address us.

He said we, the "Special Forces Soldiers, will soon be the principals in the fight with the world's oppressors of freedom." During his speech he mentioned our recently approved, by him, "Green Beret," worn officially from this day on. He said to us, "the Green Beret is a symbol of excellence, a Badge of Courage and a Mark of Distinction in our fight for Freedom."

The next time I was to be in his presence, was when I stood as a member of the "Death Watch" detail in the White House East Room, sometimes known as Blue Room. We stood a night and day vigil over his remains. The President lay in a closed bronze casket draped with the American flag. His immediate family and members of the Catholic clergy surrounded him. President Lincoln had lain in the same room some 100 years before.

In the late morning of Saturday, November 23, 1963, Col. William "Pappy" Grieves, and Sergeant Major Francis F. Ruddy of the US Special Warfare Center notified us all, that the US Army Special Forces were to be the official Honor Guard at President Kennedy's funeral services. The family and widow of the late President, Mrs. Jacqueline Kennedy, personally made that request.

Special Forces Honor Guard chosen to participate in the funeral of President John. F. Kennedy. Albert is in the middle of the 1st row.

This was a very unusual request, as all five services have "Special Ceremonial Honor Guard Units," permanently stationed in Washington, DC. and they are tasked with this duty. We understood that all heads of the five branches of services were opposed to this request. But never the less, Mrs. Kennedy's wishes were granted.

The details for our commitment to this special duty assignment had many elements. At noon, at another formation, each of the Special Forces Group's was asked to provide a number of volunteers.

To the best of my recollection, we who volunteered were vetted as a prerequisite to be chosen. We were asked a series of questions as to being a combat veteran of WWII, or Korea and about our awards and decorations. The rest of the prerequisite questions, I do not remember. Except that preference was given to most combat decorated senior sergeants. The selection took just about one hour. The number of selected personnel was 42. We would serve as members of Special Forces Presidential Funeral Unit. In addition, Colonel "Pappi" Grieves, and Sergeant Major Ruddy were designated as the Special Forces Liaison Officers with the Kennedy Family.

We were to travel to Andrews Air Force base outside Washington, DC. Each member was to wear fatigue uniforms while traveling. Each member would carry a complete set of Class "A" uniform, jump boots shined to a high gloss, our "Green Beret" headgear, a pistol belt, and an M-1 rifle. All of us had two hours to get all things together. At approximately 2:00 pm we departed Fort Bragg aboard an Air Force aircraft for Washington, DC. Before our arrival at Andrews AFB, four members of our group were ordered to get into class "A" uniforms, to be picked up immediately upon arrival and taken directly to the White House. I only remember two of the men: Sergeants First Class Boyette, and Ben "Jaws" Taylor.

Col. "Pappi" Grieves and SSM Francis Ruddy accompanied them. The rest were taken to Fort Myer, and lodged at the military barracks for overnight. It was Saturday night. On Sunday afternoon, if I recall correctly, sometime in early morning I was on duty at the White House and later returned to Fort Myer. The President's body was moved to the Rotunda for public viewing. Having slept a couple of hours, I awoke to see on the barracks television, the shooting of Oswald by Jack Ruby. I was not involved in any other kind of activity for the rest of the day.

On Monday, 25 November 1963, the entire Special Forces Contingent was moved by bus to the outside of the Capitol's Rotunda building. As I recall, four of our members were selected to march alongside the horse drawn caisson carrying the flag draped casket of our President. The rest of us, were formed into a marching unit led by Maj. Hefti. We followed the caisson, and marched to the steps of St. Matthews Cathedral. After a short religious ceremony, we resumed our long march following directly behind the Cortege consisting of a horse drawn caisson bearing the flag draped body of the President. This was followed by Black Jack, a rider-less horse as a symbol of a lost Leader, led by a single soldier, a member of the 1st Battalion, 3rd Infantry, the Nations' Honor Guard at Ft Myers Va. Directly behind was the US Army Special Forces Contingent and last the detachment of the Scottish Black Watch. The long funerary march continued from St. Matthews Cathedral, over the Arlington Memorial Bridge, across the Potomac to Arlington National Cemetery.

At a point just short of the burial site, the Cortege stopped. The Special Forces Contingent broke ranks and moved forward forming the "Cordon of Honor" along the footpath of a green slope leading directly to the grave. There we stood at "Present Arms" at ten feet intervals on both sides of the footpath leading to The President's final resting place. This was our final salute to our beloved Commander-in-Chief.

Here we were to witness a great many of the world's leaders as they passed in front of us. Joining the Kennedy family were kings, princesses and presidents from nearly all the countries in the world. Personally I was impressed mostly by two of these: first, a small stature of a man, with the incredible name, and title, His Majesty Haile Selassie. The King Emperor of Ethiopia, claimed to be a direct descendant of Queen of Sheba, who, to me, actually looked very much a royal and carried himself with a great dignity. The second, was Charles de Gaulle, President of France, who actually stopped in front of me and asked me to explain the meaning of the four rows of ribbons/decorations worn on my uniform. As all passed before me, I was very much impressed by being a living witness to see in person most of the World Leaders of my time. And witnessing the official graveside ceremony followed and attended by the Kennedy family and all the international dignitaries. For us there would not be a more moving moment.

When, upon termination of official ceremonies and after the eternal flame was lit at the gravesite, there came for me a most unforgettable, personal, and poignant act. Sergeant Major Francis F. Ruddy who, as a part of Kennedy Family entourage, had taken his green beret and placed it next to a family bouquet on the grave of our President. We of the Special Forces Contingent remained at gravesite for a while, mingling with family members. Then upon order by Sergeant Major Ruddy we fell into ranks and marched off . . . . to fight.

Lauderdale man guarded JFK's coffin

By NANCY SAN MARTIN
Staff Writer

FORT LAUDERDALE — Albert Slugocki isn't a flamboyant man.

Slugocki

His military memoirs — 15 medals, pictures from Vietnam and a letter summoning Slugocki to the White House to watch over President John F. Kennedy's coffin — are tucked away in a bedroom at his Fort Lauderdale home.

The summons became the highlight for a soldier who served 21 years in the U.S. Army.

That memory unfolded 30 years ago today.

"I remember sitting in the hall where we had just had lunch when someone, a sergeant I think, walked

■ Where were you when JFK was assassinated? **1D**

in and said the president of the United States had been shot," said Slugocki, 62. "Of course, all of us turned the radio on full blast. But there were no details.

"I remember being very frustrated," he said. "I wanted to know: Was he killed? Was he wounded? What happened? Where?"

The answers came two hours later. The president was dead. And the base, Fort Bragg in North Carolina, was put on alert.

Later that afternoon, Col. William "Papi" Grieves walked into Slugocki's room with a message: "The Kennedy family has requested that special soldier forces bury the president," Grieves said. "I'd like to ask you to volunteer."

Slugocki was No. 12 on a list of 43 soldiers chosen for the honor. The next day he went to Washington, D.C., and was among four picked to guard the coffin in the Blue Room at the White House.

The job was called "Death Watch." The assignment entailed standing at attention, rifle in hand, for 30-minute intervals.

The president lay in a dull metal coffin set in the middle of the room. The top was closed. There were no flowers, no sense of splendor.

"It was very serious, very sophisticated," said Slugocki, who joined the Army in 1950, five years after he escaped from his native Poland

South Florida Sun Sentinel,
Nov. 26, 1993 Newspaper article about
Albert Slugocki as an Honor Guard
At the funeral of President Kennedy

CHAPTER 10

Berlin – The Good Life & Movies

It is late winter now and snow is falling. I am waiting for the weather to clear, which looks very unlikely. In another couple of hours we will be unable to fly out of here from the International airport called Tegel, which is in the French Sector of West Berlin. I am sitting in the airport's departure lounge drinking. It's getting late and our flight was now delayed nearly three hours. There are many people waiting for the weather to clear so we can start our journeys to where ever that may be.

I am going all the way to JFK airport, New York. My flight from West Berlin will take me to London's Heathrow airport, a couple of hour's flight. Then the real voyage begins all the way across Atlantic to the good old USA. I am on my way back all the way to Vietnam with a thirty days' leave squeezed in between, in Providence, Rhode Island, where I would be a guest of my good friends, Wilk Wilkerson, and his wife Joanna.

**Albert on special duty in Germany
On a S.F. clandestine assignment.**

I am looking through the lounge windows at a grey dark late afternoon outside and am thinking about my fourteen-month tour with a highly classified assignment as Special Forces intelligence operative with the USSF Detachment A in West Berlin and think of the parting words of my commanding officer Maj. "Bouncing Betty" Johnson. "Albert, we all wish you luck. But think about your luck. This will be your third combat tour in Vietnam. Weigh your chances."

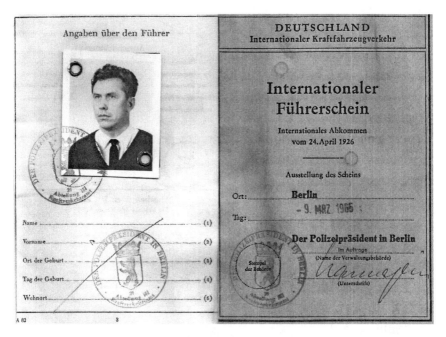

Berlin, Germany. I.D. and driver's license is issued to clandestine intelligence operatives by "Der Polizei Preasident". No name or address—just a photo.

Further he said, "I hate to lose you. Life in Berlin has been good to you, You could have stayed here with us for at least two more years." Maj. Johnson and I had known each other Since Laos 1959. The "Bouncing Betty" nickname had nothing to do with Major's gender. It happens that the Good Major while in Laos, had stepped on an antipersonal mine commonly referred to as *Bouncing Betty*, which for some strange reason failed to explode. As my mind wanders, I thought of all the wonderful people I knew, my military SF Contemporaries and my German friends.

While in West Berlin I made a maximum effort to integrate

myself with all these folks initially because of my clandestine work assignment to successfully blend in with local population. But in doing so, after time my relationship with local Berliners became very personal in nature and more so since language was not a barrier with me. In West Berlin and among its people, I felt very much at home. While in Germany there came a time that could have changed an entire course of my life. It all had its start with meeting some different and unusual people at one of my hangouts, a bar cabaret named "Madrid." It was here that I had a privilege of meeting a famous English Movie Director Terence Young of Pinewood Studio's England, and his girlfriend Nadia Gray.

Albert Slugocki as a language advisor to movie director Terrence Young.

It so happened that Terence was in W. Berlin working on directing a movie for ABC German Film Studios. He and Nadia came early and well before the actual shooting, to get the right feeling and catch flavor of this very unusual place full of intrigue and uncertainty. A city under siege located deep within the communist East Germany, divided between four world powers, with four different administrative sectors. Three of which were by Western Powers: Great Britain, France, and the United States. The fourth sector, as a part of Russia's Iron Curtain, further divided by the ill-famed Berlin Wall, had minefields and armed east German and Russian guards.

Terence and I would normally meet nearly every day and spend the day riding its underground U-Bahn and S-Bahn rail lines visiting different neighborhoods, parks and city attractions. He would take all this information like a sponge to water and make notes. But above all wanted to know all about me, which all his questioning regarding my person, I would somehow try to avoid. Finally I told him that since I cannot tell you the truth, what is the point to lie to you, just let it be. He, being an intelligent person, finally gave up and we got along just fine. One of his favorite places was a bar named "Korale" located on a street by the name of Uhlanstrasse and off Kufursterdamm. This place open at 10:00 PM gets really going after a midnight and closes at daybreak. I am very much of a regular and feel at home in this place. Its owner, Simone Korda, is an Austrian Jew of an uncertain age. Her lover is a Polish man without documents.

Korale is that place where everything is just fine. It comes alive after midnight and the clientele is everything from pimps, first-class whores, actors, actresses (real and imaginary), members of the former east Prussian nobility, high time hustlers, spies and counter-spies and master pick pockets. The amazing thing is that whatever your profession is from above menu, once you are inside Simone's salon you are safe and secure. No one is abused, robbed, or hustled. Never, during my time that I frequented this wonderful place, was there any trouble.

Everybody was expected to be on his or her best behavior. Terence quickly became a cause célèbre simply because of his film making fame. Terence and I were always surrounded by very beautiful women even in the presence of Nadia. And our drinks were happily paid for by Simone or somebody else. For all three of us, we became real bon vivants at a Free Loader's Ball. After about a week of all of this I accompanied Terrence to the offices of ABC Studios and it was suggested by him to one of the studio's executives to use my services as a language coach.

And so I was immediately hired for the production time period of a film named "The Secret Agents" which was going to be produced in Italy and in West Berlin A sort of cloak and dagger bullshit thing with real world famous actors. James Mason came from England, Terence from Pine Studios in London, and Robert Ryan and Henry ("Call me Hank") Fonda from the USA. From France a wonderful actress by the name of Annie Girardot, from West Germany came Mario Adorff, and a real "bug-eyed weirdo" by the name Klaus Kinski. Actor's wise, it was a full house. Naturally I had to report all of this to my boss, Maj. Johnson, and Sgt. Major Pilkington. "Unbelievable" said Maj. Johnson. Sgt. Pilkington was very anxious to find out how it all happened, and gave me two weeks off and marked it down as "on duty training."

My services as Russian Language Coach, was very limited to only two sessions with Hank Fonda at his hotel room in the Berlin Hilton. He was only interested in the Russian accent and after two lessons his Russian accented English sounded very convincing. After that I became a sort of "Steppin Fetchit" man for Terence. Of course I invited the whole cast to Simone's Bar. Maj. And Mrs. Johnson were formally introduced to all these lovely people at a cocktail party given by the French film producers at a famous Kempinski Hotel Golden Room, on Kufursterdamm in Berlin.

During the film production we were shooting a scene on location at Tempelhof Airport It was late evening and one of the minor German actors managed to piss Terence off. He was escorted off the set. Terence then spoke to Robert Ryan and asked him "How about Albert—do you think he could do these few lines?" Ryan said "Let's try it". And presto, I became an actor on the first take! In another few days of shooting, we were finished. There was a big party and then everyone went home. I got a big surprise as ABC paid me $ 975.00 Dollars in salary. In about two months' time I received a telegram from Pinewood Studios in Great Britain.

Albert Slugocki in a "walk-on" part in the film with movie star Robert Ryan.

Mr. Young requests your presence in Casablanca, as his assistant for production filming of "Station Sahara." Fourteen days on the set. Off I go to see my commanding Officer, good old Maj. Johnson and I ask him for permission and leave time to go to Morocco. This time, however, Maj. Johnson good naturedly and with a smile asks me "well Sgt. Slugocki, do you want to continue to be a soldier or you want to switch careers and be an actor?" (I think he said a movie man). It's a tough question. I immediately tell him, "Soldier is what I am, and will be."

He then calls the Sgt. Major and tells him to issue me a two-week International ordinary leave. So off I go via Frankfurt aboard Iberia Spanish airline on direct flight to Casablanca. Upon arrival at the Mohammed Airport in Casablanca I retrieved my luggage and immediately was mobbed by a great many hustlers and taxi drivers. But out of all this bedlam I was almost immediately grabbed by a skinny little fellow wearing a red fez, also named Mohamed, who had a little sign with my name on it and was, by his own admission the owner of a beat up French Citroen car. Since it was early morning, he insisted on immediately driving to our destination, the Moroccan City of Ouarzazate (War za zat).

It was a ride of some eight hours from Casablanca airport. Ouarzazate was then known better as Movie City, was unknown to many, and was located at the end of the civilized world. The city supposedly was built by some Hollywood Mogul in 1960 and now was being used by Americans and European filmmakers as a perfect desert location for many of their films.

With its cheap labor and exotic location, it offered a perfect setting just south of the high Atlas mountains in a barren desert plateau. The city, with its ancient casbah and souk, represented a real setting straight out of the 19th century. I was told by my driver that the entire city was now owned by Atlas Film Studios, which was located just on the outskirts of town. We arrived well into the evening after traveling on some really rough roads and checked into a very nice hotel by the name of (I think) "Hotel la Perle du Sud." I had something to eat then went straight to bed.

The next day after breakfast, I went searching for Terence Young at Le Berbere Palace Hotel and found him drinking his morning tea. We talked. He had a very small role for me, almost without spoken lines, but offered me a personal acting exposure in a production of a film to be entitled "Station Sahara." The part was that of a bad guy that kills a good guy and then good guy's friends whack me, the bad guy. In about three days we went to the already built set and commenced working. I had a coach teach me how to fall down and learn other technical aspects of acting. But I did what I was told with minimum takes and received good grades from the cinematographic crew. After about one week of shooting I was paid and was anxious to get back to Berlin before expiration of my leave.

All of these events were surreal to me. Africa was another world, an exotic place and the good-life! A couple nights before leaving, I met with Terence, who really put me between a rock and a hard place with an outright offer of a real honest to goodness role in a forthcoming film titled "Lord Jim." He told me, that I am wasting my time being a soldier or spy or, whatever the fuck I was doing for a living. All this unhinged me. I went to bed unable to sleep and stayed awake until morning. But somewhere in late morning, taking the 14+ years of military service into consideration, I decided the best thing for me would be to stay in the army and serve my country. Upon hearing of my decision, Terence, who served with great distinction as a British Officer with the rank of Captain of an Armored Corps and had participated in the Normandy invasion in 1944, informed me that somehow he knew that this would be my decision. Above all he said that he appreciated my friendship, my personal conduct, and demeanor, and bade me farewell. As he was very busy with his work, we never again had a chance for a further conversation. As a quick goodbye, but in a very special way, I saluted him and he, in a proper military manner, returned my salute. I left for Casablanca and the long journey back to Berlin.

On a personal note, I found Terence to be a man of great intelligence and very much the proverbial English gentlemen with no bullshit attitude about life. After WW II, he became a successful filmmaker and director. Terence directed the first and second of the James Bond films, *Doctor No* and *From Russian with Love*. As *the xhighly respected* man that he was, it was rumored that prior to his distinguished military service, he was a member of the British Intelligence Service, the famed MI5. Perhaps this was a consideration when he was selected as the director for the cold war era films.

Sometime during the long trip back to my base, I decided that I should not stay in Berlin or engage in the so-called *"Cold War"* which was all cat and mouse bullshit. I decided to go back to the real fighting in the mountains and jungles of Viet Nam. That's where my Special Forces Soldier's skills were needed most. And so upon my return to Berlin I immediately put in an official request for transfer to the Republic of Vietnam. This was almost immediately approved and I'm on my way to join with my Special Forces Brothers, to do what I know the best.

Vietnam

CHAPTER 11

The Ghosts of Duc Lap – 1966

The time was spring 1966. Having arrived at Than San Nhut International Airport in Saigon, I was met by Maj. Terry, an Old SF hand who immediately informed me that there is absolutely no need to report to headquarters at Nha Trang. All arrangements have been made for my in-country assignment as an SF Field Intelligence Operative in and out of Vietnam and Cambodia. The unit commanded by Major Terry was officially known as Operational SF Detachment B-57 with operational base headquarters in Saigon, in the so-called "Safe House."

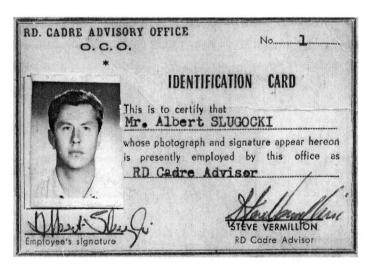

I.D. card issued to para-military operatives while on clandestine assignments for the C.I.A. in Vietnam.

My working partner was to be Master Sergeant Paul Sobol who was well known in our ranks as an outstanding, experienced Special

Forces Operative. As a team we were to be engaged in a clandestine operation to be launched into Cambodia's sparsely populated wild jungle area of Mondul Kiri Province, which bordered directly to the East of Vietnam's Province of Darlac. The Mondul Kiri Province of Cambodia was covered with impenetrable jungle forest in a remote area laying east the Mekong river and sparsely populated by half naked natives still practicing the slash and burn method of agriculture. This entire province had only one old paved French colonial road to Cambodia's Capital city of Phnom Penh. Mondul Kiri remoteness, however, hid two very important strategic objectives.

First, it recently became a very important infiltration route into Vietnam by North Vietnam's communist forces, soon to become famous worldwide as "Ho Chi Minh Trail." Secondly its jungle mass hid and sheltered a number of Rhade Montegnard tribesmen, formerly of the Vietnam highlands who, had revolted against the Government of South Vietnam forces in 1964. Their failed revolution was led by their hereditary Chief named Y-Bham. It was estimated to be 2500 men in strength, fully armed and ready to fight another day. Together with their families they made their way across the border into the depths of this remote region of Cambodia. The name of this failed revolutionary movement was FULRO. Members of FULRO were originally trained, armed, and even led by US Special Forces in the war against the communist forces of Vietcong in the highlands of Vietnam. These tribesmen had established a very close relationship with their American leaders and mentors, who lived and fought alongside them and always taking their side in their very strained relations with Viet's, who always discriminated against them as their inferiors, and referred to them as MOI or savages.

The original plan of action was for Paul and me to infiltrate into the Mondul Kiri area and make contact with our former allies the FULRO, and then somehow induce them to cooperate with us in Mondul Kiri by collecting intelligence information and armed interdiction against North Vietnam's forces of infiltrators along the Ho Chi Minh trail. The whole thing to me sounded a bit crazy and made me a bit uneasy about success of such an undertaking. Personally, I had a pretty good grip on South East Asia and more specifically the former French Indochina. I had spent some 18 months in this area in the years of 1959 and 1960 and then again in 1963 when I was assigned to the Office of US Army Attaché for Intelligence as an operative between the countries of Phnom Penh, Cambodia, Vientiane, Laos, and Saigon Vietnam. In the winter of that year I also was assigned as a Special Forces intelligence operative.

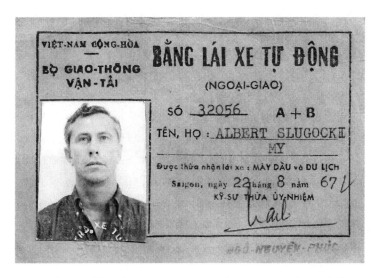

I.D. card issued by Vietnam to para-military operatives while on clandestine assignments for the C.I.A. in Vietnam.

By traveling continuously between these three countries I had good general knowledge of these countries. My knowledge of the French language helped also. The down side of the whole situation was that the Cambodian Ruler, Prince Norodom Sihnouk, in 1963/64, had thrown Americans out of Cambodia. Therefore no matter what cover we would use as an Americans in attempt to travel by road or river within Cambodia, we would meet with failure and maybe personal demise.

Having said that, should my superiors decide to use my services in this mission, other proposed operational aspects immediately scared me. It was proposed that only I would enter Cambodia from Bangkok, Thailand, as a third country national with a phony Polish People Republic passport and with all of my personal documentation prepared for me by an unknown agency of the US Government. I fought with all my might against this idea. While in Bangkok we met with some DIC (Defense Intelligence Agency) people in Bangkok, and were lodged in one of the smaller hotels while awaiting the arrival of Maj. Terry. Upon his arrival, briefings sessions commenced shortly thereafter and with strong recommendations from the DIC people, the entire idea of going to Phnom Penh, Cambodia was scrubbed.

Shortly after we returned to Vietnam under the cover and documents identifying us as employees of a large US Construction Company, Brown & Root, which at this time, was working on a variety of construction projects in Vietnam and Thailand. We both checked in at a hotel and waited for orders. The whole mission began to stink. Paul informed me that he is sick and tired of all this crap and wanted out. He quickly accomplished all this by getting in touch with Col. Pappy Grieves, now retired, was now employed by US-AID, and was heading a new project, the organization and training of Vietnamese Field Forces Police and he suggested Paul join him, as a Civilian Paramilitary instructor. Paul already had twenty years of service and could retire. Pappy immediately pulled some strings got Paul retired from active service.

During our time together Paul and I became friends, and the loss of his company kind of unbalanced me. I was now alone living in a hotel in downtown Saigon waiting for God knows what until one day a civilian accosted me in the hotel's elevator and ID himself a Capt. Snyder of US Military Intelligence Unit attached to Special Forces. It appeared that MI (Military Intelligence) had taken over further planning of a now Secret Mission named FULRO CONTACT and although B-57 continued to exist my new CO was to be Maj. Murray.

I also was instructed that the next day I was to check out of the hotel, proceed to an address in Saigon and report to my new commanding officer for further instructions. When I arrived I was told to surrender my B&R construction outfit's documents and was told to await orders to put me back in uniform as a Master Sergeant in US Army Special Forces. All this took a while, but once all orders and documents were in order I received a very detailed mission briefing from my new masters.

My new mission briefing turned out to be very professional and Major Murray came through to me as a well-versed professional intelligence officer. The mission remained the same, but the implementation was completely different from original plan. It was determined that the insertion would be launched from a Special Forces detachment site located almost on the border of Vietnam and Cambodia and directly opposite to Mondul Kiri Province. It was to be assigned a couple of indigenous assets and as a three man team be deployed on foot over the fence from the close vicinity of the SF detachment site at the newly opened SF camp named Duc Lap, some four kilometers from the Viet and Cambodian border.

Upon hearing the name and location of this camp I immediately recognized this area and its past significance. Just two year before I was located in the same area. No more than six kilometers from Duc Lap, was a former location of a Special Forces detachment in a place called Boun Sa Par. In 1964, a horrible atrocity had taken place there. The revolting FULRO Montegnards, trained by the Special Forces team, have ordered the American trainers to leave. Once they were gone, they gave an ultimatum to Vietnamese counter parts of the American team (LLDB), to lay down their arms, and depart from camp. The rest is kind of hazy, but it came about that some shots were fired (by whom I don't know) and some of the Viets were shot. At least eight remaining Viets were taken prisoner, brutally murdered, and thrown into the depths of the camp's latrine.

The perpetrators of this crime were primarily Rhade tribesmen of the FULRO revolutionary movement. Right after this incident, the Montegnard soldiers, for a time, waged an open warfare against Vietnamese, however soon to be defeated. The remnants of this force of some 2,500 in strength, well trained, armed, and together with their families under their indigenous commander named Y Bham, crossed into Cambodia, to lick their wounds, regroup and fight sometime in the future.

Their location in Mondul Kiri was known to us but not to our Vietnamese counterparts. Again our mission was to contact this group and somehow entice and convince Y Bham and his people to use his forces as and interdiction force to stop, or at least impede, the flow of North Vietnamese supplies along the so called Ho Chi Minh Trail. A very dangerous undertaking since it would definitely piss off our Allies, the South Vietnamese Government, and create an international problem with the now neutral country of Cambodia.

Prior to departure from Saigon, through Ban Me Thout to Duc Lap, I was introduced to two of our assets that would accompany me across the fence. The first was a Rhade tribesman, Mr. Char Ang Nhe. He was a tough looking man, dark, slightly grey, broad shouldered, and a former French Colonial "Garde Montegnard Commando" and a native of the Buon Ma Thuot Area. He spoke a fair English and French. The second man was an ethnic Cambodian and also a former soldier of the French Colonial forces, with a rank of Sergeant Chief in a Cambodian Commando Unit, with some 20 years of service which was mostly combat time. He was very neat in appearance and visibly a professional soldier. His name was Chau Thiem. He originally hailed from a Cambodian town of Lomphat in the Province of Ratankiri, an adjoining province to Mondul Kiri and was very well acquainted with the jungle area of our objective.

Both men, to my estimation, were very well suited for this mission. Whoever was responsible for the recruitment had done an excellent job. For the next few days before our departure from Saigon we would meet together at several different safe houses, and received detailed target area briefings. There was talk at this time regarding the team's communication capabilities and a strong possibility of another member for our team as a communication man, joining us, in the immediate future.

Flying from Saigon and viewing from above it looked like a great carpet of green jungle entirely covering the great mountain spine of land, which is geographically known as Chaine Annamatique extending from north Hoa Binh area all the way down to Bin Phouc province of Vietnam. We had left Bien Hoa military airport at noon and have been flying continuously ever since. Finally one of the two pilots came back and informed us that we should be landing at Buon Ma Thuot Central Highlands airport in another thirty minutes time. Further, they asked me "would it be possible for them to spend a night at Special Forces B-23 Camp in Buon Ma Thuot?" as they did not fancy flying at night all the way to Saigon. I said "no problem with that." A routine landing followed and the pilots were picked up by SF people.

We, in turn, were picked up by the RD Cadre folks (CIA) and were taken to a "Safe House". The next day I reported to Special Forces B-23 Detachment, for transportation to the A-Detachment site at Duc Lap. The two indigenous assets remained in a safe house at Buon Ma Thuot. I, upon arrival, immediately merged in with the team's activities. The exterior of the Duc Lap camp was still under construction. Its inner perimeter of defense was already finished. The time was just before the coming of the rainy season so there was an incredible urgency made to complete the camp's outer perimeter of defense and the construction of the indigenous living quarters. The last project was the clearing of local vegetation, trees and shrubs at the base of the hill where the camp was located.

This was the first time that I heard from the A-Detachment's team members how it came about that this particular camp was built. Since the previous S.F. camp at Boun Sa Par was abandoned after the FULRO incident, there was an urgency to have an operational base close to the border and close to the Ho Chi Minh trail. Still the only operational airstrip, capable of accommodating air cargo, was located some 6 kilometers away at Boun Sa Par. Whom-ever was responsible for the exact selection for the location of the Operational Base of camp at Duc Lap had not taken into consideration that this strategically located hillock, where the new camp stood, was considered a very special and holy place by local tribal people, the Mnong. This was their burial place since time immemorial and considered "Beng Yaang" (Forbidden Place). The whole area, including the trees that grew upon it, was also considered sacred.

The local tribal Shamans of the "Mnong Gar" (People of the Forest), the Americans and the Vietnamese military were warned, in the strongest terms, not to disturb this holy site or to cut its spirit trees for by doing so it would invoke an evil curse for all that would dwell there. The Chief of Mnong Gar and his sorcerers pleaded with Americans and Viet authorities, to no avail. The trees were cut and the top of the hill leveled to accommodate the future camp. There was an immediate reaction from the local people. The newly recruited unit for military service, were tribesmen known as the Civilian Indigenous Defense Guard or C.I.D.G. They had just completed their basic training and had then deserted en masse. And so it was that the camp became operational. Some two weeks passed and I became a semi-permanent resident and bonded with the S.F. detachment folks, while getting acquainted with the local terrain by participation as a member of the Security patrols in the immediate area of Duc Lap.

Then one night, about midnight, I was awakened by small arms fire coming from the northern part of our inner defense perimeter. I went very quickly to my assigned defense position and almost immediately realized the firing was outgoing from our positions. After a short time the firing stopped and several illumination rounds were popped, and then . . . . silence. Thinking one of our troops got nervous and started all this, I went back to my bunker.

In the early morning the firing was attributed to nervous troops and all returned to normal. There were some comments made by indigenous troops that someone was throwing rocks from outside of perimeter at our troops on night watch. End of the story? Not quite. The next night the same thing happened. This time the rock throwing incident was witnessed by a member of our counterpart, a Vietnamese S.F. Sergeant who swore that someone was throwing rocks. Further, the rocks came from a very close range and from a very narrow level spot just outside the wire.

The area was thoroughly searched but there were no footprints found. The area, from where the rocks were believed to have been thrown from, was between a minefield and a barbed wire fence. All of our mines were found to be in their place. The third night at about 0300 hours, several rocks were thrown from the same location within our perimeter! This now precipitated a fusillade of small arms fire from, by now, very nervous indigenous troops followed by bright illumination of this area. Troops actually had seen rocks coming from a narrow strip of packed earth between the minefield and the inner perimeter barbed wire fence, landing in our trench. I actually have not seen this, but one of the Americans stated he had seen this with his own eyes.

By afternoon of that same day, a delegation of our indigenous troops confronted Camp Duc Lap's commander, demanding an immediate sacrifice of a buffalo, saying the rock throwing incident was indeed the work of evil spirits, or the so-called "Yaang Beng Brieng". The sorcerers and shamans of the Mnong Gar people want revenge for the desecration of this holy place and sacred burial grounds and for the destruction of holy trees. They believe this is a place where evil deeds, violent deaths, and pestilence will always dwell. In a few hours the tribal Mnong Gar shamans and their sorcerer arrived and, after prayers, chanting, drinking from wine jars, and the playing of sacred gongs, the sacrificial killing of a buffalo ceremony took place.

In the end, the Mnong Gar announced they were unable to remove all the wrongs, and predicted a great many misfortunes would befall Duc Lap, including death and pestilence. The morale of the local troops fell and many desertions followed. Personally the whole thing made me nervous and upset.

A couple days later I was picked up by a "slick" (helicopter) and I was off to Buon Ma Thuot. Upon arrival at the RD Cadre House, I had a quick conference with B57 MI people from Saigon and I was issued new orders that I, as an American, cannot cross the Cambodian border (with a big lecture about neutrality of the Kingdom of Cambodia) because, if I was caught or killed within its borders, it would create an international incident.

Therefore It was decided I should remain on the Vietnam's side of the border and act as Launch Officer for the FULRO contact operation. My two indigenous friends are approved for insertion into Cambodia. The launch site changed from the vicinity of Duc Lap to an area just north, and close to the abandoned village of Don Dak Nam La, which was very close to the border area and just off the seldom-used French Colonial Road #14c.

The security for the launch site was provided by a small unit of Nung tribesmen (mercenary soldiers of Chinese tribal minority from North Vietnam) working for RD Cadre people in Buon Ma Thuot. They were already inserted into the Launch Area, and presently engaged in reconnaissance and security of the Launch Site. One Sunday, in late April 1966, both operatives were inserted into Cambodia's Mondul Kiri Province. We remained in the Launch Site overnight then walked some distance, and were picked up by two Slick's off Hwy 14c and taken for a short flight to Buon Ma Thuot where we dropped off the Nung security people and returned to Duc Lap immediately.

Upon my return Lt. Amadeus Ihli, the Operation Communication Officer for Special Forces Detail B57, made radio contact with the inserted team. Ihli, who was recently promoted from NCO to the rank of 1st Lt, was perhaps one of the most qualified Special Forces Communication Specialists. A real professional in all phases of Special Forces operations. He, at this time, assumed operational control of the inserted team consisting of our two operatives, Char and Thiem.

We were able to maintain good communication with both of them for two days and on the second day of insertion Char and Thiem were successful in crossing the most dangerous part of their journey, the main area of the Ho Chi Minh Trail in Cambodia. We kept good track of their progress figuring that in another day they should be reaching the FULRO encampment. All looked good. On the third day we were unable to communicate with them. We had tried to reach them on several occasions during the next day and night, all without success. And so it went for next few days. The air of gloom prevailed amongst all of us involved. The possibility of a failed mission became a probability.

On the sixth or seventh day, the Duc Lap security and reconnaissance patrol found a North Vietnamese Army canvas rucksack hung from a tree branch not far from our camp. Upon checking it for bobby traps it was removed and brought back to Duc Lap camp. It contained the severed head of Mr. Thiem. What really happened will never be known. After a short radio report contact with B57 in Saigon, and RD Cadre people in Buon Ma Thuot we were ordered to immediately destroy any and all documents pertaining to this mission. Lt. Ihli was ordered to remain in Duc Lap. I was ordered to return to Saigon by the first available aircraft for debriefing. A very sad end, to say the least. My departure on the next day was very low key. Most of the members of SF Detachment at Duc Lap, were not informed as to what happen.

Since the nearest fixed wing operational airstrip to Duc Lap was located some half an hour away by jeep ride at the village of Boun Sa Par, the road between the two locations was considered to be unsafe and contested territory. These trips to the airstrip required mounting of a security patrol consisting of at least of platoon strength, from DUC LAP camp. These were indigenous troops under the command of a US Special Forces NCO. The security of the actual airstrip, however, was the responsibility of local Vietnamese Regional Forces.

After a safe arrival at the airstrip, Sergeant First Class Hernandez, the NCO in charge of security, checked with the VN Regional Force people regarding the security of the airstrip. He was given an OK and radioed the incoming CV-7 (Caribou) aircraft, "all secure," and directed it to land. The aircraft, upon landing, taxied to our location and, with its engines running, opened its aft loading ramp. I then ran up the ramp and boarded.

It was then that I realized it was full of Vietnamese soldiers, women and children. The visibility inside was poor due to swirling red dust entering through the rear ramp door. The aircraft accelerated and with more dust clouds swirling, taxied down the dirt runway for takeoff. The next thing I felt was the Vietnamese soldier sitting next to me who fell into my lap. Both my legs and crotch were soaked and wet. Thinking this man was puking all over me, I grabbed for his head. It was then I realized my hands were full of this man's brains and gore. Unable to detach his safety belt, I kind of pushed his body aside while becoming totally soaked with his blood. This madness was almost surreal; the red dust, screaming and roaring engines, it was a nightmare! The aircraft had been shot up on takeoff. Towards the front of the plane many Vietnamese appeared to be dead or horribly wounded while still strapped into their seats. The red dirt still swirling inside made it a very weird and scary scene, a picture of living horror. The cabin deck was red with blood, body parts and scattered personal belongings. With this the aircraft became airborne and the red dust cleared.

We continued flying at tree top level to give the enemy a minimum target, we flew for I don't recall how long before making an emergency landing at Dalat airport. In shock from all this carnage, I don't know how I got off the aircraft. The American crewman opening the ramp door had been shot and fell dead as the ramp touched ground. I was covered in blood and in shock. Thinking that I was wounded, rescuers placed me on a stretcher and I was evacuated to Dalat's Catholic Mission Hospital.

I suffered no physical injuries, but in my mind to this day, I remember clearly this bloody carnage. Subsequently I arrived at Saigon's Than San Nhut airport and reported for debriefing of our failed mission. After a day decided I had had enough and to stay out of these "half-assed" badly conceived missions. Upon calling my friend Sergeant Major George W. Dunaway of the 5th Special Forces Group HQ in Nha Trang, I was ordered to set everything aside and catch the first available flight to SF Headquarters in Nha Trang for further assignment. As Team Sergeant, Special Forces Detachment A-242 at Dak Pek, the most northern, most remote hill top Special Forces camp in the Second Corps area of Vietnam. I was quite happy about my new assignment and eager to go.

CHAPTER 12

A Family Affair

Upon my arrival in Nha Trang Special Forces Headquarters, I was informed that my next assignment would be as a Team Sergeant of detachment A-242 at Dak Pek, the most northern, most remote hill top Special Forces camp in the Second Corps Area of RVN, reachable only by air, and close to the Laotian border. I was somewhat familiar with this camp as it was at one time, two years before, where a good friend of mine, Master Sergeant John J. Self, reigned supreme. Shortly after I was on my way to Dak Pek, for the next four or five months. Then came a day after two days of leading a large security/combat patrol into the jungle hills surrounding our camp, I dropped to the ground and lost consciousness.

Thank God the other American member of the patrol was our team's medic, Sgt. James R. Phillips, who somehow got me evacuated from this highland's dense jungle area. It was a major task. It took the combined efforts of the helicopter crew, indigenous members of our patrol, and of course the life-saving efforts of Sgt Phillips. I found myself evacuated to a large US Army medical hospital in Pleiku, Central Highlands. Where, after several days it was determined I had suffered from a sudden pericardial heart attack (a swelling of the heart lining) caused by an unknown viral infection.

Shortly after I had returned to full duty status at Dak Pek I was told to pack my bags and return by "first available aircraft" to Nha Trang. Thinking that because of my recent medical incident, some very bad news awaited me. Nothing of the kind. It was however, an immediate "out of uniform" assignment with a paramilitary CIA clandestine organization. My assignment was personally arranged by

CIA regional Director, Mr. Ernie Sparks. This assignment required me to attend a two weeks orientation & briefing, at the sea resort town of Vuong Tau (in French colonial times known as Cap St Jaques). The original name of this newly minted clandestine counterintelligence unit was to be known as Counter Terrorist Program or, in abbreviated form, known as the CT Program.

Its mission was a straight forward organization responsible for identification, infiltration and destruction of the communist Viet Cong organizational infrastructure, and identifying and destroying its secret cadres membership, at Village, District and Provincial level. The recruiting for this mission would be primarily from the ranks of recent volunteers from the Chu Hoi program. This consisted of communist prisoners of war who switched sides. They were mostly former members of North Vietnamese or local Viet Cong forces augmented by locally selected recruits.

A bold and dangerous mix of people, to say the least, to be trained and led by folks like myself, responsible only to South Vietnam Province Chiefs (Governors) and their personal and trusted intelligence members, and to folks like Mr. Sparks. The program was inaugurated in four provinces (States) of the Republic of Vietnam.

However, it was very short lived, as it was seriously compromised by one overzealous member of an operational team (Navy Seal) in the Delta Region province of Camau, who brought in the severed head of the local Vietcong Chief Political Cadre, to the CT team house. Immediately word got out to International Press Corps, first in Saigon, then worldwide including Newsweek, Times magazines and others. All this happened when the program was beginning to be a great success. We were paralyzing Vietcong's logistical, political, and intelligence activities. To keep this successful operation going it was time to change the name from the CT program to PRU. (Provincial Reconnaissance Unit).

At this time I was already deployed with an active PRU outfit in Tay Ninh Province in order to gain personal field deployment experience under the command of a very professional operative, Special Forces Lt. Freeman. (KIA in 1967) while waiting for my posting in the capitol city of Qui Nhon, in the Province of Binh Dinh in central part of Vietnam. After a couple of weeks I felt comfortable in my forthcoming position as commander of Binh Dinh Province PRU team. I received a communication to move to Qui Nhon, and immediately commenced with the recruitment, and training phase of our PRU operatives. In the Qui Nhon CIA Operations Station, one of the principal station officers was my former old buddy from Special Forces days, Joe Vaccaro. He was now a career CIA Officer.

Albert on patrol of the Ho Chi Minh trail at the Laos border area. April 1967 and 10 days out from Dak Pek.

I had recently returned from a lengthy leave to Europe, awarded for a six months extension for combat service in Viet Nam. While in Europe I married a long time sweetheart, Joe's sister Margaret. All done legally in the city and garrison town of Gibraltar, United Kingdom of Great Britain. And so the whole operation now became a "Family Affair".

I must add that during the training phase, all conducted on an offshore island and away from the ever watching eyes of Viet Cong, there came the time to arm our group and to spend much time on an improvised firing range with our indigenous folks who just a short time ago were in the ranks of the North Vietnamese armed forces. Now members of a clandestine combat/intelligence unit, they were deathly dangerous to their former communist masters who were now sworn to allegiance to the Republic of Vietnam. All volunteered in order to kill their former brethren. Need I say more. As the only "round eye" in the group it made me uneasy and nervous especially at night, always questioning myself. Will I wake up the next day? My charges, however, became loyal and courageous and we wrought much havoc, and destruction to the communist infrastructure in the Province of Binh Din.

At times I felt there was a sort of perverted pleasure present on the part of our operatives when, dressed and acting as Viet Cong tax collectors, or intelligence agents and political cadres, or uniformed Communist North Viet Nam soldiers bearing their AK-47 rifles. They were about to depart on their deadly nightly missions of double cross.

It is now 1967 and from that time on I served two more tours in Vietnam and returned home in late 1970. As an afterthought, I must say that in my many years serving in combat as a member of the United States Army Special Forces in Vietnam, I became very much emotionally attached to the mountain tribal soldiers, the Montegnards.

The same goes for the Ethnic Cambodians and Nungs of North Vietnam. All good soldiers loyal to the U.S. Special Forces. In the end we Americans, however, betrayed them all for they gave everything to us by putting their faith, lives and loyalty by courageously fighting alongside us, and putting their lives and their families in mortal danger. The relationship between these mountain tribes became very personal. Their loyalty was to us as their leaders. In truth, they became nothing

Sergeant Major Slugocki of the Special Forces— January 1970.

Gen. Johnson decorating Sgt. Maj. Slugocki with a Bronze Star medal for heroism in Vietnam. January 1968.

more than pawns of this war. First during the French Colonial war of Indochina and later in the American conflict they were abandoned. The Americans left them to suffer incredible horrors at the hands of the Communist victors.

CHAPTER 13

The Story of the Beehive Buddha

From October 1969 until February 1970, the district of Triton, An Giang Province, the Republic of Vietnam, was the scene of bitter battles as US Special Forces and our mercenary troops fought Viet Cong forces for control of Nui Co Tho, a mountain in the remote border area between Vietnam and Cambodia. This region is known as the Seven Mountains, three of which are within the geographical boarders of Vietnam. The others lie across the border in Cambodia.

Early in the same year, US Special Forces had secured and, to some degree, controlled the two other mountains within Vietnam, Nui Giai and Nui Cam. Viet Cong guerillas, reinforced by North Vietnam's regular forces, decided to fight and defend, at all cost, Nui Co Tho. Combat raged through November and December 1969. The local US Special Forces unit, Detachment B-43 of the 5th SFGA Vietnam, its Operational A Detachments, and the 4th Corps Mike Force Battalion (a mercenary force) were the main forces taking part in the battle.

I was then serving as a Sergeant Major in the B-43 Command Detachment in the village of Chi Lang, located in the foothills of Nui Cam. This was our operational area. Throughout my entire year in Chi Lang I dedicated just about all of my free time to helping local villages and the inhabitants, who were largely ethnic Cambodians, living within the border areas of Vietnam. The lingua franca of this region was Cambodian, and the ethnic Cambodians of the region were officially known as Khmer Krom, or South Cambodians. Seeking to win the hearts and minds of the people was expressly part of my mission, and I had considerable US government funds at my disposal to help me accomplish this.

The predominant religion was Buddhism and Buddhist temples, small and large, dotted the entire area. Here, as in the rest of Southeast Asia, the faithful practiced Theravada Buddhism. The differences between this and other branches of Buddhism are akin, for example, to those between Baptist and Catholic in the Christian religion. The roots are the same, but the actual faith differs in its ceremonies and beliefs.

Some ten years previous to my deployment at Chi Lang, I had personally become interested in Theravada Buddhism during a visit to Laos. I had been intermittently deployed as a Special Forces operative in Southeast Asia since 1959, bouncing back and forth between Saigon, Phnom Penh and Vientiane. An acquaintance of mine, a pilot for Air America, offered to let me fly with him to the Laotian spiritual capital, Luang Prabang, which was also where the Laotian kings resided.

Following my frequent visits to Vientiane, I always, or at least, time permitting, would visit Luang Prabang and commenced to visit its magnificent pagodas. My favorite was the most beautiful Vat Xieng Thong. I befriended one particular monk who spoke fluent French and passable English. While visiting Luang Prabang I began to seriously pay attention to Buddhist teachings, its basic tenets, precepts and philosophy of Therevada Buddhism, all of which appealed to my personal spiritual thoughts. When it was time for my semi-annual leave of two weeks, I chose Luang Prabang as my destination as opposed to R & R (rest and recuperation) places like Hong Kong or Singapore.

And so I went again to Vat Xieng Thong to seek further religion enlightment and was admitted to the Vat's humble accommodations, sharing monastic life with others (except for the daily task of begging for food and the wearing of monk's robes) by shaving my body hair. My spiritual guide and teacher was the English speaking Monk Sen.

Although I never became a practicing Buddhist, I began to follow its sacred teachings and do so to this day.

At the time of my initial ten day visit, old King Sisavang Vong died, and his son Savang Vatthana ascended the throne. There were many celebrations and although I had no idea of their meaning, I became enchanted with the beauty of the ceremonies.

Given my own attraction to Therevada Buddhism and the deep belief of the indigenous Cambodian inhabitants of Chi Lang, I decided to dedicate the funds at my discretion to rebuilding the area temples. This project was a major undertaking. Many hundreds of bags of cement, pallets of bricks, stacks of lumber and other building materials were scrounged and appropriated legally (or otherwise) for the projects from the entire Delta region and delivered to us courtesy of various pilots. Continental, Air America, US Army Aviation units, and anyone else who wanted some sort of "atta boy" pat on the back, were in on it. The materials were then delivered to the Abbots of the area temples. Our efforts were received with open arms. The local people, being religious and industrious by nature, immediately went to work on the monasteries and temples. As a result, we were very successful in our endeavors.

All of the native soldiers and Ut Soul knew of my devotion to the Buddhist faith and of my undertaking of repair and reconstruction projects. I became involved not only as my chosen faith but also to promote good will between the U.S. Special Forces and Cambodia. On occasion I would go to temple with my friend and counterpart, Sgt. Maj. Lem, a devout Buddhist. He was from the Hoa Binh area of North Vietnam. Ethnically he belonged to the Black Tai minority. Other times I would go to temple by myself to meditate.

The Therevada Buddhism is sometimes referred to as the most pure of the Buddhist faith. Its followers are simple people. Therevada doctrine holds that to achieve Nirvana (Heaven) you must work out your own salvation with vigilance. In other words, it is up to each individual to find their faith. Therevada Buddhism is the religion of Burma, Laos, Thailand, Cambodia and Sri Lanka (formerly Ceylon).

The Mahayana (large vehicle) holds that an individual should forego Nirvana until all human kind is ready for salvation. The ultimate goal is to become a Bodhisattva (Saintly person). The beauty of Buddhism is its simplicity. There are prayers to be said and sacred litanies of verses sang by the monks. When praying, each person is talking directly to God. What has drawn me to the Buddhist religion is its honesty, purity and beauty of its faith and the peace that it brings to one's heart.

On one particular day, the date escapes my mind, a prominent Buddhist Abbot requested to see me. He was an old man, skinny and wrinkled with his yellow robe, worn with age, wrapped tightly around his frail body. Two novices accompanied him, bearing large metal bowls filled with water and flower petals. I was able to speak Vietnamese, but my Cambodian language skills were limited to military orders and terminology, so our camp interpreter joined us. The Abbot blessed me with holy water from the bowls while the novices placed flower petals all about me.

Albert Slugocki at the Buddhist Xien Huang Pagoda in Luang Prahbang, Laos.

I thought that the old monk had come looking for more lumber or cement. But as it turned out his visit was for a very different reason. After the blessing, the Abbot began to tell me the story about a holy image of Lord Buddha that had been abandoned in one of the small temples located at the south base of Nui Co Tho Mountain, the contested area that the Viet Cong was defending. The name of this statue was "The Sacred Beehive Statue of the Seven Mountains." Legend has it that the honey of the bees that lived in the hollow statue had miraculous powers of healing. Who really knows?

The temple was located in no-man's land, controlled by our forces by day, but at night the front lines were the scene of frequent firefights. The old abbot begged me to recover the statue, and I promised him I would ask permission of my commanding officer, Lieutenant Colonel Richard "Dick" Stanier, to mount a small combat patrol with a mission to recover the holy Buddha.

And so, within a few days, with Colonel Stanier's blessing, I had mustered a small force, all volunteers, including Sergeant Major Lem, my VN Special Forces counterpart, a Platoon-sized group of our Cambodian mercenary soldiers, and myself. Mounting two trucks, we set off at daybreak first driving across a small mountain pass to the south of Nui Cam, a contested area where Viet Cong forces sometimes would ambush road traffic. Upon approaching the pass, we dismounted our troops, and tactically deployed into two elements on the left and right sides of the road, sweeping the high ground on both sides. We then remained in a road security position while driving through the pass. Sometime later we arrived in Tri Ton, a small district town and drove west about two kilometers to a location in close vicinity to Co Tho Mountain.

Dismounting, we advanced on foot in tactical formation toward the bottom of its southern slope where our objective, the Buddhist temple, was located. We met no enemy in our advance and secured the immediate area. Sergeant Major Lem, myself, and a group of soldiers entered the temple. Partially burned, the building bore many scars of war, and even the parts unscathed by fire were in ruins. Miraculously, however, the Buddha had survived. We discovered it intact among the shambles, sitting on the temple altar, full of cobwebs and covered with dust and dirt. Its right forearm bore a bullet wound from an AK-47, but otherwise it was in good condition. The statue's right hand was on one knee, with the hand pointing down toward earth in the Bhumispara position, which is usually interpreted as Buddha calling the earth to witness his good deeds. There was beehive residue on the small altar.

Wasting no more time, we withdrew with the statue and returned to camp. On the way back to Chi Lang our troops were in a very festive mood, passing the statue from hand to hand among themselves with great respect, like the holy thing it was. When we brought the statue to the local monastery and presented it to the abbot, the local Cambodian villagers started a great celebration, which lasted several days. Then, as time went by, the whole affair was just about forgotten—or so I thought.

I was just wrapping up my fifth tour of duty in Vietnam, and my time was short. It was now December 1969. One Sunday morning shortly before Christmas, the old abbot appeared again at the main gate of our camp. He wanted to see me and asked for permission to enter the camp. He was followed by a great number of villagers, some of whom carried on a flower-bedecked platform the statue of Lord Buddha that we had recovered.

I met him accompanied by our interpreter, Mr. Phong. The abbot said that he had had a vision about bad people from the North. He did not know when, but he believed that the Viet Cong would win the war. He was certain that a sea of blood would run in Cambodia and Vietnam and that the communists would destroy all the Buddhist temples, kill all the monks and destroy the statues of Lord Buddha. Knowing the great love I had for the Buddhist religion, the abbot said that he was commanded by his spirits to give me the statue. He wanted me to take the holy image with me to America for safekeeping in my home. I was very much surprised by his statement and request, and humbly accepted his gift.

Over the next two months, I kept the holy statue by my bedside on its pedestal, along with photographs of my wife and infant son. The Cambodian soldiers and camp workers brought weekly offerings of fruit, incense and flower garlands to adorn the Beehive Buddha, and my bunker soon came to look and smell like a Buddhist temple. And then another strange thing happened. An old Cambodian woman with a shaven head, all dressed in black, began to spend the night at the entrance to my bunker. She was a war widow and a Buddhist nun. She became a watch-person, sitting outside while I slept.

It was said repeatedly by the local population that a giant black cobra watched over me as well and that it could be seen at night coiled on the front of my veranda. I never saw it, although the very thought of it made me nervous, especially at night. The local people firmly believed this tale. Although we had never suffered serious casualties at the camp, on some occasions we had experienced small probing attacks and three or four mortar attacks with several mortars landing within our inner perimeters. While the statue was in our camp, however, we were never attacked.

In February 1970, I finally left Chi Lang and Vietnam, and the statue went with me. Soon after I left the B-43 camp it came under attack on a regular basis by the Viet Cong. The mass killings by the Khmer Rouge soon began in Cambodia and in some border areas of Vietnam. Throughout this entire border region, between 1975 and 1978, Khmer Rouge guerillas regularly crossed over into Vietnam and slaughtered local people, including their own Khmer brothers. Buddhist temples were burned, and a special hatred extended to Buddhist clergy, who suffered torture and death at their hands. The Khmer Rouge and Viet Cong were allies for a while before turning on each other and brutally wiping out thousands of innocent people, mostly Cambodians. To ethnic Vietnamese, they showed no mercy. In the ethnic Vietnamese border village of Ba Chuc, for example, the entire population of over 3,500 people were annihilated—man, woman and child. Such was the carnage that Master Ut Soul had accurately prophesized nearly ten years before.

Many years later, in the winter of my life, I found myself increasingly reflecting on the past. The statue of the Lord Buddha from Nui Co Tho still adorned my modest home in Florida, and had been in my family for over forty years. During this time, the Beehive Buddha survived another conflagration, again seemingly by miracle. In 1973, my house was hit by lightning, and the fire destroyed an antique devotional altar I had purchased in Macau, which was mounted just above the statue. The Buddha was charred in some places by the fire but I was able to have it restored and today it bears no trace of the fire.

Throughout the years, I had often wondered if it would be possible to return the Sacred Beehive Statue to its original home. I had never considered myself the rightful owner of the statue. But the question was, did

The "Beehive" Buddha statue—recovered from a destroyed pagoda in Vietnam.

the same Cambodian people still live in the Seven Mountains region? And would there be a safe sanctuary for it? Although I had tried many times to remember the name of the pagoda near our camp at Chi Lang, but it escaped me, as did the name of the Abbot as well. Nor could I recall the name of the Buddhist nun who kept her nightly vigil outside my bunker, although I did remember the sad story of how she became a widow during the French Indochina War, subsequently losing her two sons in the American vs. Communist conflict. Thirty-some years has dimmed my memory. How could I find the answers to these questions? I did not know, but I was certain that the Lord Buddha would give me a sign as to what course of action to take.

On October 10, 2003 I boarded a Singapore Airlines flight from Singapore to Than San Nhut Airport in Saigon, today known as Ho Chi Minh City. I was on my way to the Seven Mountain Region, returning to Vietnam for the first time since the war. It was time to make my peace with God and myself. After an uneventful flight across the South China Sea, the familiar sight of the southern-most part of the Mekong Delta, the Camau Peninsula, came into view. Flying low over a half-drown world of mangrove swamps, I gazed down at a thousand canals full of brown water emptying into the deep blue of the South China Sea as our plane neared the final approach to Than San Nhut.

Upon landing, we taxied past long-abandoned US helicopter concrete revetments overgrown with weeds to the brand new and very modern looking airport. All immigration and customs procedures went smoothly, including the greeting, in English, no less, by Vietnamese immigration officials: "Welcome to Vietnam!" There was no luggage inspection. Outside the terminal, the driver for the Hotel Majestic was waiting for me, holding high a small sign bearing my name. This is when the memories of the war really hit me: the good times, the bad times, the loss of friends, and many other events that had happened long ago.

Our car dove into the incredible traffic of automobiles, mopeds, bicycles and pedestrians, all bobbing and weaving. The people looked the same, the city bore no change, and the smells of the street food were just as I remembered. It was as if time had stood still. The only difference was that the old Saigon was now officially named Ho Chi Minh City. But it was all still one big, chaotic outdoor soup kitchen with street vendors competing at every corner of every street, avenue and square, offering every imaginable Vietnamese dish. The commingled odors of food, gasoline fumes, hot peppers, human sweat and excrement were overwhelming. Our destination, the Hotel Majestic, was a famous landmark from French colonial times, and still represented the long-gone French legacy, having been in operation since the early 1920's. There it was, with uniformed doormen in all its glory, looking as elegant as ever at the foot of the street known in French colonial times as Rue Catinat, during the Republic of Vietnam as Tu Do, and now as Dong Hai. The street faced the Saigon River, curiously still officially known by its old name. The grand, oversized rooms at the Majestic gave me a special feeling. The passing of time and war had never really affected it. It was a comfort to me and after having a Singapore sling at the rooftop bar, I relaxed and retired to my bed.

The next two days were spent busily making travel arrangements. It was not an easy task to organize my visit to the Seven Mountains Region. The proposed trip became somewhat complicated, primarily since the destination of my quest was the Province of An Giang, where I hoped to find the Theravada Buddhist temple from which we had rescued the Beehive Buddha, and to seek more information about the current situation of the region's Cambodian inhabitants. Although I was still unable to remember the name of the temple, I knew that it was located in the District of Tinbinh, adjoining the District of Triton. Both were immediately adjacent to the Cambodian border, outside the designated tourist destinations in Vietnam.

Nevertheless, thanks to the excellent services and political connections of a local tour operator, Ms. Kim of Ho Chi Minh City, I received a special police permit to visit the area. It carried, however, a special provision: In addition to my Vietnamese interpreter and driver, a third member, a Mr. Thu, would join our expedition to act as a guide and provide security. I was told he was originally from the area and spoke Cambodian.

Thus it was, on the third day of my stay, we departed on our journey. After driving for approximately an hour, we entered the outskirts of town and drove into the Mekong Delta. Passing through numerous small Delta towns, we came to and crossed the Mekong River bridge at the town of Vinh Long and continued on our journey northwest, following one of the main Mekong channels, the Ba Sac, all the way to the border river town of Chau Doc, where we stopped overnight.

At Chau Doc, I was happily ensconced in luxury in at the four-star, French-owned Hotel Victoria, on the banks of the Mekong River. Nevertheless, unable to sleep, I sat out on my balcony overlooking the darkened river. It had been over thirty-three years since I had left this area, and a flood of memories overcame me as I thought about the hardships of a long-past war and of all the friends, American, Vietnamese and Cambodian, I had made and lost in South Vietnam over some five years there as a Special Forces soldier. I now began to have serious doubts, questioning the real reasons for my return to the place where so many of my friends had died.

And then, in the midst of my soul-searching, the exact name of the pagoda and its abbot came to me. It was the Chua Tot Pagoda, and the abbot was the Most Reverend Ut Soul. The exact location of the pagoda, including local landmarks along the way, also vividly appeared in my mind. Could it be the sign I always believed the Lord Buddha would send me? How else could these names and precise images have suddenly come back to me, as if in a trance, after so much fruitless searching? It was as if he were literally showing me the way.

After this sleepless night, nervous and excited, I left Chau Doc with the rest of my party, heading out on a well-kept dirt road. This took us west, directly parallel to the Vietnamese-Cambodian border along the Vinh Tre Canal, to the outskirts of the large village of Chi Lang. As we passed numerous houses built directly next to the road, I noticed immediately that the occupants were Vietnamese, not Cambodian. I asked Mr. Thu what had happened to the Cambodians. "They were resettled from the border area," he replied.

In front of us on the horizon appeared the largest of the Seven Mountains, which I immediately recognized as Nui Cam. Now I knew exactly where we were. As I was pointing out various terrain features to my two interpreter-guides and our driver, the trio became rather nervous. From the tone of their voices I determined that something was not right, and it was upsetting my companions. Finally I asked

Mr. Thu, who had so far acted as spokesman and leader of the three, to explain. He said they were very nervous to be so close to the border. Although we had permission to visit the area with all the necessary documents from the Ho Chi Minh authorities if we were stopped by the border police we could still find ourselves in very serious trouble, including the possibility of detention. This was especially the case since I had shown them such intimate knowledge of the region and admittedly was a former member of the American military who had fought their government's forces in the area.

And so we continued down the road for a very uneasy half-hour. Mr. Thu was quite amazed at my memory, and all the more so when I told him that at the next turn of the road, on the left, there would be a large sugar palm grove with some mango trees. Incredible as it seemed, up ahead on the left side of the road our destination appeared. A grove of bamboo and mango trees. It showed no sign of a pagoda or any other buildings, but seemed to be an abandoned grove in the middle of rice paddies. However, once we got closer, we discovered a concrete-framed entrance with a well-traveled road leading to the interior of the grove.

Mr. Thu's expression changed from apprehension to a smile of complete surprise as he informed me that the weathered sign at the entranceway, written in Cambodian script, read "Chua Tot Pagoda." We had arrived! As we entered the inner area of the monastery, to our right, as if time had stood still, there was the pagoda. We parked in the large clearing and were almost immediately approached by two people, one a young Buddhist monk, the other a man who turned out to be the temple groundskeeper.

Our Mr. Thu now appeared to be unable to communicate in the language he claimed to know. Luckily, the grounds man knew both languages, for he turned out to be the only Cambodian speaker there who also spoke Vietnamese. A conversation ensued, during which I explained to all concerned the purpose of my visit. I said nothing about the statue of the Beehive Buddha, but I did tell both of them that I was the American who had helped them rebuild the pagoda in 1969.

When I mentioned the abbot's name was the Reverend Ut Soul, even before my words were completely translated into Cambodian, the young monk immediately fixed his eyes on me, expressing great surprise and interest. Taking my hand in his, he led me to a small building across from the temple. There we sat down on the veranda where he offered us tea. He recounted that Ut Soul had passed away some years ago, either during the civil war of 1978-1980, or shortly thereafter. He next went into the building and then reappeared carrying in both hands a small clay urn, stating through our interpreter that it held the ashes of Ut Soul. At this point, he began to pray. After the prayer, he handed me the urn. Quite frankly, I didn't know what to do with it. So I stood still, silent for a moment, and then passed it back to him. He then went back into the building with the urn. By this time, a small crowd of elderly Cambodians had gathered on the temple grounds.

Returning, the young monk again took my hand and we walked together to the pagoda. Once inside, still holding my hand, he kneeled facing the altar, and I did the same. As he chanted his prayer, I prayed in silence. Next he took me to the right side of the temple to show me a strange scene painted on the wall. It depicted a gray-haired man with obviously Caucasian facial features, wearing a green-colored shirt and trousers that resembled a uniform. Both of his hands were extended in a gesture of giving what appeared to be a gift to a Cambodian woman. This was a reference to a mystical female deity who sometimes appears in Cambodian legends. Pointing first at the mural and then at me, the monk indicated that the painting was of my person. I was utterly amazed. With a couple thousand sacks of cement, a new floor, some beautiful tiles and the industry of the local populace, we had managed to restore the pagoda. I had thought these acts had been forgotten, and was deeply moved and humbled by this unexpected depiction and commemoration of the temple's restoration.

By this time, the temple had filled with the local populace, most of whom were elderly or middle-aged. Curious as to what was going on, they all approached as I stood in front of the wall. A loud conversation ensued between the crowd and the interpreter, as they urged him to give them more information. He explained to me that they were amazed by my presence, and further stated that they remembered an American soldier who had given money and building materials to the Chua Tot Pagoda. They also said that Master Ut Soul had often spoken of the mysterious American as their benefactor and he continued to do so even after the Americans had left and it became very dangerous to mention anything about Americans, the war, or the former government of South Vietnam.

The young Cambodian monk who met us on our arrival turned out to be the present abbot of the Chua Tot Pagoda. When I asked him his age he said he was thirty years old, and had come from Cambodia where he had been ordained, to tend his local Buddhist brethren in Vietnam. There were no older monks in either Cambodia or the border areas of Vietnam because they had almost all perished in the carnage at the hands of the Khmer Rouge Army between the late 1970's and 1980's. In 1980, most of the survivors were transported to Cambodia by the Vietnamese government. When I inquired about any knowledge of the statue of the Beehive Buddha of Noi Coto, none of the people now gathered in and outside of the temple knew anything about it. This really caught me by surprise.

Now Mr. Thu, supposedly our security man and Cambodian translator, came to me privately, and with great emotion on his face told me that he was a member of the national police assigned to keep an eye on me during my visit. However, he said that as a devout Buddhist, his religion came first, and he felt very bad about his assigned duties. To prove his point, he showed me a picture I.D. claiming this was his police I.D. card. Still showing great emotion, he said that he was also deeply touched by my story of the holy Beehive Buddha and very impressed by the wall mural. He then stated that his report would not mention anything about the painting, or any further details regarding the nature of my visit.

By now the pagoda grounds had filled with many elderly Cambodians, all anxious to know more about me. A couple hours passed in conversation with the local people while Mr. Thu and our driver were at the town market, where I had sent them to buy bread, rice cakes, candy, soft drinks and cigarettes. Soon Mr. Thu arrived loaded with all sorts of goodies, and a good time was had by one and all. When evening fell and it was time to go, I gave a parting gift of a hundred dollars, the local equivalent of three months' wages, to be used for the up-keep of the pagoda and its grounds. As I left, I promised everyone I would come back next year.

Albert Slugocki re-visited the pagoda that he helped to re-build during his active duty in Vietnam.

And so I did. On my return trip in 2006, while en route from Ho Chi Minh City, I stopped at the Mekong Delta Town of Vinh Long. There I met a good friend of mine, now a very successful businessman with much influence in those parts, who lived in the area and owned one of the largest manufacturing plants in the Delta. Over lunch, I asked his thoughts about trying to bring the statue back to the Chua Tot Pagoda in Chi Lang village.

His answer completely surprised me. Good intentions, he said, might very well be misconstrued by the Vietnamese government and judged to be politically incorrect by the authorities because the old hatreds between the Cambodians and Vietnamese were still very much alive. There were problems with the Cambodian minorities living in the Seven Mountains area adjacent to the Vietnamese border. Further, I might be accused of stealing a religious object of art from Vietnam and illegally transporting it out of the country, and now be attempting to return it under false pretense. Moreover, the history of the statue made it a national treasure, and most likely it would be confiscated upon arrival in the country. It would probably either be placed in one of the national museums, or be stolen outright by corrupt officials. All this meant there was little, if any, probability of returning it.

Taking my friend's advice to heart, with a weary feeling I departed Vinh Long for the long drive north to Chi Lang and the Chua Tot Pagoda. A big welcome awaited me on arrival including a large gathering of the Cambodian population. We all went to a newly constructed meeting hall, where the monastery monks commenced with chanting prayers. Upon entry I was informed that the prayers were meant for my soul and those of my family. Against the back wall of the building stood an altar. In front of it stood a large stone-carved statue of Buddha. From the looks of it, it was newly carved. On its pedestal was inscribed my name, Albert Slugocki.

I was overcome with emotion as a small musical ensemble began to play ancient Cambodian music. All this was followed again by a trip to Triton, where we purchased loads of food and goodies, which we distributed to the assembly. We all had a memorable visit with these wonderful, yet very sad and impoverished people. The Khmer Krom people in Vietnam had always engaged in agriculture. A year after the fall of South Vietnam, the new rule came to their region, the government declared that no one was allowed to own property and all Khmer land was confiscated, causing them to lose their only means of making a living. The stolen land was then given to former members of local Viet Cong as a reward for their service in the 2nd Vietnam War. The government also encouraged ethnic Vietnamese to resettle from densely populated areas to the border area, almost completely displacing the Khmers; banned all traditional Therevada Buddhist activities; and restricted the use of the Khmer language to home use only; neither in the country where they actually lived, nor in their mother country, just a stone's throw away.

We left before dark for our lodgings in Chau Doc. Driving back to Saigon, my thoughts were full of doubts about returning the statue of the Buddha to the remnants of the Khmer population in the Seven Mountains region. A population explosion of the Vietnamese was taking place in the entire Mekong Delta, and it was obvious that the rapid Vietnam-ization of the Seven Mountains region would shortly erase the ethnic Cambodians completely from the area.

Ut Soul, Reverent Abbott of the Buddhist Monastery at Chi Lange—murdered by the Khomer Rouge.

I still do not know what I will do with the statue. If I could, I would build a shrine for it, so it could not be stolen. If I were to try to repatriate the statue, I would advertise in a Vietnamese newspaper that I was returning it to the Vietnamese and Cambodians to promote peace. As Vietnam has the status of most favored trading partner with the United States, I think it might be possible to return the Beehive Buddha in this manner, but I do not have the required funds. It remains to see the next sign from Lord Buddha.

Civilian Life

CHAPTER 14

A U.S. Marshal – The Wrong Choice

It is spring, 1971 and I am now honorably discharged from the U.S. Army Special Forces at the rank of Sgt. Major, after twenty plus years. At the time of my retirement, I have been assured in writing of immediate employment with the CIA. However, it never materialized. All they offered me was a temporary, one-year assignment to Southeast Asia, in the country of Laos. I would act as a special operations advisor to a mercenary unit fighting the communist forces, known as the Pathet Lao. This was unacceptable to me. Especially, since my wife Margaret just gave birth to our daughter, Lonnie. Leaving her again for one year's time was completely out of the question.

I then received and accepted employment with the Department of Justice, U.S. Marshal's Service, as a Deputy U.S. Marshal, in the Southern District of Florida. I was assigned to the Marshal's Office in Miami, Florida. This I considered as good luck, since, as a rookie, I could have been assigned to Alaska. All of this suited me just fine because we decided to live in Fort Lauderdale Florida, close to Margaret's family. Miami was only 28 miles to my new work place. After a short period of training in Washington D.C., I commenced with my new career. A few months later, I was selected for training and assignment with a newly organized elite unit of the U.S. Marshal's Service, The Special Operations Group (S.O.G.).

Graduation of Class #2—U.S. Marshal's Special Operations Group, in Los Fresnos, Texas in the fall of 1972. Albert is in the left front kneeling.

This new organization was responsible for special assignment on sensitive federal law enforcement missions within the continental U.S.A. and its overseas territories even though I was based permanently in Miami. During the years from 1971 through 1977, I participated in countless missions as an S.O.G. operative in the U.S.A. and overseas. The highlight of my assignments was a three-month deployment on a rotating basis in the winter and spring of 1973. S.O.G. members were deployed to the Ogalala Indian Reservation at Pine Ridge, South Dakota. It is a national historic area, with a village known as Wounded Knee. Eighty-three years prior, on December 29, 1890, the Ogalala Sioux Indian Reservation was the scene of one of the most shame-full acts committed by the U.S. Government. The defenseless Native Americans were massacred by U.S. troops.

And now here, in the winter of 1973, I witnessed and participated, together with the Ogalala Sioux Tribal Police, in an armed confrontation with members of the American Indian Movement (AIM), led by Russell Means. We were fired upon with communist AK47 submachine guns and faced a motley crew of white "wannabe" Indians, waving communist flags, and shouting communist slogans.

I observed red flags flying from the village's historic church steeple. The big problem with Mr. Means was that the so-called Indians were in fact recruited from the skid rows of Minneapolis, Denver, and Chicago. They were the folks who robbed the village of Wounded Knee and its Native American Trading Post/Museum. They stole irreplaceable Indian artifacts and then sold them in Denver and other southwest hockshops. Adding insult to injury, the AIM members burned a beautiful, historic church.

Later that same year, while assigned to S.O.G., I was in charge of a special security detail responsible for the Soviet's delegation staff of visiting General Secretary of the Soviet Union, Mr. Leonid Brezhnev. This particular security detail was probably the most demanding and difficult, with chaotic working conditions. Protecting the safety and wellbeing of the members of a tyrannical communist regime on American soil made me sick to my stomach. The security of all those people became a very serious matter, as Mr. Meir Kachane, an American Jewish extremist/dissident, issued some very serious threats against the safety of Mr. Brezhnev and members of his staff.

I spent more than six years with the Special Operations Group. I had assignments that had taken me, at a moment's notice, to all over the 50 states, and at least 5 different countries. In 1977, my services in S.O.G. were officially terminated. The reason cited in the written termination notice read as follows: "personal problems and a propensity for extreme violence". This became evident while participating in assignments that required the use of physical force.

I continued to serve with the U.S. Marshals. And in 1978, I was assigned to the highly classified Federal Witness Protection Program in the Southern District of Florida. My new duties dealt with the personal security of protected witnesses and their families, whose lives had been threatened by criminal elements. During an assignment that year and in the middle of the night, I was to immediately move a protected witness from her residence, to an established "Safe House." The protected person insisted on taking her television with her. In my attempt to help her and while carrying her TV set, I tripped and fell down a few steps, still holding on to the TV. I suffered serious injuries to my back and was placed on light office duty by a government doctor for an unspecified period of time.

Finally, it was determined I was unfit for further service as a deputy U.S. Marshal, and was medically retired. As for my propensity for violence, this plainly said I was unsuited for police work. I attribute my violent mental state to my military service, and specifically to actual combat conditions. I was trained to kill or take prisoners. This was a real and valid reason I should never have been a law enforcement officer. Even well before my discharge from the Marshal's Service, I began to have nightmares relating to my wartime traumatic experiences, first as a child during WWII, and then as a combat soldier in Korea, Vietnam, Laos and Cambodia. In addition, there was my participation in many clandestine military operations that had violent outcomes. I was, as they say, in a complete state of denial as to my mental state of mind. After my retirement from the Marshal Service, I felt useless as a man and a failure in my life.

I became afraid to sleep at nights, as the demons of my past came to me much stronger now, in the form of horrible nightmares. I felt ashamed and worthless, unable to deal with these serious mental problems. After all, I was once a good and brave soldier. Now I dreamt of my fellow men that died alongside me, blaming myself for still being alive. I kept all of that to myself while feeling unmanly, yet too proud to admit my problems. How could I be a Special Forces Sergeant Major? And to this day, the best America has.

How could I admit all that, and to whom? The answer, at that time, was nobody! Just suck it up and forward March. It is now 1980, and I am slowly realizing that I have some serious problems with my life. To make life for my family more miserable, I began to drink to excess, sometimes having a complete blackout. I became abusive to my family, and, frankly, I still do not understand why my wife, Margaret, stood by me all that time, after what I had done to her and our children. The fact was I did not have the slightest clue. What was I suffering from? Today it is well known to all as Post-traumatic Stress

Disorder or P.T.S.D. It was a dirty word to all my contemporaries and for all professional combat soldiers who fought our wars. Right or wrong, I prevailed and kept going on.

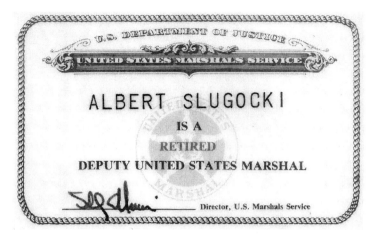

Albert's I.D. card –after retirement as a deputy U.S. Marshal.

Brazil

CHAPTER 15

The Amazon River – My Life's Choice

There came a time when I meet a very nice gentleman by the name of Hector Salazar who was visiting a mutual friend and member of his family in Miami. He was from Peru, and lived permanently in the Amazon River town of Iquitos, Peru. We became friends, and had many conversations about the town he was from and of course, the subject of the Amazon River kept coming up all the time. I became very curious about the Amazon jungle and its native peoples. Somehow it dawned on me that I must travel and see for myself, what this magical place was all about. Having nothing better to do with my miserable life I went and visited Don Salazar in Iquitos.

Thus I was hooked by this mighty river and its mysterious jungle. During my stay in Iquitos I was introduced to an American by the name of Paul Wright who was the owner of a large river passenger vessel named "Amazon Queen" and a jungle tourist camp not far from Iquitos, where I was invited to spend a few days. After several days and peaceful nights at Paul's place, I managed to sleep, without pills or getting drunk. The surrounding jungle was a friendly place where birds were singing while I went for long walks into the jungle with no one shooting at me. There was peace. As a self-confessed misfit I found that I was in the right place without really knowing why.

The beauty and the majesty of the Amazon jungle did a number on me. Upon my return home to my family it gave me a different look at life and I developed a strong longing for peace like I had found in the Amazon jungle. I knew I would have to ask Margaret to let me go for a while, to find myself again. I did not know for how long. I did not know how to ask her. I also was fully aware that I would be forsaking my responsibilities as a husband and father of my two children for not being there with them when they needed me the most. Never the less, finally I did ask. Surprisingly she agreed. Somehow, as an intelligent person she knew of my state of mind and took a gamble on letting me go. She even gave me the necessary funds to buy a riverboat in Manaus, Brazil.

A wonderful woman she was, and still is. So this Amazon adventure became my personal redemption from futility, a beginning of release from the hell of my nightmares and a sort of self-cure of mental anguish of my past. By living a life of a river man and sometime jungle dweller I have learned to live in close communion with Amazon nature's beauty and its wonders. During my time on the river, I was very often asked the same question, over and over again: What made you come here, how did it happen that you are here, the perfect example of people's natural curiosity to ask and their wanting to know. For the Amazon rain forest and its rivers is an unusual place to be. Some times when asked these questions I even felt a touch of hidden envy. I always found it hard and difficult to deal with these simple questions.

CHAPTER 16

Brazil to Peru – The Long Voyage – Manaus Nights

Sitting at a prime table at the Hotel Monaco rooftop restaurant in Manaus is like sitting on top of the world called Brazil, especially when you're drinking a perfect Caipirina, concocted of Brazil's finest sugar cane liquor, native lime juice, and other mysterious ingredients. Such was my great indulgence and pleasure one evening in winter 1983, after a day of great success. I had been lucky enough to obtain a dry dock space at the boatyard of Cordeiro-Regio Ltd., located on the Rio Negro on the left bank of Manaus in the well-known slum of Educandos.

This particular evening was a double pleasure. Sitting beside me also sipping a Caipirina was Paul Hittscher, a long-time friend who had just arrived that afternoon on Cruizero do Sur Airlines from Iquitos, Peru. Paul had come to advise and assist with major repairs needed aboard my riverboat, the 90-ton river vessel, *Cidade de Natal*, which I was converting from a general cargo vessel to passenger service. A native of the tough waterfront of Hamburg, Germany, Paul had survived the extensive Allied bombing of his city during World War II. He joined the German Navy's Submarine Service at age sixteen, waging a deathly game of war from 1943 until the German surrender. In 1945, he and his U-Boat crew found themselves prisoners of the French in the Port of Toulon.

As prisoners of war, they were forced to work for almost a year disarming and clearing sea mines from various French ports, during which time Paul witnessed the death of his shipmates on an almost daily basis. After the war, he somehow managed to get to the United

States where he worked as a seaman, shipping out of ports on the Pacific coast for several years.

Paul was now quite a celebrity in Iquitos. In the early seventies, he had become captain of the M/V *Destiny*, a U.S.-flagged pleasure yacht owned by a famous Las Vegas millionaire named Krekorian, who in turn sold it to South American Travel Company, Inc., which operated out of Riverside, California. The *Destiny*, re-baptized the M/V *Amazon Queen*, ferried passengers on the Amazon River between Iquitos and the tri-border areas of Leticia, Colombia; Santa Rosa Island, Peru; and Tabatinga, Brazil. For quite some time Paul remained captain, sailing with his Peruvian crew over river and sea from Los Angeles via the Panama Canal all the way to his home port in Iquitos—an incredible voyage of over five thousand miles.

Paul and I first met in Iquitos when he and his Peruvian wife Edelmira were the owner-operators of the El Tropical, which was the best restaurant in the city. The M/V *Amazon Queen* and its owner, Paul Wright of Amazon Tours and Cruises Inc., had continued to operate on the customary route for a couple of years without Paul at the helm, and then the vessel sank under very mysterious circumstances, going under with some or all of its crew. Yes, Paul was very much the type to fit into "The Misfits," the select circle of those I called true friends.

So here we were, sitting on top of the world drinking, ruminating on things past, talking about the Amazon River and the latest gossip from the Iquitos waterfront and contemplating the choice between hitting the sack early or figuring out what to do next.

We sat there for quite some time, enjoying the fresh breezes in the open-air restaurant on top of the Hotel Monaco, built on the highest point of the city. Much later, when the place had almost emptied, we decided to spend the rest of the balmy night at The Cathedral, a famous nightclub located in the bowels of our Amazon City of Sin, Manaus. At the entrance to this subterranean refuge of local and imported scalawags, pimps, whores, dope dealers, and other elite members of Manaus society, we were warmly greeted by a human giant black doorman named Otoniel, who, recognizing Paul, gave us both a vigorous *abrazo* or embrace.

After this endearing welcome ceremony, Otoniel ceremoniously ushered us into the underground den of sin and pleasure, a cavernous space consisting of several large rooms connected by wide, arched openings. It was now after midnight, and life was just beginning to stir in the packed interior. We were quickly seated at a small table very close to the large, slightly elevated bandstand—combination-dance floor. The action began with a small band playing one of those sad, slow, hauntingly beautiful sambas that evoke something special in all of us and the Brazilians call a "Saudade"— the sadness of one's soul. It is the sort of music that really pulls at your heartstrings. There were three musicians, two of which were non-descript, with exception of their musical mastery. The third, the bongo player and lead singer, was a young, good-looking man with a *café-au-lait* complexion, dressed in an outrageous black shirt with large white polka dots. As he sang, his sad ballad of lost love was barely audible above the noise.

Many Cuba Libres were delivered to our table, and things had begun to mellow out, when the band changed its rhythm. The music became faster, an intensely gyrating samba tune, and the dance floor, until now empty, filled with girls dancing. They danced with no one in particular, but for their own pleasure, expressing the emotions, passions and desires coursing through their veins. They remind me of tropical birds or butterflies, dressed as they were in colors of the same, vibrant and beautiful, with glittering skins—the beauty and wonder that is Brazil. Occasionally, or I should say often, these Birds of Paradise visited our table. We bought them Cuba Libres, in which they would indulge as a matter of course, sitting with us briefly. Then, as if possessed by the seductive rhythm of the samba, they would fly away back to the dance floor.

Then—I had heard it many times before—there was a sharp sound as if someone had cracked a whip, followed by the strong smell of cordite. The crack was repeated, and Paul and I dove for the floor, amidst a crash of broken glass and hundreds of screaming voices. "Paul, are you OK?" I heard myself hollering. "Stay down!" My face was now pressed to the Coca Cola-soaked floor and I heard more shouts. The music stopped, a girl screamed next to me, then—silence. Paul and I stood and looked around, with one thought in our heads—"get the fuck out of here"! On the debris-strewn dance floor, almost directly in front of us, with both hands grasping at the floor, lay the body of the *café-au-lait* singer in the outrageous polka-dot shirt, the blood slowly seeping from his handsome face. A stampede ensued, as everyone panicked in the effort to get out, jumping over overturned tables and chairs, rushing for the door.

Paul and I headed in the opposite direction, to the back bar area, where we stood in state of shock. Paul, the first to recover, ordered us both a drink from the stupefied bartender. The police arrived on the scene, taking some people away, asking questions of others, but completely ignoring us. Julio, the proprietor of the place, came over and talked to us in English and ordered more drinks. It was all unreal, as if in a movie. Finally the police left, taking the body of the dead man with them.

We decided we were still alive. I went to the smelly bathroom and puked, then Paul and I left. At the door, the black giant of a man Otoniel stood crying.

CHAPTER 17

Brazil – Port of Educandos, Manaus

About ten days later, Paul went back to Iquitos. The *Cidade de Natal* was out of dry dock and in water, and I was seriously thinking about moving out of the Monaco, as it was eating away at my budget. It was not that it was so expensive on a daily basis, but the long-term costs of lodging and meals were quickly adding up to a considerable sum.

Before he left, Paul had given me some very good advice concerning reconstruction of the boat, but the outfitting and construction had really dug into my finances. That's the way it is with boats—there's always something to do that you had not figured on doing. I had just been informed that it would take another week to complete the construction of eight double-bunk cabins and two combination shower-bathrooms on the second (top) deck. At that point, I would be able to live aboard in my own cabin, located immediately behind the bridge. I decided to call my wife Margaret to give her a full report. In the meantime, it was time to get back to work.

I had meanwhile had the good fortune to befriend the American-Brazilian family of Jack and Edina McClintock. What a family! Jack, from St. Louis, Missouri, had formerly been a Catholic Monsignor and the priest in charge of a charitable mission in the Brazilian State of Amazonas. In Manaus, he had fallen in love, left the priesthood, and married his Brazilian sweetheart, Edina. They now had two grown sons, one a local businessman, the other the manager of their popular family-owned restaurant in Manaus, the Panorama. Edina also managed the rooftop restaurant at the Monaco, which is where I met her and became acquainted with her family.

Through Edina, I met the owner of the Monaco Hotel, Mr. Manuel da Silva-Rodriquez, a very well-known and politically connected attorney. When I say it was my "good fortune" to meet these people, I really mean it, for without their gracious patronage and their help in handling the Manaus Port Captain's Mafia, I would never have been able to obtain the documentation I needed to operate my vessel. Had I been without personal local connections, the authorities would have politely received me, given many promises, and then done absolutely nothing. This was all the truer because, as an American, I looked to them like a big, fat, juicy steak.

In this instance, Manuel politely advised me to have my *despechante* (port's shipping agent) pass an envelope containing two one-hundred-dollar bills—new, without pen marks, tears, or gambling stamps—to the Port Captain's Office. Once this was received, I passed all the port inspections with flying colors. Again, if I had not had such friends to guide me through the labyrinth of corruption, I would never have survived, and would probably have ended up on the bottom of the Rio Negro.

I called Margaret and we had a nice conversation, catching up on the kids and other news from home. Above all, she was concerned about my personal safety. Then—bang! Margaret told me she was sending more money by a courier, whom I was to meet that Saturday as he debarked from the Miami-Manaus flight on Varig Airlines. The courier would be somebody I knew very well, but she would not give me his name. "Well, we will see," I said to myself, happy as can be, and looking forward to meeting the mystery courier.

Needless to say, on Saturday I was at the Manaus Airport, scrutinizing the arrivals as they emerged from Customs and Immigration. Out came my big surprise in the person of Captain Larkyn "Rocky" Newsome with a big smile on his face. Rocky was a good friend from my days as an operative with U.S. Army Special Forces in the South East Asia, and even before that time from our service together at Fort Bragg, North Carolina, and in Germany. Our friendship had continued after Rocky retired from service and became a pilot with Air America in Laos and Continental Air in the Republic of Viet Nam. By hook or by crook, he had always managed to keep in touch with me and now, suddenly standing before me in Brazil, was this legendary soldier and pilot, at one time my mentor and superior, whose professionalism I had always respected and whose friendship I would always cherish.

"Hi Slugger," he greeted me, using my Special Forces nickname from long before. Seeing the great surprise on my face, he said, "I'm here to help you. I'm not working for the government." It was a short taxi ride to Manaus proper, and we were soon ensconced at the Monaco's rooftop bar. As we were enjoying a friendly drink, he surreptitiously passed me an envelope containing a very substantial amount of money.

Over the next few days, Rocky helped me outfit the riverboat. Everything went smoothly on that end. While Rocky was at the boatyard, I was busy looking for cargo to defray the cost of the very long trip from Manaus to Iquitos—some 1,100 river miles. I discovered it was not going to be an easy thing to do, as the changes made aboard to accommodate passenger service had seriously limited my cargo space.

After many days of trying to come up with some cargo, I received a message from the Honorable Louis Ruiz-Beltran, Consul Republic of Peru in Manaus, requesting my presence at his office. Having no idea what it was about, I presented myself the next day at His Excellency's office and was immediately granted an audience. With great surprise, I was much pleased to find out that Mr. Beltran's own curiosity about my person had led him to call me before him. He wanted to know all about me and my commercial undertakings in the region. In the end, he offered his help. His diplomatic status as Consul enabled me to meet some notable Peruvians residing in Manaus, all of which led to the procurement of cargo bound for Iquitos.

The cargo, the property of a small trading firm from Iquitos, consisted of cooking oil, all neatly packed in 24-unit cardboard cases. There was a total of four thousand cases—quite a lot weight. This meant that every crook and cranny of space aboard would be loaded with cargo. By accepting to transport it, I was taking an awful risk from the point of view of safety. I then discovered that the cargo was consigned only to the Brazilian border town of Benjamin Constant, located only a stone's throw from the Peruvian village of Islandia. Upon arrival at Benjamin Constant, I was to contact a local man who would provide me with a cargo manifest for the Peruvian Port of Iquitos, some 268-river miles away. All this amounted to a little bit of smuggling. I was instructed to do this to avoid the payment of export taxes to the Brazilian border authorities at the official border control port of Tabatinga, which lay just two hours upstream from Benjamin Constant.

I was game, as I had been game for this kind of thing before and I knew my way around the tri-border areas and their great maize of small, navigable channels. A couple of days later, I was contacted by two Peruvian business ladies (a.k.a. smugglers) who had purchased a quantity of ladies' shoes, underwear, and other items from a textile manufacturing plant in Fortaleza, Brazil. They were anxious to find a cargo boat captain bound for Iquitos to safely carry their goodies. I agreed and rented them two of our recently constructed passenger cabins.

While all this was happening, my friend Rocky was slowly getting acquainted with the goings on. He balked at the amount of cargo I had obligated myself to take on. Categorically stating that we would surely sink and drown all concerned, he brought to my attention the seacock located at amidships at the center bottom of the riverboat's hull, which he believed had a faulty installation. "You put this under the pressure of too much weight, and this son of a bitch is going to blow!" he insisted. He truly believed the *Cidade de Natal* would sink on her maiden voyage.

Additionally, I had discovered that Rocky, at age sixty, had some serious health problems. He was suffering from gout, and was having a terrible time with climbing twice a day up and down the 102 steep steps between street level and the river shore. He was also not very happy about having to shit and wash himself in the Rio Negro. He was too much of a man to complain about any of this to me, but he did complain to Edina at the Monaco. Of course she told me right away. She further told me she was very concerned about Rocky's health. "What kind of friend are you, anyway?" she berated me. "You should take better care of your friend."

This put me between a rock and a hard place. I didn't have the time or money to affect further repairs, much less to take the boat out of water and put it back into dry dock in order to fix the seacock. My agreement to carry the cargo had committed me to a sailing date. This was the unwritten law of the river. I needed to get out of the Cordeiro & Regio boatyard as soon as possible, as they were now charging me for berthing. Rocky then gave me an ultimatum: either fix the seacock or count him out. He would not go with me on the journey to Iquitos. "We might sink and we might not," I told him, "but I have got to go."

So it was that Edina and her sons made travel arrangements for Rocky to fly back to his home on Tavernier Key, Florida. I felt shitty about the whole thing, as I valued our friendship, but it was his decision. Rocky left, and I was sad, but maybe that was just our Karma. Meanwhile, the *Cidade de Natal* would soon be moving from Cordeiro & Regio to the official river port, located almost in downtown Manaus. In a week, we would be bobbing up and down with a hundred other riverboats all tied one to other at the floating port of Escadeiria (the Steps). As I attended to the remaining details I lived aboard, making daily forays to the many local ship chandlers to make my final purchases before moving to the cargo dock.

One evening while we were still at Cordeiro & Regio's floating dock, I was playing around with my most recent purchase, a small generator that had just come aboard that afternoon. I was making small adjustments of its mounting in the engine room below the main cargo deck. Night had fallen, but a bit of fading daylight lingered on.

Suddenly I felt as if I were not alone. I stopped work and listened very quietly. There was a muffled sound, like footsteps on the deck above me. Someone was definitely aboard. To my left, at about eye-level, an open side air-intake window about twelve inches tall ran along the engine room wall. Looking over, I saw a pair of bare feet walking quietly parallel to the narrow opening toward the fantail of my boat. I froze, sensing immediate physical danger, grasped the large monkey wrench with which I had been working with. The narrow opening prevented me from seeing anything more than the bare feet of the person stealthily moving above.

The next instant, I sprang forward toward the rear ladder, and practically flew up to the main deck. I was suddenly face-to-face with a super-surprised man. He obviously had not seen or heard me in the engine room and I appeared so suddenly on deck that I almost ran right into him. Regaining some of his composure, he rapidly wheeled towards me, saying something in Portuguese. As he was moving in, I sensed or heard another person behind me on the fantail. I pushed and kicked my assailant with all my might, causing him to half fall to the deck. Instantly, he sprung again. I saw the flash of a knife in his right hand as he lunged, and swung my wrench, managing to hit his forehead. I kicked him again, and he screamed and stumbled backwards. Evidently stunned from the blow to his head, he lost his balance and fell overboard with a loud splash.

My assailant fell from the cargo deck amidships between two deck support stanchions, where there was no security chain railing. Realizing that there still was somebody else aboard, I ran for the fantail, only to hear the splash of someone jumping into the river. Turning around, I ran again to the place where the first man had fallen, but found nothing. There was nothing to see and nothing to hear but the dark, lapping waters of the Rio Negro.

All became very quiet. I could hear my heart beating rapidly. My chest was hurting and my hands were trembling. I sat down on the main cargo hatch and took stock of my situation. I was all alone. My boat was the last in a row on the floating dock, almost on the main stream of the river. The whole Educandos District of Manaus well knew that I lived aboard, alone. I had been seen carrying a considerable amount of cash on my person as I made my daily purchases for the trip to Peru, and I paid in cash for the extra work at the boatyard. All of this made me a walking target for the 1,001 thieves and other assorted criminals in my neighborhood—the infamous *Favela de Educandos* slums.

With all these thoughts running through my mind, I got up and carefully examined the starboard side of my boat, where the poor unfortunate bastard went overboard. I found a considerable amount of what looked like blood spots marking the exact spot of my man's exit. A flood of thoughts rushed through my mind. Did he drown? As I had practically thrown him overboard, was he able to swim away bleeding? What about the local piranhas? Peering over the side, I could see nothing except for glittering black water, and the distant harbor lights of Manaus. No sounds, no clues, no anything. Looking at my watch, I found it was 10:00 p.m. Total darkness enveloped me and my boat.

All sorts of thoughts were racing through my head. Suppose the man overboard had drowned. Should I notify the police? Now fully aware of the danger of my situation, I looked up high to the cliff above to the well-lit streets of Educandos. There was not much choice. I had to reach the safety of the streets, the presence of other people, and friends. Whatever the cost, I had to leave the boat immediately.

The streetlights were my immediate objective. First, however, I had to cross a snake-like raft loosely connected by bits of anchor chains, cables, manila rope or what have you and perpetually moving with the current and the small, choppy waves. The crossing, of course, had to be accomplished in total darkness. At that point, I would reach the terra firma of the junk-strewn Cordeiro & Regio boatyard, where anyone might be lurking. Then to climb the wooden steps attached to the nearly perpendicular cliff, through the piles of garbage thrown there and everywhere. I clearly remember the 102 steps on that hanging staircase. All of this was unlit and looked very menacing.

Back at my cabin, I found my nighttime visitors had stolen most of my stuff, including a nice flashlight. In almost total darkness, I was nevertheless able to find my switchblade, which they miraculously had missed hidden under my mattress. Then I was off for the safety of the streetlights. How I managed to reach the door, I do not know, but I found myself on the street, out of breath and sweating profusely.

I quickly headed for Doña Antonia's one of my favorite haunts. Friendly faces met me, and my fears quickly dissolved. I recounted my tale of woe, and was given all sorts of friendly advice from my river rat friends— none of it very encouraging. Leoncio Vasquez, a well-intentioned street hustler and numbers runner, told me it was unlikely that the drowned man's body would surface. The denizens of the Rio Negro, piranhas, were in large number and since the man was bleeding; . . . well, you know. On the other hand, the other man who jumped into the water could report everything to the police and could make a lot of trouble for me with both the authorities and the local criminal gangs.

I was in a no-win situation. I could claim self-defense but then, what with the Brazilian Federal Police, local cops, investigators, pay-offs, crooked lawyers, and corruption— not to count ordinary red tape— I would lose a couple years of my life fighting. Not only that, I'd be doing it all from a jail cell. Should you be accused of a criminal charge in Brazil, you go to jail while proving your innocence. Leoncio, friend that he was, volunteered in advance to bring me everything I needed during my incarceration.

As all these discussions were taking place, my friend Wilton, Doña Antonia's son and an extremely ugly, fat, but wonderfully good-hearted man who ran the joint for his mother, called for a celebration in my honor. Looking towards the sky, he thanked God for my good fortune in still being alive. I swear there were tears in his eyes. I was deeply moved— here I was, an American gringo, living among Brazilians whom I really didn't know very well who had, nevertheless, been kind to me and were worried about my safety and well-being.

"Thank God," I said, and went over to Wilton and gave him a hearty *abrazzo*.

Wilton then did something unimaginable— he bought a round of beer for the house. Not to be outdone, I ordered Calderada de Tucunare, a hearty dish of local bass and vegetables worthy of a Sunday feast, for everybody— a dozen or so people. Happy shouts and laughter prevailed. Even Marixenia came over from her corner by the lamppost to see what was happening. The others told her my story, embellished with plenty of extra flourishes, and she planted a big juicy kiss on me. This she followed by a tremendous hug, pushing my head and face deep between her gigantic tits. As she was doing her number on me, and I was struggling to escape her grasp, she started to dance. All around me, people were having fun. It felt good and comforting to have such friends. Joao, a welder at Cordeiro & Regio's, then appointed himself the guardian of the good boat *Cidade de Natal*. He finished his Calderada with a great gusto, went into Doña Antonia's kitchen, and emerged with a gigantic kitchen knife. Thus armed, he disappeared into the bowels of the boatyard to assume his duties as guardian.

At this point my face was hot and flushed, and I felt very tired. All my friends in unison came to the conclusion that police should not be involved in any of this, accepting as fact the dubious possibility that my unknown assailant swam away. My friends offered to keep me safe while I remained in Educandos, and Doña Antonia invited us all to leave. It was well past midnight and time to close up and go home.

The coolness of night descended on Educandos as the streetwalkers, no-goods and no-accounts disappeared from its corners. The street lamps were smothered with fried bugs of gigantic size, the smell of their burning flesh hanging in the cool night air. Marixenia begged me to take her with me for the night. Looking at her, I felt filled with compassion. Her face was all puffed up and swollen beneath the paint and rouge. Her pimp Otoniel, the little prick, had done a number on her face. We called a taxi man who charged me triple fare. Too tired to protest, I just paid him and slammed the taxi door off its hinges. We entered the Deodoro, a typical flea-bitten hotel, and went to the front desk. The night clerk gave me the look known all over the world to any man and woman asking for a room late at night and in we went. Without even undressing, I lay down and passed out into oblivion. And so went another night in Manaus on the Rio Negro.

CHAPTER 18

Brazil to Peru – A Voyage to Remember

I am still docked at, Estailero Cordeiro Regio. There are still things to be done like welding and installation of a 750 gal fuel tank. For sure sometime late the next day all will be in order and ready to move to Port of Manaus at Escaderia. Tomorrow I am taking on a crew of five, all with the exception of one are Brazilians, the fifth member and most important one is Peruvian, who will sail with us as river pilot with official title of Contra Maestre Fluvial. His name is Victor Rios-Cahuachi a Peruvian citizen, an old time river man with some 20 plus years of experience in river navigation. Victor has been in Manaus six months, without a job. He came to Manaus aboard a Peruvian flag Tugboat, which was seized by Brazilian authorities and after six months' time is still rusting away on the shore of Rio Negro.

As for the prospective Brazilian crewmembers I don't have much choice and in accordance with laws of the Brazilian Maritime Syndicate, the Port Captain is to provide me with fully documented crewmembers for my voyage. This is where my problems began., The next day, five prospective crew members report to me, of which Motorista Fluvial (Engineman) when hearing of our destination being Iquitos, Peru, immediately resigns. Back to Port Captain's office pleading for help, I got lucky and signed on a real good engine man in the person of Manoel Daimurcho-Paichao Yoss. This young man, later on during our voyage proved to be a real hero.

As for the other three Brazilians, the Contra-Maestre(River Pilot 2nd Class), Jose Barbosa Maciel proved to have a serious problem with his eyesight. Can you imagine, a river pilot who cannot see! I complain immediately to the Port Captain, but to no avail and I am forced to take him. The other two, River Man 1st Class Raimundo Rogeiro Oliveira and Joao Ludgero Ferreira, the cook, are OK. All crewmembers to come aboard next day, as we are moving to Port of Manaus to receive our cargo. In addition I just found out from our Despachante, there are several prospective passengers looking for a passage aboard our vessel, plus a small used car, and three new refrigerators. This is not counting the high value cargo of assorted ladies things already aboard in two cabins, locked securely with great big padlocks on cabin doors plus the cabins windows, while still in port, are nailed shut. All starts the next day with no problem. The crew all are aboard and with fond farewells from dockyard crew, and all the good people of Educandos we move to our berth at Manaus Port, The Escaderia. The Port Captain Inspector comes aboard and finds us without fire extinguishers in the engine room and on the second deck. After some money passing, we are issued an official clearance to sail the next day. In the afternoon my newly found American friend in person of Mr. Gilbert "Gerry" Miller, comes aboard. It so happens he found himself in Manaus doing whatever, who decided to come with me, all the way to Iquitos, Peru. Now Gerry is really a "piece of work" as they say in New York.

He is small to medium in stature with a curly head big-bugged eyes and a permanent smile on his face and a good sense of humor., Certainly an intelligent person aboard is very helpful, and easy to live with. I am happy to have him aboard. Next comes aboard a real strange guy, an American expatriate bearing Brazil's residency documents, but also identified with an American passport, which shows his place of birth as Chattanooga, Tennessee. His name is Van May, James. He asks to many pointed questions, like, how is it that I, as an American, am an owner and Patron(Master) of a Brazilian flagged commercial vessel, followed by some other personal questions. At this point I should have denied him passage because taking him, later proved to be a big mistake. His destination is Tabatinga, a Brazilian border town with Colombia. Two other passengers are Brazilian citizens bound also for Tabatinga, Brazil.

One of the two Brazilians is the owner of a small car, now securely aboard. As for my cargo consignment we take aboard cooking oil. All of the cargo comes aboard on the backs of bare foot stevedores. With our cargo loaded and boat all secured for the night and to prevent theft, I engage the services of two local policemen as overnight guards. We are almost ready to sail the next day early, but were delayed until 11:30 AM by an Agent of Fiscal Police. Some money passed hands and we cast off for our long journey to Peru. Almost immediately we encountered bad weather with poor visibility, after some hours of being underway, we leave the black waters of Rio Negro and enter the main channel of Amazon, strange as it sounds

The worldwide known river as Amazon, in Brazil it is officially named and known as Solimoes, it was named after some obscure Brazilian admiral a century ago. After a few hours of sailing with Victor at the helm and still encountering heavy rain and poor visibility, the night falls. We are now some two more hours away from a small river town of Monacaparu. Rios reports having a problem with the steering. It appears to be the steering pulleys so we must slow down and somehow make it to the safety of Monacaparu. Now both of us are on the wheel, plus Barbosa Maciel, the blind Brazilian pilot, mans the super bright (500000 Candle strength) searchlight, sweeping the dark River ahead of us. We know well, that just before the mouth of Monacaparu channel there are ill famed "Roques" a series of rocks right in the middle of shipping channel. We are now desperately trying to avoid the rocks, which we did as we passed them on our port side, half an hour later, and entered Monacaparu channel safely. It is night now almost midnight and with a running time of eleven plus hours, we are safely secured at Monacaparu harbor.

Next day early the local mechanic found our problem to be with the steering chain improperly installed, and of the wrong size. We installed the proper sized steering chain and depart at noon. Ship responds well to adjusted steering problem and clip along at 9 knots per hour. Good weather, good visibility, but encounter very strong current, with much debris in water. We must slow down and proceed with the greatest of caution, and initiate a nerve-wracking maneuver to avoid hitting all the flotsam, debris floating rapidly with river's current, especially dangerous are half-submerged tree trunks. Slowing the vessel down to half speed and use of all three crewmembers as a team, a combination of four sets of eyes watching what is ahead of our vessel. After a while the flow of that garbage clears and we are able to navigate safely. Just Passed mouth of Purus river early, and continue running all night.

The river at his point is extremely wide like a couple of miles wide if not more. It's like driving our boat on an ocean. Traveling All night and day under way, we doing well and making up for the lost time. Rios at the wheel, towards the end of day. Had to stop, the engine temperature high, problem with water intake pump pulled over to one of many small-unnamed islands. Mosquitoes swarm all over, departed one hour later, all is well is upon us as we continue. Aboard our food is very simple, mostly beans, dry beef, fresh fish with plenty of rice.

The crew at every meal, lace their rice heavily with Farinha (a cereal like small kernels) made from a local vegetable called in Portuguese Mandioca (Spanish Yucca). In mornings we have fresh fruit juice of maracuja, eggs with dry biscuit, with plenty of strong brewed black coffee (Cafezinho) make for our daily diet. In evening, besides food we serve our passengers a small glass of dark cane rum, and small bottle of Pepsi Cola. This is when I started noticing that our American passenger Mr. Van May from Chattanooga Tenn., apart from consuming his daily ration of rum, dips nightly into his own reserve and drinks himself into oblivion every night.

This bothers me, but as long as he is not bothering rest of our passengers, so I don't say anything to him. The early morning found us close to small river town of Cadajos. I decided to have a little break for crew and passengers. As we have been underway for at least 20 hours' time we stay three hours tied to shore, some went for walk, and crew rested aboard. Resumed our journey in the afternoon with weather rapidly changing to high winds and rain with visibility almost at zero, we were however, forced to continue to our destination at a medium sized river port town of Coari. We arrived at the municipal pier of Coari at about 8:00 pm. All secured aboard.

The crew asks for beer money and permission to go ashore is granted, before they leave however, something told me to take extra precautions with the safety of vessel and make the crew double the ship/shore lines both at aft and fore. Victor making small jokes about it, but, never the less, it is done. The crew departs for the town, to raise a little hell. I hit the rack, sometime later I awake to pelting rain, with wind howling, the waves begin to hit us broadside and vessel although well secured to pier, begins to slam against it.

The god-dammed crew failed to hang fenders (Truck tires) at port side opposite concrete pier like they were supposed to. I hurry with four big tire fenders, not an easy thing to do, and curse my crew. It's already early morning, the storm subsides and I am exhausted from all of this. There was no sign of my crew. I found out cook never left, stayed aboard and slept all night through last night's raging storm, and now is smiling saying "Bon Dia Padron" is handing me a hot cup of coffee. Finally the crew came back and, to my great surprise, are being accompanied by, or practically carrying our good passenger Mr. Vann May with them, still drunk. No need to argue or talk sense to a drunk, I say nothing, but find out from crew he paid for all night boozing and whoring for my crew. I am pissed off to say the least.

I will have to have a showdown with this American prick, and set him straight. We take on extra diesel fuel, and depart at about noon. So much for Coari. We pulled away from dock and into the midstream channel and head for our destination port town of Tefe. Sometime later, the vessel's steering responds poorly. I began looking for an island or any other place where we can secure and see what we can do. Tied to a high river bank we make an inspection and find the trouble is with the port steering cable, which we fix and continue underway. The vessel responds well. The weather is nice with sunshine and a cool breeze blowing.

The river looks clean of all debris with no islands in sight. About noon I decided to give our Brazilian pilot a chance at the wheel. Mr. Maciel, while at the wheel almost rams our vessel head-on into a sand bar. At the last moment our Motorista Manoel Paixao, who happen to be on the bridge, grabs the controls and put's the vessel in full reverse. The whole boat shudders but stops just before being beached. Immediately after I relieved Mr. Maciel of all duties aboard. I order him to his cabin and inform him that upon arrival at our next stop in a port town of Tefe he will be discharged, paid, and placed aboard next available boat going back to Manaus. This man has been nothing but trouble for me since we left our port of departure. I feel sorry for the old man, but obviously he not capable to perform his duties as River Pilot.

We continue, and at about midnight are able to see on the night's horizon, the distant lights of Tefe. We arrived at dusk and had to wait until morning to take a few things aboard. I engaged the services of a Brazilian river pilot but at departure time, we have a no show. Guess he changed his mind. We leave harbor at about noon, with only one qualified pilot aboard, Victor. While in Tefe we made some food purchases, and now have plenty of fresh meat and vegetables aboard. Our biggest problem throughout this voyage has been obtaining diesel fuel. Our single engine's power had been strained to maximum with the heavy load of cargo and upstream, going against strong river current.

Our single diesel engine, an 8 cylinder, air starter, 275 HP Japanese Yanmar, although powerful in pushing power, consumes a lot of fuel at 9 gal per hour, and is pushing a 90 ton vessel against 3 to 4 miles per hour against the river's current. At a maximum 8 to 10 knots per hour speed, its raw water intake pump is getting fouled up with debris in river water and getting sucked up into main water pump, is real rough on single rubber impeller, which had been replaced already on two occasions.

The price of diesel fuel rises in price, as we are getting further away from major towns along the river. Anyways we forge forward, hopefully we get to Peru soon where diesel fuel is three times cheaper. It is night now and we encounter torrential rains, visibility poor. Dangerous travel, but can't waste any more time, I am going to bed with one eye open, with every hour or two looking out my cabin door, checking our progress. Victor was driving and Raimundo was working our search light. We were running at half speed, hugging the starboard side of shore—all this in a total darkness. Daylight breaks, still raining, the weather clears some, as we arrived at the small river port of Fonte Boa, we. Went to purchase some plastic fuel hose. Our cook is scouring the local market for vegetables.

At this point, we will have to take a break from river as Victor and Raimundo are completely exhausted from last night's navigation. We notified our passengers that we will resume travel at 2:00 pm sharp and Invite them to go ashore until then, stressing he point of punctuality of our departure, stressing the importance of a timely departure to each passenger. Sometime close to the hour, most folks return, missing are James Vann and one of the Brazilians, Jose Lucio Passoa. We sent a crewmember to bring them back. The crewmember returns, without the duo, stating they are drunk and refused to come back aboard.

Both were found drinking at a local bar. We waited another hour then our engine-man volunteers to bring them back. Shortly thereafter they are back and very drunk. The American was totally drunk and turned abusive. I had warned them that from now on should they desire to continue to travel with us they are forbidden to go ashore until we reach our destination, the Port of Benjamin Constant in Brazil. At that, they both became very agitated and quarrelsome. I offer them that they should consider perhaps catching tomorrow's local passenger riverboat making a stop at Fonte Boa, which might be more suitable for their travel.

Hearing this, they both decide to get off. I then ordered the crew to put their luggage ashore, return their fares and personal documents and off they go as we pull away, both of them screaming all sorts of obscenities in three different languages. Good riddance I say. As required by the Admiralty Laws of Brazil, I made out an official document of this incident, entering it in the vessel's log, to be filed with the Port Capitan upon my arrival at Tabatinga, Brazil, which later proved to be a very wise thing to do. Again we are under way for the rest of the day and night. That evening we encountered strange weather. It turns hot, and muggy with no wind and, although we are traveling in mid-river channel far from terra firma, a swarm of mosquitoes is upon us. There are millions of them. All our passengers are secure in their screened cabins but we on the bridge are suffering. It's dark now and the mosquitoes, as suddenly as they came, now disappear.

It's past midnight and the mosquitoes return. We are passing the large village of Foz do Jutai and a confluence of the Jutai river. Somewhere near here I know the time changes, but we don't' know where. With the first light, our cook discovers Vann May's American passport. He found it in the crew's head on the main deck. The weather is clearing with some breeze and the day is passing quietly. I am in my hammock with a bad cold. Later in the afternoon we pass another small river town of Belo Horizonte.

It is my estimate that, since Manaus, we have travelled well over a hundred hours. This slow progress is attributed to a very strong current and the incredible load of cargo and our vessel rides heavy in the water. The countryside has changed considerably from down river as we make our way up river. Up until now we passed riverbanks empty of jungle forests. The riverbanks are showing extensive cultivation and pasture land with small cabocle (native) villages along the shores. These are poorly constructed shanties with rusty tin roofs. Now, we begin to see more second growth jungle and the shore areas are much greener. One gets the feeling we are slowly getting away from civilization.

I estimate we have already traveled over 900 miles upstream from Manaus, which is a little more than three quarters of the way to Iquitos,

Peru. It is late afternoon as we pass the large village of San Antonio de Ica, and the mouth of a river of the same name. The river Ica is one of the major tributaries of the Amazon. It really has two names. In Brazil it's Ica and up river, as it crosses the Colombian border, it becomes el Rio Putumayo, where it later creates the geographic border between Colombia and Peru. It is considered very wild and dangerous to navigate yet it is navigable all the way northwest to its last navigable port, Puerto Assis, Colombia.

The weather clears and we have a full moon. It's now the eighth day since we left and we are more than three quarters of the way to our destination. The remainder of the night passes without incident. At sunrise we continue, arriving at Sao Paulo de Olivencia, a large Brazilian Port City. We need to purchase diesel fuel but there is no fuel to be had. We are in trouble to say the least.

We try to purchase fuel from the local riverboats in the harbor but finding nothing. We are told by the Port Captain to try up river at Santa Rita do Weil. We depart shortly after and are bound for Santa Rita, two hours away. I'm keeping my fingers crossed that we will be able to get fuel soon. We arrived three hours later and were able to buy only 70 gallons at triple the price normally charged. We pulled away from a fuel barge but the purchased fuel has water in it, and our brave engine's fuel injectors sputter and spit, but somehow the engine keeps going. After about three hours we hailed down a Colombian tugboat pushing a fuel barge and bound for the Putumayo river, a 12-day journey to the Colombian port of Puerto Assis.

I had met the tugboat Captain, a wonderful Colombian fellow by the name of Cesar Barroso who I invited to have lunch with me. Incredible as it seems, when I tell him I am American he tells me a story of a longtime ago when, as young man serving in Colombian Army, he was a member of a Colombian Infantry Battalion composed of all volunteer's that fought alongside the American 7th Infantry Division in 1951 in Korea. The same war and at the same time as I was there. Well, as you can imagine, we were immediately engrossed in re-telling our respective war stories. He was so much moved by the miracle of our meeting in the middle of the Amazon, that his eyes were full of tears. By the time we parted we knew it was a very rare and emotional experience for both of us.

As a parting gift he gave me two 55-gallon drums of diesel fuel. A God sent gift for me and all concerned. As we pulled away the weather again turned nasty and for the first since I have been on this river, I see whitecaps. The river, at this point, becomes immense in width and the feeling of being at sea returns to mind. The weather clears and as we travel at full speed, Raimundo, our helmsman, runs us aground on a sandbar. The engine-man gets nervous and shuts the engine down. Good Lord, here we are on a sand bar outside the true shipping channel that, through the negligence of Raimundo, had managed to get us stuck. I order the engine-man to start the engine but he, because of his nervousness, he fires all the air from our two compressed air bottles, which are needed to start the engine. It doesn't start and now we have a serious problem, as there is no other way to start the dammed engine and back off the sandbar. It is night now. We light emergency kerosene lanterns both fore and aft and spend the night stuck in the middle of the Amazon.

Night falls, the mosquitoes arrive with incessant buzzing and they are all over us. Morning comes with all its glory. Some boatmen arrive from shore but even they realize our helplessness. There is nothing we can do, except to put up a red flag on the foremast and wait for a passing boat. About noon, we get lucky and a large tugboat pushing a barge arrives at the scene and offers help. I notice the tugboat belongs to a river fleet owned by a Brazilian friend of mine, Mr. Alvaro Maghaleis of Benjamin Constant, Brazil. We fill our compressed air bottles and start the engine but discover that the propeller is jammed against the rudder. We can fix the propeller and in short order it is done.

We cannot fix the steering rudder and steering column. The tugboat, after a short conversation with Alvaro's office via radio, offers to tie us alongside the barge and with our engine on and together with both engines running, we make it for the last leg of our Brazilian journey. The Brazilian river port of Benjamin Constant is located right smack on Peru's border, a stone's throw away. All is well and my friend Mr. Maghaleis has made arrangements with the local Astelleiro (dry dock) in Benjamin Constant to fix the damage.

Off we go and very fast at that with an extra engine going full speed. We almost fly. It really comes down to having a rotten crew. Enough said! At the speed we are now traveling we should reach Benjamin Constant this evening. At 7:30 PM we are passing Colonia Fejoal and, after a while, we see the flickering lights of a large Ticuna Indian village. The visibility is poor and we continue moving at full speed into the infinite darkness. The tug people do not use nightly illumination as offered by me claiming it ruins their night vision. How in hell do they know what's land and what's river? I see nothing but darkness ahead of us. Its midnight now and we are pulling into the B. Constant docks.

We are safe and secure, neatly tied to a municipal pier. Within half an hour a man, who looks and acts like a Mafioso type from the movies, appears at the dock demanding to see me. Come to find out he is, in fact, the true owner of my cargo of cooking oil. He asks me for the official copy of the Port of Manaus manifest and, upon receipt, gives me a phony international cargo manifest from Benjamin Constant, Brazil to Peru's port of Iquitos. The whole thing takes no more than ten minutes. He leaves me with a smile and a message of "Good luck and I will see you in Iquitos."

The crew demands an advance on their wages to get drunk. At first, I say no but then relent and we all go to the local bar for some beer. Tensions disappear. It's midnight. In the morning, the three Brazilian members of our crew demand to be fully paid and discharged, as they do not wish to travel to Peru. I agree, but tell them I must travel to Leticia Colombia, an hour away by local speedboat, to get money.

Finally, it was decided to take our vessel and its cargo directly to the port of Tabatinga, get rid of our passengers, unload the car and three refrigerators, then go to Capitania dos Portos, Tabatinga to discharge the crew. As we pull away from the dock, the vessel fails to respond to the wheel and we drift aimlessly about in the river current. Finally, a small boat comes along and takes us in tow to a nearby ship repair facility where we get the bad news that our rudder is loose and the rudder flange is bent double and the propeller is misaligned with two of the three blades bent to the point of being useless.

I leave Victor at the shipyard and return to B. Constant where we catch a local ferry to take us to the Port of Tabatinga where, upon arrival, we all go to the Office of the Port Captain and proceed to discharge the Brazilian crew. Immediately, a fight ensues with my crew as they demand double pay and are now making a big scandal in front of the office staff at the Port Captain's facility. The whole thing does not look too good for me. Finally, we settle and I am able to get rid of the dammed crew. There are no handshakes because I can't stand the bastards.

As soon as I am finished with the crew, I and my, by now good friend and passenger Gerry Miller, the American, are off to the adjoining town across the border to Leticia Colombia. We change some money to pay bills and buy more diesel fuel. After this, we now must get back to B. Constant. The afternoon ferry left some fifteen minutes ago. We immediately engage a small speedboat, loaded already with a couple of passengers. The speedboat is overloaded and we almost don't make it crossing a very choppy five-mile wide river. We finally catch up with the ferry and arrive at about 7:30 pm in B. Constant in total darkness.

Surprised, we found our vessel back to the municipal pier all spick and span with a smiling Victor awaiting us. What happen during the day was amazing. Victor and four workers from the boat yard had spent almost all day diving and fixing our boat's problems. The most amazing thing is that they removed the bent propeller under water, repaired and re-installed it and did the same thing with the rudder. Now, we all get drunk. Early the next day we finally get underway to the Port of Tabatinga. Upon arrival at the dock, we are met by a Brazilian Coast Guard Officer. A young lieutenant who informs me that, upon examination of my documents and manifest of my vessel issued to me in Manaus, there are several discrepancies and we are to remain at the Port Captain's dock in Tabatinga, until further notice.

This asshole, in order to prevent us from sailing, orders his man to remove one of my fuel injectors and I am stranded In Tabatinga, which is located only a stone's throw from the Peruvian border. While aboard, thinking what possibly more could go wrong, two Brazilian civilians board and identify themselves as members of Brazilian Federal Police. They ask me to accompany them to their office adjoining Port Captain's building. Once inside, they ask me for my personal papers and the ship's documents. I show them my passport and also other personal documents. Then, I am ordered to empty my pockets, which include my wallet where they find my US Armed Forces Retired ID card, Florida Driver's License and Special Forces Association membership card.

A series of personal questions are asked and while all this is happening, my interrogator, a young friendly looking man, tells me that there has been an official "Denuncia Oficial" filed against me for making a seditious derogatory comment and remark in public against Brazil and its Government. After two hours of interrogation and after rummaging through contents of my wallet, these folks realize that I am a victim of someone's wrath, and nothing more. The whole situation changes and now I am served a nice cup of coffee and the rest of the officers are very anxious hear of my wartime past with US Special Forces in Vietnam. So we talk about the Viet Nam war and my time there. Now they tell me that an American countryman, Vann May, made this denouncement against me. They apologize and let me go. It's late in the day. I return to my boat and think I am stuck in this place. I have had enough of this fucking boat, this fucking river and the whole fucking world!

I'm spending a night aboard with an armed guard outside on the dock. Early the next day, I am summoned to the Office of the Port Captain. Upon arrival with all my ship's documents, passport, etc., I am ushered directly into the Port Captain's office and asked to take a seat. The Port Captain then speaks to me in a rapid Portuguese. I answer in Spanish saying that I am having problem understanding Portuguese. He smiles and in perfect English, asks me some personal questions. Then obviously being already briefed by The Federal Police folks, asks me about my military service. To my surprise tells me that had spent two years as a Brazilian Naval Exchange Officer, and was stationed in Washington DC. The bottom line of all this is that he calls in his subordinate, the same nasty bastard that had detained me and my vessel. To my surprise, the Teniente is ordered to replace the fuel injectors taken from my vessel. Further, in my presence, he tells him to immediately issue a Port clearance for my departure. As a parting comment he tells me "Capt. Slugocki, you certainly have had a very interesting and adventurous life, I wish you luck."

I really don't believe this turn of events and I ask permission of the Port Duty Officer, if I could leave my vessel at the Capitania's dock until I am able to muster a sufficient crew to take it to Peru. He answers affirmatively but gives me only a twenty-four hour permit as a large Brazilian ferry from Manaus will be arriving the next afternoon and I must be gone by then. I tell Victor to take charge and leave immediately via speed boat for B. Constant to speak to my friend Alvaro Maghaleis about borrowing a couple of river men for the rest of my voyage to Iquitos, Peru which is still some 286 river miles away from the tri border area.

After a short meeting, I thank him profusely for towing me with his tugboat and, at the same time, ask him to loan me at least two Marineros, one as Motorista, and the second as an assistant to my principal river Pilot. He kindly loaned me a Brazilian crew and, after a couple of hours waiting, the two appear. B. Constant's Ferry is ready to go. Nilo Morreira, the Motorista, suggests he would like to take his girlfriend Marixenia as our cook. I immediately agree. The second new member of our crew arrives and we wait another hour plus for the new cook. She appears and off we go. This time I engaged a speedboat to get us to Tabatinga. We all arrive safely and are all aboard.

Taking stock of the situation, I decide to move our vessel away from municipal dock to Santa Rosa Island across the Amazon and on the Peruvian side of the river almost directly opposite Brazil. This place is still referred to as Puerto Ramon Castillia, a former Port of Entry for Peru, now completely abandoned as the last year high water flood washed away the entire post, its buildings, port's wharf along with its people, leaving nothing but half destroyed and abandoned structure that used to be Peru's Port Captain's office. The Peruvian side on Santa Rosa Island is unfortunately located on the low side of the Amazon and subject to annual flooding. It is here we move to just in case there's a change of mind by the Brazilian authorities.

Early the next day, we dispatch our small dinghy across the river to Brazil's commercial port where there is large open-air market. Marixenia does the food shopping for our voyage. The dinghy, upon return, takes me to the Colombian port town of Leticia, adjacent to Brazil's Tabatinga, a ten minutes trip. Here I look for a friend of mine, an American expatriate by the name of Mike Tssalikis, originally from Tarpon Springs Florida and a longtime resident of Leticia who is commonly referred by the locals as the unofficial 'mayor' of this small Colombian port city. Mike knew everybody in this tri-border area. Mike's business used to be exporting fish to Colombia's capital of Bogota. He also became a tourist camp operator and hotel owner. There was even an American documentary film made of his exploits in this area of Amazon.

The reason for my visit had nothing to do with our friendship. It would be through him and his personal contacts that I would secure a safe passage from Colombian drug pirates and mafia based in Leticia. He arranged for me to a pass, without any problems, through the Amazon river area from Leticia up river, all the way past Puerto Allegria. We were cleared on to Chimbote and all the way along the Colombian side of the border on the Amazon river to Isla Tigre and the mouth of the Atacuari river, which forms the political border with Peru.

This area was, and I think still is, a man-made island where the Amazon river provides the natural border of the two countries. The small islands in this area belong to neither Colombia nor Peru, creating a natural haven for all kinds of bad people either Colombian or Peruvian. Mike would have to vouch for my person, and crew as not being members or agents of the American or Peruvian Police or drug enforcement people. As to the piracy operations, we had already paid them for the ship's safe passage in Leticia.

You might call the whole thing pre-paid life insurance. With proper payments made, we returned aboard. This evening we sail. We pulled away from Ramon Castillia late that afternoon in bad weather and hugged the port side of the river, a territory of Peru. We hoisted the Peruvian Flag on the foremast and kept clipping along all the way to Puerto Allegria, a new Permanent Port of entry in Peru.

Its late evening. A drunk, wearing the uniform of the Peruvian Customs Police staggers aboard. He demands whisky for himself and his girlfriend. The girlfriend turns out to be under arrest by Peruvian Customs for smuggling a kilogram of "Pasta from Iquitos" (a raw base form of unrefined cocaine). She is presently in the custody of my new drunken friend. An incredible situation develops. The girl, also drunk, engages me in a conversation and tells me that she was taken off one of the riverboats serving the route between Iquitos and the tri-country frontier. She admits having the dope on her person, stating that now she is awaiting transportation back to Iquitos. In the meanwhile, she is forced to fuck the entire police station in Puerto Allegria.

Do I believe her? I don't know. The drunken customs man, after examining my documents and cargo manifest, says it is all wrong and that he will put all my documents in order. We are getting ready to leave the next morning and true to his words, all my Peruvian documentation is in order and neatly arranged in a manila folder. My friend now asks me about a "Propina" for all this service. I pay him fifty dollars. Nothing is free you know. We take a woman and her child aboard, bound for Iquitos. This is a courtesy as the woman is the wife of one of the border police officials. We pull away from the dock at about noon and immediately, the weather turns and, after two hours underway, we seek the shelter of shore, tied well to a large tree on the riverbank. We stay put here until the weather improves. After a couple of hours, we venture from this safe place and start our journey. All the channels are choked with floating debris. It is a very dangerous situation but, as we are five days behind schedule, we take a chance and go on.

Victor and I are almost permanently on the bridge. One steers and the other works our powerful spotlight. With the exception of our passengers we are all up including the cook who keeps us in coffee and also takes her turn with the searchlight. In order to avoid the main shipping channel of the river where all that shit is, we take a chance and enter an alternate channel between Isla de Cacao and shore. On the port side of us is heavy jungle on shore and we find less heavy flotsam but encounter large logs floating just at the water level, and difficult to see even though we navigate with our illumination. The situation on the bridge is very tense. The woman with her baby is told to wear a life jacket and stay in her enclosed cabin next to the mess table on the second deck. Gerry, the American, helps with the search light duty. We should make it to the large village of Caballo Cocha in a couple of hours where we plan to spend the rest of the night.

At exactly 23:56 PM we strike a floating tree. The vessel shudders as the tree and its branches makes an awful noise as it passes under our keel, then breaking our steering protector flange and dislocating our rudder. We immediately are thrown to starboard, striking shore. Thank God its muddy flats cushioned our impact on the shore. But all is well and we did not sink and the tree passed under our keel and did not puncture our hull. Victor enters the water, which is only chest deep. We are stuck in mud, all safe and sound. The engine room deck is free of water and the main cargo hatch, at keel level, is dry. I announce, "let's go to bed and sleep, and tomorrow we will see what must be done". After just a few hours of sleep we are all up with first light to asses our damage.

Checking the propeller, its shaft and stuffing box will require getting into the water and these muddy, turbulent water back channels of the Amazon are extremely dangerous to humans, as they are the primary places where the most dangerous and feared creature makes its home and feeds on unwary fish or humans. Its Brazilian name is Cundiru and in Peru it is known as Carnero (the butcher). This tiny fish, no longer than two to three inches or even smaller, and 1/8" in diameter, enters a fish through its mouth or body cavity, gets into its stomach area and consumes its insides then bore's out of the fish's body. This kills the fish. In humans it can enter any cavities including the ears, nose or rectum. It can actually enter a body through a person's urinary stream, then feeling trapped, open up its side knives, like two sharp fins and cuts into human flesh. It can only be removed by surgery. A horrible thing. The next danger is the ever-present piranha.

We enter the water wearing underwear, long pants, with cotton stuck in our ears and nose and take our chances. We dive down into this watery mixture of mud and water armed with large two large six-pound hammers. We try to straighten the propeller arms by taking turns with myself then Victor then Nilo, the engine man. The other Brazilian crewmember is afraid and refuses to dive or enter water. Our Gerry Miller, "El Americano," jumps in to help. What balls! Out of nowhere appear two local Indian folks, who were fishing nearby in their canoe.

They join us and shortly there is a loud scream from one of them. One of the Indians holds on to his ear, his face showing a great pain. He continues to scream. Victor is nearest to him. He looks and hollers "Carnero!" We all rushed to help him. But to help how? Looking into his left ear we are barely able to see a small fish tail. Victor jumps back aboard down into engine room and comes back with small pliers, reaches into the man's ear and grabs the tail and pulls it out. It's a bloody mess! It looks like he pulled out not only the carnero, but also a great bit of flesh. We rush this guy aboard, load him up with pain and penicillin pills and put sterile dressing on his ear. We want him to stay aboard but he declines, jumps into their canoe, and furiously paddles away. Oh my God, what next!

There are five of us able body men in the water pulling a stout manila rope securely tied to the boat's stern. We pull to the right and then to left. This goes on for about an hour of maybe more. Slowly, it seems, the boat begins to float free. How it happen we don't know. Victor remarks that this was because the water had risen with all the rain we been having. Anyway, the rest is quite easy, for we now have a spare propeller aboard. With all of our combine strength we place the rudder back into its stanchion rod base. Changing the propeller takes at least two hours.

Again we are underway and pass the mouth of the black water channel that would take us to Caballo Cocha. We pass an entry to Caballo Cocha and continue to sail in the Isla Cacao channel, now desperate to get to Iquitos, which is still some twenty hours away. In a while we are almost at the end of the Isla Cacao channel, and are about enter back into main channel of the Amazon, when we encounter another storm. When it struck us it immediately blew our supper off the upper deck dining table with a clatter of broken dishes, then next went the chairs. One of the chairs flew against the cabins rear wall and broke the sink's mirror to smithereens. Birds seeking refuge flew about wildly and if they smashed against our dining room bulkhead, were killed and fell to the deck. We head for the shore. Victor and I are holding the wheel to hard starboard and somehow we make it. As we closed in to shore, Victor, in a desperate effort, jumps ashore and is able to tie us down to a stout tree. Its lower limbs hit and break two of our starboard deck support beams and one of the smaller branches breaks and enter the passenger cabin door.

The whole place looks eerie. With all this destruction while being heaved back and forth against the riverbank, we hold secure. I just hope the tree and the rope holds. It held and after a short time all is well and the storm passes. When Rios takes the wheel I notice his hands are trembling. We enter the main channel of the Amazon and in a short time we arrive at the Peruvian border outpost at Chimbote.

Here after some uneventful formalities, we meet the family of my friend in Iquitos. Sr. Oliveira, the last of the so-called "Patrones" of the Atacuari River. His son Pedro and his family of three teenage kids, all bound for Iquitos, ask me for passage. Of course I agree as Pedro is an excellent river man, and will help at the helm. The second reason is that the Oliveira family is one of the strongest family clans in this area and virtually controls the entire area of a border river of Atacuari and Isla Tigre. So you see I could not refuse. All is now well and at late evening the entire surface of the Amazon is covered with floating debris, and drifting trees. As the river is now in a full flood, it becomes too dangerous to navigate in the dark so we stop.

Bugs, bugs, and more bugs. All attack our two lights at the open dining room area topside. We all watch in amazement as they fly in continuous circles around the light bulbs, getting closer and closer until being fried by the heat from the bulbs. The stench is overpowering. Finally we are forced to switch our generator off. All lights off. Everyone up at early morning, hot coffee while pulling away from the bank, temperature cool and visibility good. In late afternoon we arrive at a Piuyal Military Control outpost at the mouth of the small Amazon tributary, the Ampiyacu. Thank God we have the Oliveira' family aboard.

Thus escape the hassles and attempted shake down by the sour looking, ill tempered, members of the Peruvian military, which its members most likely are garrisoned here at this shit place, as punishment for God knows what bad deeds. We are underway the whole night with bright moon lighting the river channel. We decided to stop after midnight and take a break. All up the next morning and our routine follows and we are underway on our last leg before Iquitos. But on late afternoon we notice our fuel consumption soars as the river now is in a flood stage with current strengthens to its maximum. I estimate its speed to be at least 3 to 4 knots per hour. We will definitely need more diesel fuel before Iquitos. As there are no major villages of river towns between this point and our destination our only hope is to find fuel at small sawmills along the way. We got lucky at Yanamono channel and were able to purchase 25 gallons of diesel. It's still not enough to reach the Port of Iquitos. We stopped for the night and. tomorrow, God willing we reach our destination.

We are all up early for our last day of travel. At some distance we make for a large village of Indiana, where with luck we are able to purchase 26 more gallons of fuel. We will be in Iquitos before nightfall. I feel relieved and take a nap. We arrive late in afternoon. It's after 5:00 pm and we are docked at the Port of Iquitos the Capitania. We are at the Harbor Master Station, waiting for port clearance and an hour later an Officer of The Peruvian "Guarda Costa" comes aboard and gives me permission to disembark our Peruvian passengers. He orders me to stay at the Harbor Station Facility for the port entry inspection tomorrow because M/V Cidade de Natal is a foreign flag vessel. This marks the end of my journey. Tomorrow I will be able to meet with my shipping agent, Mr. Percy Zevallos, will clear Port, move to Iquitos Muncipal pier and disembark my cargo. It has been a long journey of some twenty long days and nights. The hell with regulations, the bright lights of Iquitos calling, my friend Gerry the American and I sneak out and have a nice dinner at El Meson restaurant and then some Cuba Libre's to calm our frayed nerves.

Peru

CHAPTER 19

See No Evil – Hear No Evil

In the early time of my days on the river, I primarily worked with M/V Margarita in cargo trade without getting involved with passenger and tourist charters and all that. There were days spent in Iquito waiting for something to happen as the boat did not have work all the time. These days, waiting for bookings, were treated by me as a sort of vacation. I did not do much and the crew worked only in the morning hours in boat maintenance, with the cook doing breakfast. Lunch and evening meals were at a local restaurant.

Quite frankly, I sort of avoided the up river trips and preferred the tri-border destinations of Peru, Colombia and Brazil. Well, Brazil only to its two border ports of Tabatinga and Benjamin Constant, not the interior. My riverboat was built primarily as a river cargo vessel. After refitting in Manaus now offers a limited facility for passengers with cabin accommodations, plus it required extra crewmembers, like a steward and an extra deckhand. On one of those afternoons while tied up to a giant mango tree at the City of Iquitos Puerto Malecon located directly at the foot of Putumayo street. In the last 20 years the river has changed its course and the former City Port no longer exists.

On this particular Sunday afternoon two strange men came aboard, and finding Lisandro my crewmember sound asleep in his hammock on cargo deck, barged up the ladder to the second deck without announcing their presence. This managed to immediately piss me off.

First it was Sunday afternoon, secondly, it was my time to take a couple of hour's siesta, and thirdly, both came aboard with dirty, muddy shoes and walked aboard onto a freshly scrubbed deck and without the common courtesy customary to receive shouted permission to board. Enough of that. Then they were standing right next to me, somewhat apologetic for their Sunday afternoon intrusion. Never the less, I invited both men to sit at the mess table and asked "what was the purpose of their visit." At this they produced their U.S. Drug Enforcement Agency's credentials and assured me there was nothing for me to be concerned about. They then politely asked me if I was a citizen of United States to which I replied yes and then did I mind producing my passport? I went to my cabin and brought it to them.

At this point of fun and games, one of the two rattled off all kinds of personal information pertaining to me. This pissed me off to no end. If they knew my name and all the personal stuff about me, then what was the purpose of their request for my passport? But I kept my mouth shut. They knew all about my military service, plus my years of service with the Department of Justice, US Marshal's Service. They were very pleasant and proper and continued their one-way conversation. They said the purpose of their visit was to engage me as a source of information about the drug traffic. To put it plainly they propositioned me to become a confidential informer about river drug traffic between Peru and its frontier with Colombia. Further there would be financial remuneration.

They kept on talking about how valued my cooperation would be as an Owner/Captain of a Peruvian flagged vessel engaged in commerce trade on the Amazon river while impressing on me that it would also be my patriotic duty to do so. They said that I was the best person around for this type of clandestine work. Not saying yes, and not saying no to their proposal for me to be stool pigeon for the U.S. D.E.A. Long after their departure I just sat there at the mess table, very much upset and a bit afraid for my person. I noticed that both agent's Spanish language was accentuated with a heavy Mexican accent. Question—would the DEA send two bungling Mexican/Americans as covert anti-drug agents to South America where they would not fit in in the interior of Peru? Their speech was ethnically alien to the area of the Peruvian Amazonia. Who knows. They certainly spoiled a perfect Sunday afternoon for me. With their personal appearance, and facial features, they stood out like a sore thumb among the local population. The problem now is how to decline their offer and avoid further contact with them.

Amazon River boat B/M "Tucunare".

We were to meet the next day to talk further about my involvement, at a specific and predetermined time in the Belen City Market area of Iquitos, at the rear entrance of Importaciones Osvaldo Perez Srl, a large commercial wholesale house located on the most crowded side street and next to a huge monster like the Iquitos Central Market. At this time of my meeting with them, I would either agree or turn down their proposal. Having taken all things into consideration I did not appear at the prescribed time. The reason quite simple, I was afraid, and had serious concern for my safety. I was not sure if they were for real. The Town of Iquitos at this time of year is full of people making big money being involved in illegal drug traffic. So much so that you never knew who you could be talking to.

The local criminal organizations working in the illegal and very lucrative drug traffic business were well organized with many paid informants on their payroll always looking for police spies, and just a hint that I was working with the Police, could spell the end of me, period. And on a late Sunday afternoon, together with Lisandro my crewmember, we pulled away from my downtown anchorage, motored downstream where we later entered a small Amazon tributary of the Nanai river, heading for a hiding place at Morona Cocha, a small lake on the outskirts of Iquitos.

There I remained for several days while I would travel surreptitiously to town in the early morning or very late evening hour. I got my crew together and immediately informed my Shipping Agent/Cargo broker, Senior Percy Zevallos, to look for cargo to take to the frontier, as soon as possible and get out of town. In a few days I got lucky. Percy arranged for a cargo of potatoes, at a very reduced rate, covering only the price of fuel, food and crew. I changed our port of departure from Iquitos proper to a small port located at a community adjacent to Iquitos called Bella Vista. It must be noted here that Percy was briefed in full by me about my contact with the so-called DEA agents and their proposal. Cleared by the Port Captain's people, and armed with all official documents, we departed in late afternoon for the Peruvian border village of Islandia on the Yavari river, which at this time was used for a trans-shipment point for all legal and not so legal cargo destined for Tabatinga, Brazil and Colombian Port of Leticia Colombia.

Coming back to the drug situation in this part of the world—it was such that just about everyone in Iquitos knew of or had friends who were involved in the illegal drug business. Attesting this was a small construction boom in the city of Iquitos on the river. We began to see very expensive, large outboard engines mounted on high speed speedboats, restaurant and bars full of people making merry and on the streets one noted a great number of brand new American pickup trucks, in a City which is located in the middle of the Amazon jungle whose longest road was twenty kilometers long leading to nowhere. The time I am talking about was in the early 1980's.

As to all those newly found riches, some said it was because of the oil boom in the jungles and in the foothills of the Andes, and the Peruvian Amazon basin. True to a point, as the town was full of gringo oil field workers with pockets full of hundred dollar bills. But that was only partially true. The truth being that the famous Amazon River at this time became known by the locals as the "The Cocaine Highway".

The proposition made by these two men forced me really think about how dangerous my situation would be while running a riverboat as the only foreigner "Patron" (Master or Owner) of a Peruvian flag river vessel. Not only that, were the two DEA agents, really what they purported to be? Or were they members of the mafia and were phony, DEA agents and a part of the same international drug cartel, attempting to ensnare me, and cause my demise? All this could result in just another corpse floating down river. My forced involuntary trip was not without some excitement and without some perverted fun. As for cargo of 10,000 kg of the best Peruvian Andean highland potatoes consigned to my Cargo Agent, an old friend Sr. Nilson Maghaleis at port of Islandia further, to be conveyed to, I don't know who.

This voyage of some 268-river miles from Iquitos, had taken us two days and two nights running, including mandatory stops at a Peruvian Military Control Point at Piyual, located outside of small river town of Pevas, then once more down river to the next Military Control Point of Chimbote, and finally at the Peruvian Border Control Port at Puerto Allegria. On the first night of our voyage, as we were passing river channel of Isla Canton, we were hailed, stopped, and boarded by a Peruvian National Police speedboat. As usual the cops were more interested in getting a good supper than inspecting anything aboard, and since M/V Margarita was well known for its good food served, it was all because of Doña Maria our cook. A small table was set on the mid-ship cargo hatch, and police had a good meal including a beer. After small talk, as it was late, but before pulling away from us, this standard question:

"Did we see any suspicious looking boats running without lights, or hear outboard engines along the way?" The standard answer was given: No. However, this time we were also warned of pirate activities in the immediate area of Peru and Colombia. With this warning we went off into the night. The next afternoon we sailed close to the Colombian—Peruvian border. At this point the river is at its widest. We noticed, some three miles across, a small speedboat leaving the Colombian village of Tigrillo at high speed and approaching us. This could be a good or very bad situation for us if this speedboat belongs to Colombian river pirates who regularly rob passenger riverboats out of Iquitos that are bound for the frontier.

Certificate issued by the Peruvian government to designate Albert Slugocki the rank of Captain (Capitan Fluvial) of an Amazon River boat.

M/V Margarita, painted white and very impressive looking, could be mistaken for a passenger vessel. As the speedboat approached we realized it was a drug smuggler's boat out of Isla Tigre. As its four occupants tied alongside our port side, and boarded, they were found to be well known to us from our occasional visits to Leticia. They knew of our neutrality and non-involvement with anybody. What they desperately needed were outboard engine spark plugs and oil for their boat. While aboard they asked if it would it be possible to get a decent meal and they were willing to pay for it out of their pocket. Doña Maria again did not disappoint, and a good meal was served. Our guests were served at the same table, sat on the same chairs, as did the Police a day ago. Then they paid in full for spark plugs and oil and left a good tip for Maria. Before pulling away they asked us, in a very serious tone of voice, the standard questions; "did we encounter any police patrols during our journey?" Of course, we replied with our standard "no."

We arrived at Puerto Allegria, the Peruvian Border control Point. We passed through without any further problems as we delivered a large sack of personal mail, plus we gave the Police folks four copies of Lima's major newspaper, "The El Comercio." We also had a great number of semi-pornographic, fully illustrated magazines, not counting a special type of courtesy donation to their food pantry, which was a 50-kilo sack of the best Peruvian highlands potatoes, and with smiles and farewells all around, we pulled away and continued on with our load of potatoes. Upon our return to Iquitos I found, to my great happiness, that there have been no inquiries as to my whereabouts. No one was looking for me. I was happy to be, once more, tied to a big mango tree on shore, awaiting my next voyage.

CHAPTER 20

Juan Perez Kaiapa

In early 1980's while looking around for jungle areas that would offer good sports fishing opportunities for the American fishermen, TREK International Safaris of Jacksonville, Florida, a world class sports fishing and hunting outfitter, recently became my clients. I ran into Mr. Leung, a Chinese Peruvian merchant, in Iquitos, Peru, who, besides being one of the most prominent businessmen, was also an ardent and accomplished sports fisherman angler and, when I was in the Port of Iquitos, we would frequent small cafés catering almost exclusively to this town's locals. It was in one of these places, where everybody knew each other, and sometimes business transactions were made on the premises. The name of this café was simply Pedro's, named after its owner Sr. Pedro Rodrigues. This establishment was located conveniently on the main street of Iquitos.

On one of my early mornings, while I was having my breakfast, my friend Mr. Leung introduced me to Jack Palmer, an American missionary evangelist preacher who, at this time, had spent some 25 years preaching and living with his wife Ms. Vivian in the most remote jungle areas of the upper Amazon, Peru. Jack, in addition to being a Baptist missionary, was one of the best fishermen that I have known.

Jack, at this time, made his home at a Yagua Indian jungle village located on the small Amazon river tributary by the name of Apayacu. He and his wife lived and preached the Holy Gospel to the Indian tribal people. Shortly after our meeting, I was on my way in a small skiff, travelling some four plus hours to visit with Jack and check out this area for possible future fishing in its black water jungle lakes and streams. A warm greeting awaited me upon my arrival at Jack and Ms. Vivian's house. Incredible as it may sound their house was really something to behold and something that I did not expect, for it was a real house, built on the high bank of the Apayacu River.

It was a comfortable place located a small distance from a local village named Yanyacu. To my surprise I found that Jack was not only a very good fisherman but also a very efficient "Jack of all trades," a skilled hunter, with a gas refrigerator full of wild game meat, and a generator quietly humming in his front yard. On top of all of this, Jacks house contained a fully operational short wave international radio station with capability of worldwide communication. Shortly thereafter I was being treated to a real home cooked meal. We called the US with a phone-patch to my dear and very much surprised wife Margaret in Fort Lauderdale, Florida.

Fishing wise we found many of the black water lakes or "Cocha's" and streams to fish in with a great abundance of fish to be had. At the same time a friendship developed with the local Yagua Tribe. They were very receptive to my idea of bringing in the "gringo" sports fishermen. As it was not commercial fishing in nature, it would give the village a chance to earn some money. Villagers would be paid to be fishing guides and outboard motor boat operators. Added to this they would be given all the fish needed for food and the remainder of the fish would be released. In time, the villagers became our friends, and I became a proud member of their community, the Yaguas.

Through much time passing, I became very involved in their community affairs while offering limited medical attention to their people. I would bring in things from the far-away Iquitos, including articles of primary needs. We would evacuate the sick to government clinics. In our travels we visited other Native Indian communities. The Apayacu tribe hold a special place in my heart, and during my frequent visits to this area during fishing season, I have meet many of the local people. Some worked for me, not only as fishing guides, but also as jungle expedition guides, and at times as members of my crew. There was one individual man that was above all. His name was Juan Perez Kaiapa.

From my beginning to work with local people in the Apayacu river area I had been struck with the extreme jungle skills of this one man in particular. This man was J.P.Kaiapa. Actually, even before meeting him, I heard tales from other members of the village. Lisandro, the village chief, told me stories of Kaiapa's extra ordinary skills as a hunter/gatherer.

During one particular visit, wanting to talk to Kaiapa, I was informed he had gone hunting and would be back with sufficient "Carne Del Monte" (jungle meat) to feed his family of eight for a month's time. The Carne Del Monte represents a multitude of jungle animals, including monkeys, pacybaras, deer, rat like mahas and wild birds, all hunted by local Indians in the great vastness of the Amazon forest.

Due to the Amazon forest immensity, hunting for meat was a major undertaking involving an incredible knowledge of the jungle terrain, a thorough knowledge of jungle navigation skills, the ability to walk great distances to find game, and, just as a general matter, of survival. On a personal note, having a fair knowledge of SE Asia's jungles I would rate the Amazon Jungle forest as the toughest of all. The animals of this forest, wise in their way of survival, and fearing man's encroachment of their living range, live as far away as possible from humans. As the villagers, in search of possible jungle agriculture plots, move into deep forestland, the animals retreat deeply into the interior vastness of the jungle.

Many of the Yagua, and other tribal peoples such as the Huitotos and Boras, were also afraid to enter into the interior vastness of the Amazon forests. For many, upon venturing into the jungle, were never to return and became victims of the jungle by getting lost, falling prey to wild animals and poisonous reptiles, and other accidents. There are powerful superstitions governing real and imaginary dangers from evil spirits residing in the great darkness of its nights, when strange sounds of the jungle are heard. Especially dangerous are the jungle lakes and swamps where giant Anaconda snakes dwell and attack and devour all trespassers. Sudden fevers are to be had from the depths of its evil smelling swamps.

Many frightening tales abound of empty canoes with broken paddles found in these lakes, without a trace of its owner. Many of the black water lakes are guarded by evil spirits called "Tunche's" who at night emit haunting sounds of warning against all that trespass its territories. Many of such lakes, being full of fish, were avoided with great care by local people.

Juan Perez Kaiapa then was looked upon by local people as an extra ordinary man, possessor of rare skills, a successful hunter, who was not afraid of all evil spirits and other dangers. He would enter this forbidding forest bare footed and armed only with a 16 gage shotgun and a handful of shells. He would carry a small handmade satchel containing a kilo of fried dry farinha (fried yucca) a box of wooden matches secured in a small plastic pouch, a sharp knife-like machete, no rain gear, and no mosquito repellant. He traveled in his trusty canoe, which had been carved out of a tree trunk and a wooden paddle. He would go on hunting forays for four to eight days duration.

He'd stash his canoe somewhere in the forest and then go on foot. Coming back he loaded his canoe full of smoked jungle meat. Being a dead shot would represent one shot to one animal. During his hunting forays he would use handmade traps and snares, and kill fish with a handmade spear. In time passing we became friends and I would learn the true story of this extra ordinary man.

Juan Kaiapa was born in the high Amazon jungle, the foothills of the great Andes Mountains somewhere close to Peru's border with Ecuador. The area of his birth is described generally to be between Rio Postaza and Rio Napo. He was born in a warlike Indian tribe of Achual, the dwellers of the Amazon highlands. This inaccessible wilderness was, and still is a home of the much-feared tribe of Achual and Jivaro Indian tribes who, until just a decade ago, were migratory in nature.

Both tribes were murdering their neighbors. Taking their heads and shrinking them to the size of a small coconut. They were referred to as "Reducidores de Cabezas". They practiced their grisly art well into the 20th century. As the story goes Kaiapa, for some unexplained reason, left his tribal village and joined an all American "Gringo" oil exploratory crew working in the adjacent jungle which in the early 1970's of the past century, penetrated that area of Amazon jungle in search of oil. He travelled with this American crew northwest as far away as the Rio Napo and the Peruvian border with Ecuador. There, in the border town of Pantoja, the Americans crossed the border into Ecuador and Kaiapa was left behind to fend for himself. Shortly after he became engaged by an illegal Peruvian logging outfit working along the shores of Rio Napo as, guess what?

A became a hunter, or, to be exact, their "Carne Del Monte" for the logging crew. As he continued to relate his life's story he said the illegal logging outfit consisted of an old river tugboat, a large cargo barge, an old Caterpillar tractor and the crew of some assorted eight to ten men. Armed with chainsaws they would illegally cut trees along the shores of the Napo River, as they sailed downstream and then, surreptitiously, transport them to a sawmill located on the outskirts of the Peruvian river town of Iquitos. After spending some time being docked alongside the sawmill, this group of "forest bandits" sailed down the Amazon River to the area of their future logging operations on a far and remote border river named Yavari. An estimated voyage time was two weeks. Yavari is a political border between Brazil and Peru surrounded by impenetrable jungle.

To this day lawlessness prevails. The Yavari, Galvez, and Yaquarona rivers are the most remote river areas in the entire Amazon region. A floating outfit such as this travels at a very slow pace and after some twenty four hours found itself somewhere close to the confluence of Napo and the Amazon rivers. It docked for the night on a riverbank in front of a small Ribereno village called "Brazil." The crew went ashore, and got stone drunk on a yucca alcohol called Masate. The drinking continued all night and well into next day, until about midday the Patron of the outfit decided to send Kaiapa hunting.

Kaiapa strongly protested and attempted to explain to a half-drunk patron that there really was a no place to hunt in the immediate area of this village. Patron persisted with his request. After some hours Kaiapa came back empty handed and meet the full wrath of the Patron and crew. They sailed in the late evening. Sometime during the night they entered the main channel of the Amazon, and kept on drinking.

At one point things got ugly. Kaiapa was accused of failure to provide them with food. Jokes were made about him being a headhunter, and more. Somewhere just past the Isla Salvador, about an hour sailing to the mouth of Apayacu river, Kaiapa was seized by the crew, who tied his legs, and were about to tie his hands as Kaiapa struggled. He was thrown overboard into the river and he entered the cold waters of the Amazon gasping for air. He told me he was sure he would drown but somehow managed to untie his legs and began to swim, fighting the strong current. The fact being that this happened in the month of March when the Amazon River is in full flood, with very strong currents of at least at 3.5 miles per hour, with dangerous whirlpools abounding, the river's surface full of floating debris, logs, and parts of trees with branches. A very dangerous situation to say the least. He managed to swim from one floating clump of vegetation to another, getting closer and close to the river's bank.

Finally reaching the shore by holding onto some tree branches, he passed out from exhaustion. With daylight a local fisherman found him. Thinking he was dead he threw his casting net on his body, tied the net to his canoe and started to paddle away towards the mouth of the Apayacu river. The net dragged Kaiapa under water where he came to and started to scream. This is how he was saved and found his way to the Yanayacu village, settled down, married a local Yagua woman, had a multitude of kids, and became a member of this village.

Shortly after Kaiapa's recount of his life adventure, I became engaged in series of commercial contracts with Iquitos merchants to carry cargo to and from the tri-border areas to Iquitos. These folks paid me well, and our cargo was clean, no contraband. Just merchandise manufactured in Brazil, like clothes garments, comestibles like sugar, salt, beans, flour and just basic things like this. All nice and clean. The downside of all this was a danger of local Colombian bandits who plied their trade at the level of the mouth of a small river named Atacuari where Colombia and Peru meet. Paying off this area's bandit boss, Sr. Ramon, didn't always work. The Peruvian military outpost located at the mouth of Isla de Cacao channel, and Peruvian Customs and border outpost at Puerto Allegria, were of no help either.

The type of cargo carried aboard M/V Margarita offered a very lucrative target. Starting at Isla Santa Rosa's departure port, we would never announce our departure time or date. For example upon receipt of the Port Captain's clearance to sail early in the afternoon, we would not sail until the hour of darkness, which, at this latitude, almost always was 6:30 pm. Then after a respective distance all navigation lights were put out and closely hugging the Peruvian side of river we would sail in complete darkness.

Every half an hour on the hour we would stop our engine and listen to any sounds of outboard motors, as no person in his right mind would run a speedboat at night, except "Bad Guys". Upon entry into the Isla de Cacao channel, a narrow deep-water channel separating the main navigation channel of Amazon by Cacao Island we would dispatch one of our skiffs equipped with an outboard motor and high-powered searchlight looking for anybody lurking thereabouts. The person aboard the skiff was always Sr. Kaiapa. The skiff would run for a few minutes and then shut down. Then Kaiapa would listen for any noise ahead of us. For Kaiapa had an extraordinary sense of hearing. In addition to being our human hearing aid Kaiapa became my personal bodyguard during our border runs.

As the time went by, my visits to Apayacu river area became more rare. We were now travelling more, and more upriver and all the way to the Ucayali and Maranon rivers. Now, some two years later, I was having my afternoon coffee and piece of apple pie at "Ari Burger" a well-known local restaurant located on Plaza de Armas, in downtown Iquitos. There was a local custom of sitting and watching the outside sidewalk to observe the great mass of human "flotsam and jetsam" passing and looking at us inside while we watched them outside. The outside bunch consisted primarily of street vendors, pimps offering their sisters, cocaine peddlers and out of work pseudo tourist guides. Out of this bedlam who steps into the restaurant, but my friend Kaiapa.

Glad to see him, I invited him to sit down. Kaiapa almost immediately started to tell me a sad story about his son Walquer Cahuachi who at an approximate age of 12 was sick. He was having a really difficult time breathing, was spiting blood, complaining of always being tired, and was, just this afternoon, discharged from a local regional hospital. The local doctors diagnosed him as having a very serious heart condition with a hole in his heart. The situation was so bad that the doctors declared Walquer's medical situation hopeless and that, without a very involved and difficult operation, Walquer would die. Unfortunately this operation could not be performed In Iquitos.

Due to the lack of a heart specialist, the local hospital was without the capability to perform this kind of medical procedure. Suggestion was made, that perhaps in the Capital city of Lima something could be done. But upon inquiry, Kaiapa was notified that it could happen but the cost of such an operation would be at least $15,000.00 US dollars, without any guarantee of success. He was further informed that only in the USA could they save Walquer's life. Saying all this, he asked me to help him in getting his son to USA. What an impossible task!

Quite frankly I had no idea, nor the money to defray the costs to get Walquer to USA, nor the knowledge of any hospital or medical institution that would be willing to do this kind of operation on a "pro bono" basis. But feeling sorry for Walquer and his father, as I was scheduled to travel back to USA in a few days, I said that I would try to help, but could not promise anything at this time. First things first. I contacted a lifetime friend of mine, Dr. Ernesto Salazar Sanchez in Iquitos to verify Walquer's medical condition.

Dr. Salazar promptly confirmed the worse that without immediate medical attention Walquer would die.

Further, the summary of the official clinical history by the Department of Pediatrics of a local regional hospital, indicated that Walquer suffered with a congestive heart and locally, and even in Lima, there are no medical facilities, nor qualified medical personnel available, to save Walquer's life—period. And so with all this bad news I left Peru for my home in Florida. Upon arrival and with the full consent of my wife Margaret, we decided to do our utmost to bring Walquer to Florida and save his life. In our efforts we began to write letters to a great many friends and contacting various medical institutions, Representatives of Florida and the US Congress.

Ultimately we were successful in our efforts, and made it possible to bring Walquer accompanied by his father to Florida. Here is a partial list of folks that helped us in bringing Walquer, and his father to the US and make it possible to receive medical attention at Shands Hospital in Gainesville, Florida.

1. United Sates Senator, Hon. Connie Mack of Florida
2. Mrs. Kathie de Verteuil, personal friend of Governor of State of Florida
3. Mr. Louis Garcia. Director of U.S. Immigration and Naturalization Office Laredo, Texas.
4. Consular Section, American Embassy, Lima, Peru.
5. Dr. Daniel G. Knauf, Chief, Dept. of Pediatrics/Cardiology
6. Shands Hospital, University of Florida, Gainesville, FL.
7. Ronald McDonald House, Family Facility, Gainesville, FL

I must also mention the help received from Faucett Peruvian Airlines Chief Operations Manager, Sr. Richard de La Guardia and in Iquitos, the Regional Manager of Faucett Peruvian Airlines, Sr. Serafino Otero, who gave Walquer and his father Kaiapa complimentary airline tickets from Peru to the USA with return passage to Peru.

Personally Margaret and myself, had to accept a full responsibility for them while in USA, plus for all domestic travel, lodgings, and all other costs except for the cost of the operation and his medical care while in Gainesville, Florida. That was all covered by the University of Florida and the Ronald McDonald House. The actual operation was conducted by a Shands Pediatric Dept. team. The leading Surgeon was Dr. Daniel G Knauf, MD.

The operation was a success after seven hours on the operating table. Kaiapa and I were present and actually watched the whole thing on a TV monitor. The post-operative time was 24 hours. Walquer recovered quickly and within twenty-four hours was able to walk around, much to the amazement of medical staff. During the post-operative period we were successful in placing Walquer in the Ronald McDonald House, where he and his father were very well taken care of.

Finally came time for Walquer to leave Gainesville. I drove up from Ft Lauderdale to take him and his father home. At the final pre-discharge from medical care, Dr. Knauff advised us that although the operation was a success with the repair of Walquer's heart and the replacement of a heart valve and the insertion of several stints, it was a once in life time procedure and could not be repeated.

His prognosis was that maximum functioning of implanted devices would only last, at maximum, ten years, which therefore meant that Walquer was given only ten more years of life. While at our house in Ft Lauderdale Walquer was getting along just fine until one night, we were awaken by Kaiapa crying and calling us to their bedroom. Upon entering we noticed much blood on the sheets and the adjoining wall next to his bed.

We were now faced with a real emergency about what to do. This was followed by frantic phone calls to Shands Hospital. Finally after a couple of hours we received a telephone call from Dr. Knauff, who after listening to our frantic call for help, told us not to worry as this situation was nothing more than Walquer in the process of expelling blood accumulated in his chest cavity, resulting from his operation. And so, after the past few hours of a serious crisis, we were relieved to find out, that all was well. Shortly after I put both of them on a Faucett airlines flight back to Peru, and Margaret and I, took a deep breath of relief. We had to promise each other, "never again!"

In June of 2002 we received an e-mail communication from Dr. Ernesto Salazar, its text stating: "About your patient from Apayacu river, Walquer Cahuachi, he had a stroke on the right side of his body and is now suffering severe hemipleija and aphasia (can't speak) due to an intravascular clot. His condition is permanent." A sort of sad ending for Walquer and his father, Juan Perez Kaiapa.

The entire Kaiapa family had moved from Apayacu river area, and now live in the vicinity of the Amazon river town of Pebas. One must admire the incredible love of a father for a son. Juan Perez Kaiapa is a hero to his son and his tribal brothers.

CHAPTER 21

Mayorunas – The Jaguar People

In the year of 1986 M/V Margarita was chartered to undertake photographic expeditions by members of the City of the Saint Louis Lambda Photographic Society. There was something very much different about this charter. First, the destination of this expedition, secondly a strange group of people awaiting us at the chosen destination. Sometime before the charter actually came about, we received an inquiry by the Society asking us to submit to a proposed itinerary for their people that would include the specific effort of its expedition members for an opportunity to photograph and record a way of life of native dwellers in a remote Amazon Jungle Rain Forest village setting.

We answered that we would do our best to find such localities. As we were in the process of looking for these destination areas and as we making our inquiries, an unexpected couple of very interesting people came aboard. They were members of a Local Evangelical Mission Church, presently engaged in their preaching at a newly established jungle village by the name of Nueva Colonia in a remote area of Ucayali. Populated by a Christian congregation of newly converted, semi-civilized members of the Mayoruna tribe, who recently, having been converted to Christian faith, abandoned their native forests dwellings in faraway jungle areas on the Yaquerana river and now, with guidance and tutelage of the Evangelical Christian Mission, were led to their newly established village of Nueava Colonia.

These particular Indian folks were and still are, known as the "Jaguar People", traditional dwellers of impenetrable jungles in the upper reaches of Yavari, Galvez and Yaquerana rivers, a wild and un mapped area which to this day is shown in white, as unchartered, unknown wilderness, bordering on Brazil and Peru. They always had a long history of belligerent, war like behavior against all outsiders, other tribe's including government authorities of both countries of Brazil and Peru. At one time in the not too distant past, they would mount attacks on Brazil's border villages and even in the year of 1958 or 1959, mounted an armed attack against the small Brazilian border town of Benjamin Constant. These armed attacks resulted in some deaths of local people and called for intervention of Brazil's armed forces.

The Mayorunas then retreated to their deep jungle lairs. In the years in between they would mount bride-kidnapping forays into Peru, specifically in the area of Gennaro Herera and Pumahuacua, villages located on the south bank of the Ucayali river. Many young women from these two villages having gone to tend their yucca fields close to the jungle, have disappeared, never to be seen again. Then again in 1970 determined efforts were made by the Christian Baptist Missionaries to reach and preach the Word of the Gospel to a group of Mayorunas on the remote reaches of the river Galvez. This attempt ended in a great tragedy. As initial contact was made by the Baptist Missionaries, using a light aircraft from Iquitos they flew over the general area where, on information provided to them, existed the Mayoruna jungle camp. Flying low over a jungle clearing, they dropped various agricultural tools, axes, machetes and metal cooking pots.

The next day upon returning to the same area, they noticed that all the items had been picked up. Embolden by this, they sent a river launch on a very long journey from Brazil's border town of B. Constant. Aboard were several missionaries led by a Mayoruna's Christian Convert guide named Tomaso. Some many days later, upon reaching a small river's edge sandy jungle clearing on the Rio Galvez, where the air drop of tools was made, was the last SSB (Single Side Band) radio contact with Iquitos. Then nothing for several days. The Iquitos mission folks made a gristly discovery from the air.

All the members of the expedition were murdered and their bodies were laid out neatly on the same beach where they arrived. There were Crosses carved into their chests. Their motor launch was burned. Since that time, I don't recall that any further expeditions entered the "Jaguar People" country until 1980. I might mention, all Mayoruna adult male tribe members were tattooed on both sides of their faces from each side of their mouth upwards to resemble a Jaguar's teeth. Their checks were punctured permanently and each hole was adorned with porcupine twill to resemble a Jaguar's whiskers. When preparing for war, the upper parts of their bodies were stained purple, using Witto leaves and their faces were painted blood red with the use of Achiote fruit juice, which created a very frightening appearance.

With all this background information well known to me and the crew, we are now listening to our two visitors with Reverend Tomaso Aquilar-Torre who is in charge. The reverend told me the following story. After several months passed he traveled to the headwaters of the Rio Galvez (the ancestral country of the Jaguar People) using a jungle trail from the Ucayali river village of Gennaro Herreral. He hiked through the jungle, then south all the way to the Rio Galvez area.

There he was successful in befriending a large group of Mayorunas, converting them to Christianity and enticing a great number of them to move close to civilization and a better life. There, as members of a Christian Agricultural Community, they would live in peace with local people and away from continuous inter-tribal wars, devoting themselves to grow plantains, yucca, corn and other crops, close to Ucayali, but still near the safety of the jungle area that they were accustomed to.

The entry into this new village was rather well camouflaged from the Ucayali river. One would, through a very small but deep channel, enter a large black-jungle lake called Supai Cocha (Devil's Lake). South of the lake there is a small black-water stream. Following this stream for about half an hour you arrive at a landing and next to it the Reverend's bungalow. Now the Revered makes the following proposal: that for a small payment, either in cash or goods for his folks, he would allow us on a regular basis to visit his settlement, with our Eco-tourists. Limiting these visits to a small groups and only once a month visits.

All this would bring the badly needed cash for his commune. An incredible offer and a perfect and interesting destination for us. However, I immediately asked him a very important question regarding the security and safety of the visitors, because of the past history of the extreme violence demonstrated by these people. He assured me that their former way of life had changed with the acceptance of Christianity. He was very convincing in his way.

I agreed to the Reverend's conditions eagerly and told him that it so happens I have the first group ready to go and soon after an all-female group, the Lambda Group of photographers, arrived with a ton of photographic equipment. All went well and shortly after they boarded we left on our journey, destination "Jaguar People." After a twenty-hour journey we arrived at the mouth of the entrance stream to Supai Cocha.

As it was late in the day we tied up at Ucayali, launched our expedition skiffs and went for a little ride on the stream to Supai Cocha lake, a large black-water of exceptional beauty, its shallows covered with the famed Victoria Regia, majestic giant water lilies, which were in full bloom. Our passengers were ecstatic about the lake scene and took hundreds of pictures. A very happy bunch came back aboard for overnight and we departed the next day before midday, with all four 16 feet aluminum outboard powered skiffs loaded with lunch and taking with us all sorts of things to trade. After about one hour and a half travel, we arrived at the Reverend's house. To the best of my recollection our group consisted of 15 people including myself and four crewmembers who piloted the skiffs.

Upon landing we all accompanied the Reverend and proceeded on foot, passing a well-tended plantain plantation, yucca and sugarcane plots and entered the actual living area of the Mayoruna people. The most amazing thing we immediately noticed was the great concave structure of the Maloka, a communal house resembling a giant beehive. It must have been at least one hundred feet long and made of native materials including a Irapai palm thatched roof. It was really something to behold. I had never seen such structures before, only very old black and white photos.

The half-naked distinguished dark brown man with his face tattooed with jaguar teeth design and many with many porcupine twills protruding from his cheeks, but minus the war paint, met us with a friendly smile. Using the Reverend's services as an interpreter, I greeted him and, at the same time, brought forward a great many axes, hoes and other tools as gifts to his people. He looked indifferent however until I showed him a large black flashlight with D cell batteries. He lit like a Christmas tree and was very pleased. So far so good, I say. He then made a speech but I didn't understood a word.

The Reverend translated all this in Spanish, and I in turn in English to our English-speaking expedition members. He warned us, we can look at the way they live, take photos, visit our Maloka and be free to do what you want. But don't touch any of our women, or children, and don't take any photographs inside the Maloka. With this warning the Reverend explained why "No pictures inside the Maloka"—It would disturb the Good spirits living inside as their protectors should we make them angry. In revenge a member of his tribe could die.

A strong warning, repeated by me to all concerned requiring their strict cooperation in this matter. All of our ladies went crazy taking pictures of seminude Mayoruna women and their bead like body adornments. It was rather late in the early evening when we decided to get our group back to the boat before darkness, as not to travel at night on the serpentine narrow channel of the small stream between the Reverend's place and the lake. Now, knowing that soon we must depart, many of our expedition members entered the interior of the Maloka while the Reverend, native elders and myself were outside talking about future visits, which we were all excited about. This place was something out of a movie, not real. To see these people adorned with porcupine whiskers, tattoos with jaguar teeth designs on both sides of their mouths, with their seminude women with colored beads hanging from their neck down to their waist was a rare experience.

The Maloka made was a perfect destination for eco-tourists. Minutes later we heard screams and shouts coming from inside the Maloka. Our females came running out of the front entrance to the Maloka, running past me in the direction of the landing, and behind them large number of our hosts, chasing after them. It happened that the ladies, upon entering the interior, immediately started taking flash pictures, contrary to our strict warning against it. The flash of their cameras frightened our hosts who had never seen such things before. This stupid behavior of our passengers now seriously provoked our hosts and it immediately resorted to violence by a couple of the native women who attacked our ladies, hitting them with sticks, as they were making a quick and hasty run for the landing and boats.

The situation now became very ugly as the ladies entered our skiffs and ordered our crew to depart immediately. My crew refused to do so without me and, leaving them at the landing, came running up to me to help. We were left behind to take on the wrath of these wronged people. No amount of pleading, explaining or apology helped. Looking for an escape path from these enraged people, we found ourselves completely surrounded. Now the Reverend was pleading. Evidently he said something and calm returned, but for only a moment. It was the village chief's turn as he came at me armed with a raised machete, but stopped.

The Reverend prevailed and probably saved my life. The tribe was now somewhat calmed. The Pastor announced that, in order to get out of here without being seriously hurt, we must pay the tribe for our sacrilegious act. We were to give them a 50 kg sack of rice, my wristwatch and the only two flashlights in our possession. Plus now, I don't remember what! Now it's a bit after 5:00 PM and in less than an hour it will be dark. As I parted with my Seiko watch, the sourly looking crowd thinned.

Now the only important thing left to for us to do was to get the fuck out of this place and quickly. Our boat travel could now became very dangerous, without our flashlights meant we would have to travel in the coming darkness and not be able to see overhead tree branches or floating vegetation, making it dangerous for our outboard motors if we hit a floating log. I cursed again our passengers, and gave the word to depart.

The Project Amazonas river boat "Margarita".

Soon thereafter darkness fell and now we have to navigate in total darkness, fully loaded with our passengers, we went bouncing from tree to tree, as we slowly advanced. Now, without a warning, rain came in full force and some of the women were frightened and crying. It rained really hard which made it more difficult to see. This rain and rapid change in creek's temperature did a crazy thing to all the underwater creatures. Panicked fish were jumping out the water and into of our boats and some landing on passengers. Now they screamed with fear as the fish thrashed about the boat's bottom. In these piranha filled waters the most danger to man is when they are in the boat. In this moment the leading boat driver Nilo cries out in pain as he was bitten by thrashing piranha. This creates a further danger as he is bleeding into the bottom of a boat full of people. Nilo, being a man of great jungle skills and courage, so as not to create a panic, takes the pain in complete silence, takes his shirt off and managed to wrap his ankle as he was driving the boat. Some feat! Rain stopped as rapidly as it started and we were now out of the jungle stream and on the lake, quickly making for the short channel to the Ucayali river and the safety of the M/V Margarita. Sometime well before midnight we were all aboard.

The crew, as they were cleaning and storing our skiffs aboard, found many small piranhas in all the boats. We were very lucky this time. Next we start our return voyage down river and stopped to stay overnight in the small river town of Nauta which lies at almost the confluence of two rivers, the Maranon and Ucayali, with the Amazon. Everyone sleep peacefully. We got underway early in the AM, reaching the Port of Iquitos in midafternoon the same day and transferred all the passenger to a local hotel. There are no goodbyes, no thank you, and no tip for the crew. Our lady passengers request cancellation of a farewell dinner at a local restaurant tonight. They are mad at me and the crew for endangering their lives. And so the life goes on.

CHAPTER 22

Vision of Tragedy – Night of Shenango

Much water had flown under bridge of life, still I remember meeting this fine person, who would became my lifelong friend. His name is Gerry Miller of East Haddam, CT. and we meet at the roof top restaurant of hotel Monaco, Manaus Brazil. The time of our meeting was winter of 1983. Gerry, as he liked to be called, was in Manaus visiting and working with, an American Scientist by the name Rolf Singer. Both were involved in a scientific research project that had something to do with a species of wild mushrooms that grows in the depths of the Amazon jungle. Their work had something to do with how these special mushrooms are an integral part of regeneration and preservation of the Amazon rain forest.

I might say that Gerry's meeting with me had nothing to do with mushrooms, for Gerry was looking for river passage from Manaus to Iquitos, Peru and was directed by some persons to contact me as I was getting ready to sail my vessel the M/V Cidade de Natal" to Peru. During my time in Manaus and since our first meeting we would meet often and I had an opportunity to learn more about this man. I was very much impressed by hearing of his adventures in Ecuador where Gerry lived with a remote war like tribe of Jivaro Indians who, in not too distant past, hunted their enemies with poison dipped darts, and as trophies would shrink their heads.

They were much feared and commonly referred by local people as "Reducidores de Cabeza". While living with these folks he learned their language and also became an apprentice of their Shaman, learning of their tribal customs, jungle medicine practitioners, and of dark secrets of their sacred shamanic ceremonies including the art of communication with spirits. When he joined me aboard for the long journey from Manaus to Iquitos, we shared many of his jungle tales.

During this time aboard we had many occasions and time to share our life's stories and became friends. While in Iquitos as I became busy with my jungle expeditions business, Gerry went back to the USA but then started to return to Peruvian Amazonia bringing with him his friends and other folks interested in the Amazon jungles darker side. He sponsored and led expeditions and he would always feature shamanistic practices, Ayahuasca sessions, identification, preparation and use of herbal medicines, sessions with local Curanderos and at times would include his guest's participation in Shamanistic practices.

His chosen destinations always interesting, would take us into some real weird areas, far removed from civilization, isolated jungle areas. To reach these areas of his interest, and of his clientele, most of the time he would charter my riverboat services. Over a period of years, we have developed a business and friendly relationship. He would bring his people for at least two of three trips a year and it was fun, especially for me. As for Gerry, he was very serious about the nature of his expeditions.

Then in the year 1987 Gerry came to Iquitos accompanied by a very beautiful woman named Christian Rikhaye. It so happen that upon their arrival at the Iquitos Airport the entire City of Iquito's population was celebrating one of the many holidays and fiestas and the whole town was either busy dancing, drinking or making merry. No one in his right mind would be working on this day. The designated Reception Agent representing me, after assuring me that he would be at the airport to receive Gerry and his folks failed to do so. And Gerry had a hard time finding me, and M/V Margarita. Finally with the help of Paul Wright he found me at the Port of Bela Vista.

After a few of bad words exchanged between us a real party began and we had a wonderful time dancing and raising hell with the local folks. The night fell, and our passengers, tired from their air trip, went to their comfortable cabines and had well deserved rest and sleep. Next morning before full daylight we pulled away from shore on our journey up river all the way to Maranon river, one of the biggest tributaries of the Amazon, our destination to be upper reaches of the Chambira river, a small isolated jungle stream located some 20 hours running time from Iquitos. On second day of our voyage while under way, Gerry and his "GG" (Gorgeous Girlfriend) came to my cabin to make an announcement as to their desire to be married at our destination at a small Indian Curarinas Indian village on upper Chambira river. My reply was in affirmative, except for my question as to legality of such thing. But not to disappoint the two young and in love people I set the legality question aside and said yes! The news of the forth-coming wedding is revealed only to the members of crew.

Albert, Captain of river boat.

For the rest mum was the word. Doña Maria our cook, had me stop at the small river town of Nauta where she promptly purchased all the making for wedding cake, plus other food stuff necessary for this happy occasion. So we sailed on, as our crew member Alicides, the boat's carpenter, started making a large matrimonial bed to be located extreme aft of the passenger deck. Doña Maria had sewn two mosquito nets together as a privacy curtain for the newlyweds.

The passengers noting all this unusual activities are asking questions but we say nothing. On the next day we reach the mouth Rio Chambira's, and continue up river for the rest of the day to Curarinas Indians country. At evening dinnertime while we all sit at the table, I address all with "I have an announcement to make—but maybe I'll let Gerry tell you all." Electricity fills the air. Conversations cease, with a complete surprise and delight I hear him say, "Chris and I are going to be married tomorrow at sunset." Their very short engagement party begins and a good time is had all and the crew. The next day early Leon "Brasico" our on board Shaman, who came on this trip all the way from Apayacu, plus the crew start decorating the boat with jungle flowers, pleated palm fronds, wild heliconia flowers. Our dining table covered with wide green Plantain leafs. The upper deck looks beautifully decorated for this occasion.

As the great Amazon sun sets, I stand before Gerry and Christiane, with two crewmembers, plus our shaman "El Brasico", Manuel the Pilot, and Wilson the Engineman standing at my side as witnesses. I read a previously prepared document, and officially make entries into our ship's log. They each say "I do" then kiss. All present applause and offer good wishes. A blue and white wedding cake appears, decorated with a heart, and message in white—"Felicidades a los Novios". Our cook outdid herself. After this voyage, Gerry's voyages with me became less frequent, although we would meet occasionally while in port.

Wedding and reception for Gerry Miller and his bride Christian Rikhaye aboard the M/V Margarita—February 1987. Captain Slugocki presiding.

I see Gerry and Christiane less and less, until I hear that they built themselves a jungle house in the close vicinity of a small up river town of Tamishiyacu. Now Tamishiyacu is one of those river towns with a very bad reputation crime wise and not only that, the immediate river area directly in front of town is and has been for many years, a witness of riverboat sinkings, sometimes involving a great loss of life. The local folks and mariners working these waters refer to this area of the river as "Muy Salado" (Cursed with bad luck) and many of the Practicos (river pilots) cross themselves in passing these bad luck waters.

Recently, while in Iquitos, I ran into a mutual friend of ours who informed me that Christiane and Gerry were not in town, but at their house which has recently been constructed for them by their new found friend, a local "pirato" (unauthorized) tourist guide known to all concerned as "Chino Loco", a real bad character. Trusting such a person with things like construction, plus making him responsible for registration with the Peruvian Ministry of Agriculture and Forestry, of a small jungle tract of land upon which their jungle dwelling stood was, in my estimation, pure madness. I was unable to contact Gerry in town. I soon found out that they are living in their jungle house deep in the Amazon forest. It was reachable only by two means: by boat in a small stream from the main channel of the Amazon and only during high water season, or by a "Trocha," a jungle trail about one and a half hours by a jungle walk from Tamishiyacu. I decided to pay them a visit the next day.

That night I could not sleep and when I finally fell asleep I had a bad dream, and the dream was about Shenango, an imaginary bird of prey and part of an Amazon Forest legend, calling my name and of a world without light, dark and foreboding. I don't recall the rest of my dream. The next day, late in the morning, I departed Iquitos in a small boat accompanied by my local friend Roberto Gil. After a couple of hours of travel we turned into a small jungle stream, which was narrow and winding and shortly arrived at Miller's jungle abode. It was a typical jungle dwelling elevated above ground with a thatch roof of Irapai leaves. This simple jungle dwelling, located in a deep Amazon jungle was the home away from home to our pair of very adventurous people, Gerry and Christiane Miller.

We were greeted warmly by both of them. Shortly after I expressed my concern about their safety while living in such an isolated place and my special concern was the accessibility to civilization in case of an emergency which would be a one and a half hour walk by a narrow jungle trail to the village of Tamishiyacu. At this point I was assured that their safety was taken care of by having someone to watch over them and their property; their trusted friend and "Guardiano" (watchman), Mr. Oster Rojas-Fernandez, a local man who now lived most of the time on the premises of their land. Gerry spoke with enthusiasm about this man and his jungle skills. After a short visit with both and assured by Gerry and Christiane as to their safety, I still was wary, and not completely convinced. Roberto and I left on the long river journey back to Iquitos. We did not want to be traveling at night in a small boat.

And so on the specific date of March 10th, 1995 it was a cloudy night. Outside the village of Tamishiyacu, four men armed with shotguns, their faces blacked with charcoal and strips of black adhesive tape, silently entered the jungle trail leading to Miller's jungle abode. They waited just outside the house with their 16 gage shotguns at ready, then entered the living area of their target, ready to do their murderous work, as Gerry and Christiane were sleeping peacefully in each other's arms. They were awakened by the angry shouts of their assailants and saw many flashlights moving wildly and close to their bed. Christiane attempted to talk to these people but suddenly they fired the first shot, which missed both of them. Christiane jumped out of bed and rolled under a heavy table at the same time the second shot hit Gerry just as he reached for his 38 mm pistol laying on a small bedside table and immediately started firing at the moving flashlights.

It was at this very moment he discovered he has been hit. Half of his right hand had been blown off but he kept firing even when some of the shotgun's pellets hit him just above his heart. Two fingers of his left hand were shot completely off and in the last moment of his torment, having glanced to his direct rear when seeing a beam of a flashlight, he fired his last shot over his left shoulder just as his assailant pulled the trigger. He was hit right straight thru his heart and as he fell backwards, dead, he managed to send his bullet right over Gerry's head. The flashlights disappeared, Christiane recollects someone shouting Vamonos! And with that there was some thrashing in the immediate jungle, then silence.

The whole attack lasted no more than minutes and Gerry, severely wounded and close to death and bleeding profusely from his horrible wounds, orders Christiane to run and get help from the village. They kiss and say goodbye to each other. Gerry, although nearly dead, knows that since he had lost so much blood and will not survive. But somehow, between "dead or alive" he maintains his cool. Behind their bed, dead and in a pool of blood, the cadaver of Oster Rojas Fernandez, the so-called trusted friend was shot squarely thru his heart. His face still masked with black electric tape as Gerry lies there while Christiane puts another bullet into Oster, just to make sure, then runs, screaming in the dark of ndfight along the jungle trail to Tamishiyacu firing her pistol they had somehow managed to reload, which was covered with blood. By the Grace of God she makes it to the village.

About three hours later she was back with the Peruvian Police and a large number of villagers. Gerry is stabilized by the village medic and it looks like his heart and other vital organs have been missed. Through a big hole, just inches above his heart, he is losing blood rapidly. They carry him to the village, and using the police radio, call for a medical speedboat evacuation to Iquitos. Eleven hours after the shooting, he is still alive and being well taken care of by doctors at the regional hospital. They don't believe that he is still alive, having been shot three times with 16 gauge shotgun shells. It is confirmed there were a total of four assailants. One was killed outright and two, wounded by Gerry, were found in the next two weeks as partial skeletons, less than a mile from the house. They had been eaten by jaguars, ants and vultures. The fourth man was captured that same morning by the police and is now serving a double life sentence at Moyabamba Prison, Iquitos, Peru. Gerry, although horribly wounded, survived it all. As for me, who had lived through three wars WWII, two tours in Korea and a survivor of multiple combat tours while serving with US Special Forces in Vietnam where I suffered several wounds, Gerry is my hero and carries in his soul, the courage and spirit of an Amazon Jungle Jaguar.

CHAPTER 23

Mystery Jungle Flight

While in Port of Iquitos, my German friend Paul Hittscher and myself would meet every Friday and Saturday evening at Paul's restaurant "El Tropical," located on the outskirts of town, for drinks, dinner and of course, good conversation. We usually talked about the latest happenings on the river, the comings and goings of local riverboats and other waterfront news in general. It so happens that this Saturday night, as usual, found us sitting at the so-called "Stamm Tish" as Paul referred to a selected table always reserved for the owner and his worthies. I, as a trusted friend and confidante, had a standing privilege of sharing this special place. This special table was strategically located at a covered vestibule entrance to Paul's establishment.

From here Paul would greet his clients and after exchanging a few pleasantries, Pedro Diego, his Maitre'd would usher them to their table. The local clientele of this backwater end of the world river town of Iquitos, were really not accustomed to such courtesy, and thoroughly enjoyed the attention given and flocked en masse to Paul's place. To put it in another way, Paul's restaurant was "The Place to Be Seen". The food was good and plenty, the beer cold, and rum drinks, like Cuba Libre's, much favored by local clientele, plus Scotch whisky, were copious albeit expensive.

Main dishes served, were grilled meats and fish, impaled onto long lance-like skewers and served directly from a very large fireplace like grill tended by a fancy dressed *Maestro de Parrilla.*

Directly behind Paul's table at the entrance wall, in full color, hung a giant and recent movie poster titled "Fitzcarraldo." This beautifully made movie was totally filmed and produced in Iquitos on Its waterfront and in the surrounding Amazon Rain Forest. It was produced by a world famous German filmmaker and producer Mr. Werner Herzog with its cast composed of several world-class actors. The production had taken an incredible amount of time and superhuman effort, due to almost continuous daily travel of an entire production crew to and from the actual filming areas located in the depths of the world's largest jungle, the Amazon. The logistics and transportation involved were mind-boggling. Just to give you an example, food and provisions and temporary shelter were provided to about one thousand native Shipibo Indian as extras.

Capt. Paul Hittscher at his "Stammtish" table at his restaurant "El Tropical". In the background is a poster of the movie "Fitzcaraldo" that Paul acted in.

Actually, several of the main actors quit production because of these many delays, and for various other reasons, like the main character actor, an American named Jason Robards, had to leave.

Rumor had it was over his drinking problem. The devil rum got to him. The next departed was an entertainment personality of world fame in the person of Mick Jagger who, as the local story went, smoked too much. I will not go into other actors that left however, Paul without any previous acting experience was personally selected by Werner to act in an important role of a Riverboat Captain.

An acting part, which really required a professional actor, and a very daring stunt man. The role required Paul to man the steering wheel at the wheelhouse of a large steel-hulled river vessel of some 250 ton, specially constructed in Iquitos for the filming, to be hauled, and manhandled up to the top of a small jungle mountain by a cast of one thousand plus Shipibo Indians. An incredible feat only to be sent crashing down an eight hundred feet narrow jungle stream over the famous and dangerous water falls of Pongo de Manseriche, located in the foothills of the great Andes mountains, to a river by the name of Pachitea.

The entire episode captured on camera by a filming crew of two cameramen who were strapped to the back wall inside the riverboat's bridge, with one of the German cameramen suffering serious wounds from broken glass. As for Paul, down he went, suffering many bumps and bruises. What balls! For this crazy stunt he was richly rewarded. The film finally was released in April 1983 and had its premiere in Paris, France. Tonight Paul was bitter for not being officially invited to attend this event, although being promised in person by Werner. And so he reminisces about his role in the most wonderful event of his life, he also raves about all the assholes he had meet during this once in the lifetime event. I can't help but think about my friend's past, his ham like hands horribly scarred by explosion and fire while at the tender age of sixteen when he served as a crewmember aboard the German U-Boat U-279, in the winter of 1944/45.

After war's end he surrender to the French and as a Prisoner of War was forced, with other members of his crew, to be part of a sea mine clearing crew in the French harbors of Toulon, Le Havre and Marseille. It is late into the night now, and after many Cuba Libre's,

I feel it's time to go home, home being M/V Margarita. I am awaken in early morning by my crewmember on duty announcing Paul's presence aboard. It is Sunday morning, the sun is already up. Still sleepy, I manage to get up and see Paul. Paul immediately asks me if I want to make some fast money. He sounds excited and all fired up and tells me the following story.

Late last night, at closing time a frequent client and acquaintance, came to him with a very strange and urgent request. He needed help to recover a downed small aircraft which crash landed on a river's sand bar, deep in the jungle, very close to a small Indian village of San Francisco de Pintoyacu, located on a small river bearing the same name.

Having a good idea of this particular area from my past travels, I immediately knew the exact location of this village. The proposition made by this fellow was that, using my riverboat and a small 75-ton barge, plus local help of the remote Ocama tribal people, we would recover this airplane. We would then surreptitiously transport it aboard the barge to a designated area close to Iquitos, a small lake named Rumo Cocha, which was connected by deep channel to Nanai river, also connected by a dirt road to Iquitos.

The small single engine airplane recovered after a
forced landing near the Rio Pintoyacu.

This whole thing immediately smelled of drugs and direct involvement with local *"Narco Traficantes."* For this reason I immediately rejected the whole thing, as I didn't want to get involved, however, Paul assured me that there would not be anything connected with drugs, all that would be required of us we would be transporting a crashed air craft, a personal property of his unnamed friend. The bottom line, this thing was Money, as the amount offered for recovery of this airplane was in the high four figures, plus costs covered in barge charter, food, crew, fuels. A very attractive commercial proposition, my estimated time to for completion of this project was no more than a couple of days, and maybe two nights of work., and so I accepted this offer.

It was quiet Sunday, with all folks either in church, sleeping or recovering from Saturday night fiestas. Ahead of us an immediate need to get things going, and ready for our task at hand. Paul and I jumped to get going. As I busied myself with getting ready with M/V Margarita being fueled, crewed, provisioned, Paul got the use of a small 75-ton barge from Occidental Petroleum people, and shortly arrived aboard a small tug with barge in tow. We tied it alongside starboard of my riverboat, and since we were already moored at Port of Bella Vista on Nanai river, without wasting any more time, we pulled away from dock at midafternoon and up Nanai river bound for Pintoyacu.

Travelling the rest of the afternoon and night we should be at the village very early in the morning the next day. Travel on Nanai river is relatively easy as there is a very little of forest debris floating, and hardly any boat traffic. Its navigation channels are easy to follow. Sometime in the night we have arrived at the confluence of Nanai and Pintoyacu Rivers, and sailed the rest of the night on Pintoyacu. We arrived early in village of San Francisco de Pintoyacu. Shortly upon our arrival, the entire village came to the water's edge to see what is happening, as we tied to shore.

Directly in front of us and up stream, as the river curved to the left, a long and narrow sand bar extended almost to middle of river, there in all its glory sat a small airplane, our prize. It was unreal how this single engine airplane somehow managed to safely land on this tiny sandy spit of land, since the entire immediate area surrounding this village was covered with a dense high jungle.

Miracles happen. As Paul got into immediate conversation with village chief, I walked a few hundred yards on a riverbank connected to sand bar where I found this small airplane in what appear to be perfect shape, looking new and clean. Upon closer examination I found it was an American made single engine plane with a sign of its fuselage saying Piper Tri—Pacer plus some numbers, which I don't remember now, I examined its interior, all nice and clean. Found its single propeller slightly bent, otherwise it looked ready to fly. Above all upon a close examination of its small interior found no trace or sign of drugs, airplane documents, baggage, nothing, actually it looked like someone had taken great pains to make it look clean.

While I was doing my inspection Paul was having conversations with the local folks. I noticed he and others went towards a small thatch roofed building on the opposite end of village. Eager to share my findings with Paul I hurried from the crash landing site and joined Paul and some locals walking to this building that, I was informed, was a local schoolhouse. As we got closer to it, I recognized a horrible, and familiar smell from my wartime service. The smell of death. As we stood at the entrance, I heard the buzz and saw many green and black flies.

Laying on the dirt floor side by side, and partially covered with plantain leaves, were the bodies of two men. After a quick look, I moved rapidly away from the building and the grisly sight of the two dead men. The village chief calmly reported to us that the two men were aboard the airplane, and that pilot of the airplane was alive. He was taken away yesterday morning by four men that came in a speedboat. As to who the two dead men were, we ran into a wall of silence from all the folks in the village. Only that they were aboard while airplane crash-landed. One could now see and feel a total fear on their faces. It was just too much for me. What in the world did I get myself into and why did I trust my friend Paul and did he know we would find out about these two dead men?

Obviously to me at this time, it had a lot to do with drugs, murder and God knows what else. All this thoroughly shocked me. I wanted answers from Paul, but he immediately made it known, and swore to me that he did not know anything about the dead people found in schoolhouse. And further that we were only to recover a crash landed airplane—nothing more. Still in a state of shock, we managed to get the locals to physically pick up the aircraft and somehow managed it onto the barge and tied it securely aboard.

As I was busy doing all that a violent argument ensued between Paul, the Village Chief and his people regarding the dead bodies, which according to locals, we were responsible to remove to Iquitos along with the airplane. Paul, argued that we would not take, transport or have anything to do with their removal. With both of them, Paul and the Village Chief aboard, they continued to argue. Paul hollered in English at me, standing on the bridge, to fire up Margarita, and as they were still arguing he hollered again "Pull away Albert. Full speed. Go!" I immediately pressed down on full, and turned to port with the wheel, to pull away from shore. Margarita lurched astern into the rivers channel, and at the same time Paul threw the Village Chief overboard. Downstream we went at full speed. Thank God the villagers had nothing but paddles to chase after us. Good Lord, what we have gotten ourselves into? I hope all goes well with our downriver voyage.

Just thinking, lucky for us at the time it all happen in early 1980's before there was radio or telephone. A motorized skiff's in a village was still a rarity and not available in these remote jungle villages. Traveling all afternoon and then into the night found us some two to three hours away from Iquitos. Sometime close to daybreak, and still in darkness, a beam of light from ashore, directed straight at the bridge, was followed by a small speedboat. It shined a beam of light upon the barge with its airplane, then blinked a couple times, then disappeared. Later, in the very early morning, just at daybreak, we entered the Rumo Cocha channel and its lake, which was our final destination. We did get paid but we never heard the true story about the airplane and dead people in San Francisco de Pintoyacu.

The life continued with all sorts of things happen, but nothing like this, guess I was very lucky. I continued with my friendship with Paul, and spent many pleasant evenings time in his company sitting at the Paul "Stamm Tish" talking about the comings and goings on the Iquitos waterfront, his long life at sea, his not so happy time of his youth in his home town of Hamburg, Germany. His service in the German *Kriegsmarine* aboard three different U-Boats during the Second World War.

But we never, ever talked about our Mystery Airplane Caper. Paul Hittscher lived for a few more years longer, but more and more and with each day "The Devil Rum" had taken him over. He grew morose, easily agitated, and depressed until he finally passed away. Iquitos did not mourn his passing. To its natives he was no more, and no less than any other "Gringo"—passing as Amazon River's flotsam on its long way to the far off sea.

CHAPTER 24

El Encuentro con Comendante Tiberio

It is now 2001 and many things have changed both on the river and in Iquitos, my homeport. I am seriously thinking of just hanging up this river business and retiring. As of right now Margarita Tours, Inc. works and makes a few bucks but just barely enough to support our Not For Profit Humanitarian Organization, The Project Amazonas, Inc. Business wise it's a losing proposition. Iquitos got bigger, uglier and dirtier. Its streets full of thousands of motorcar type taxis, belching foul smelling fumes. The total population swelled to an estimated half a million people mostly because of folks formerly living in surrounding jungle villages who are looking for a better life, flocked to the city and its not too bright lights. In doing so they have created a twenty plus percent of unemployment.

The new comers, without a job, are forced to live in so-called *Pueblo Joven Colonies,* all located on the peripheries of Iquitos, which in reality are nothing more than huge suburban slums, areas with no electricity, running water and no sanitation. Sad but true. Apart from that, the Amazon River had changed its course completely and by-passed the City center. The big old mango tree at the foot of Putumayo Street used to be my favorite place to tie up and it is still there. Malecon Boulevard's and its riverbank, is now a scraggly slope ending at bottom with terra firma. The M/V Margarita formerly *Cidade de Natal*, which at one time was my pride and joy, was sold by me to Paul Wright of Amazon Tours and Cruises. The boat had sunk at anchorage at Isla Santa Rosa, due to negligence of her crew. For a while I had leased a steel-hulled vessel by the name of M/V Delfin but my lease expired.

Finally in the year 2000 I, with help of my friend and very capable assistant Sr. Fernando Rios Tulumba and our faithful former crewmembers, have built a 68 foot long, 56 ton riverboat named Tucunare. She was a beauty! Constructed of the best Amazon forest hardwoods, powered by single 146 horsepower Perkins diesel engine she had capacity for 14 passengers. Her maiden voyage was very long, from Iquitos to Yavari river then up to its confluence with Rio Galvez, in the heart of Mayoruna Indian country. All went well on this 21 day voyage. Shortly after, in early January of 2001, we had received a charter request for an expedition from a group of Tropical Fish Biologists from the US that would take them from Iquitos all the way to Putumayo river's Peruvian National Rain Forest Reserve El Chambiral.

A very tall order, as it would require six days of river travel just to get there and seven days to return. It also would require an *International Dispatch* from the Port Captain in Iquitos because we would travel through Brazil and Colombia. Additional documents were required from Peru's National Police, the Peruvian Army and its Naval Command in Iquitos. The Tropical Fish folks were going after a very beautiful and rare ornamental fish by the name of Discus, a wild species found only in the Putumayo river and its black water jungle swamps of the *Reserva Nacional Chambiral*. This expedition was to be followed by another, consisting of members of a sports fisherman group from Florida. The total operational time for two expeditions will to be 14 days.

All this requires incredible logistical and administrative efforts on our part. The M/V Tucunare with a crew led by me would sail from Iquitos some two weeks before the scheduled time and will carry sufficient fuel, lubricants and dry groceries needed for the entire expedition, including the return trip. The estimated round trip is 1,200 river miles. The expedition's air support for passengers and logistics required the charter of a light aircraft from Jim Bracy's

North American Air Charter Svc located in Iquitos. A Cessna 180B with floats and from FAP (Peruvian Air Forces) the charter of de Havilland DHC (Twin Otter) turbo, 19 passenger aircraft with floats which would shuttle both groups in and out of Iquitos and the small Putumayo river village of San Martin de Soledad, located close to *Chambiral.*

All in all, a full load of details to attend to before departure. Somehow it was all accomplished and with a great many official documents and permits, boarding was allowed and we sailed with an extra engineman and 1500 gallons of diesel fuel aboard. Leaving behind Dr. Devon Graham, PhD and Fernando Rios to be in charge of all the details in Iquitos. We left on the 22nd of January 2001. After two days on the river, we crossed the Peru—Brazil border and continued down river well into the Brazil's waters.

At night, as we were passing the town of S. Paulo da Olivencia, and in really bad weather, we encountered a very large Brazilian Navy Gunboat traveling up river. Passing us at great speed and with their powerful and bright search light fixed on our bridge, our Pilot, Hernan, was temporarily blinded. Then, as it passed, created a series of great waves in their wake, almost sinking our small vessel. Other than that we continued all the way down to the mouth of Rio Ica at its confluence with the Amazon. We did not stop at its small river town of San Antonio but left the Amazon channel and entered Rio Ica and started our upriver travel. Two days later we arrived at Port of Ipiranga Brazil and the Colombian border.

At Brazil's side I was questioned for about two hours by a young Brazilian army officer who could not understand how an American could be a Master or Patron of a Peruvian flag vessel. After an SSB radio communication with his superiors we were finally allowed to proceed. Now the same river, called Rio Ica by Brazilians, changed its proper geographic name to be internationally known as Putumayo. After about an hour's voyage we entered the Colombian border port of Tarapaca. At the port's dock we were meet by heavily armed Colombian Army people with their arms at ready, which was kind of intimidating. We were told to stay aboard as they began searching as we waited for the so called Port Captain, who arrived shortly thereafter.

He was a black man of great size, afat and an unkempt looking man. He demanded to know what we were doing at Tarapaca. While he was aboard he commenced to interrogate me as to my destination, mission of our expeditions, etc. Then he gave me a warning about travel on the lower part of the Putumayo, advising me that there is a great danger of night river travel but without further explanation he let us depart.

To tell the truth, this small Columbian village of Tarapaca with its barbed wire defensive positions and nervously armed soldiers reminded me of some far away Vietnamese village getting ready for an assault by Viet Cong communist forces.

All ended well and the troops retreated to whence they came. This town had an eerie feeling about it. It was a frontier town with a sense of danger about it. It is a military outpost on the edge of a *No Man's land*. In fact, Tarapaca was the last government controlled area of Colombia for the next couple hundred miles. Sailing up river for about two hours we were still in Colombia, then as we crossed the narrow part of Colombian territory, noting only a concrete border marker, we entered into Peru on the port side and the Republic of Colombia on our starboard side (north bank) of the Putumayo River. The River is a de-facto political boundary between two countries.

At mid-afternoon, upon reaching the mouth of the Rio Yaguas, then travelling south on the Rio Yaguas, we arrived at a Peruvian Military Control Outpost, which is nothing more than a small thatch covered shack, manned by three raggedy looking barefooted Peruvian soldiers, who looked very much surprised to see us. Two of them left their post running into the jungle and in few minutes appeared accompanied by a tall very light skinned Peruvian Army Captain who was a very much out of place looking fellow in this God forsaken jungle outpost. He was very nice and extremely talkative person. He spoke to me in a Limeno accent and without looking at our official documents, asked for a beer, which, almost in a second's time, was served. Obviously this man was very much adversely affected by being in these desolate jungle surroundings.

In my mind I tried to imagine what sins had he committed to be sent here. He began relating to us some real weird stories, about unexplained lights appearing in the jungle, strange noises in his house in the middle of night and of hearing canoes on the river with their paddles slapping the water. For this man's sake I hope he would be relieved soon from this creepy place before losing his mind. But strangely enough I also noticed, half hidden by the river bank vegetation, a brand new looking speedboat with a large outboard motor hanging from its stern. What was all this about? Having left him with 6 bottles of beer and having fulfilled our obligation of reporting, we departed. At just another turn in river we came upon a Peruvian National Police Outpost where we again presented our papers, crew manifest and other required documents.

Here things were better organized, and we were asked should we like to communicate with Iquitos we were welcome to do so, all nice and friendly. In front of the Police Post were the half submerged twin-propeller passenger aircraft parts with floats sticking out of the water, looking new, and really in good shape. I was informed its owners, the Colombian drug dealers, having landed on the wrong side of the river, were ambushed by Peruvian Police, and two members of the crew drowned and two others were shot dead. In addition they showed me a couple of gold dredges seized from Brazilians operating illegally on the Peruvian side of border.

Upon departure we received a standing invitation, from the Police Captain in charge, to come back in the season of low water to help him pan for gold. While spending the night somewhere on the Peruvian side of the river, we heard heavy river traffic, all without navigation lights, moving silently up and down river, carrying God knows what. We decided to navigate only in the daytime as everyone felt navigating at night might not be prudent and would be interfering with the night traffic. We continued for another day and reached the mid-sized Peruvian village of Huapapa, a very nicely situated village located on a black lake directly off the main channel of Putumayo. At this time while having a conference with a local Cacique (Chief) and I outright asked questions as to the safety and security for ourselves and our expedition's members coming to this area via air in a few days. The answer given to me was that he personally guarantee's the safety of all visitors and further said that there are some immediate areas that we should stay out of.

When using local guides provided by the chief, or his friend from San Martin, we should not worry. We departed almost immediately for San Martin de Soledad, our proposed base of operations in this area and at night fall, tied up to shore. The next day at noon we arrived at San Martin. The afternoon is spent getting acquainted with the local area and getting ready to receive our expedition members. This village and the Putumayo Region is a strange and mysterious place, sparsely populated with small villages where you would find some even stranger people. We found families of Brazilians, Colombians, Peruvian, plus tribal peoples, living together, in a relative peace. In addition, in the village of San Martin, there is a strange little middle aged man who speaks with a very pronounced Mexican accent. He claims to be studying local herbal medicine, but who knows. The night traffic continues and when my crew makes inquiries, they all are meet with "we don't know who these night people are and we don't want to know."

The local *No See-em* biting *Mosca flies* are on us all day. It is impossible to walk around without buttoned down shirts and long pants. Another blood sucking insect is the ill-famed *Putumayo River Mata Blanca's* who attack in great swarms where evidence of their presence on your face is slight itching. When you do the natural reflex, swatting your face, your hand will be full of blood. This indeed is a God forsaken place, but with a very beautiful virgin jungle, full of birds, fish, black giant alligators, Caymans, and an evening sky full giant squawking large blue and gold Guacamayos and brilliant red Papagayos, flying to their jungle roost for overnight. Although these areas are dangerous and uncomfortable to men, its primary jungles and black water swamps are breathtakingly beautiful. In a few days our first expedition group arrives safely aboard the FAP (Peruvian Air Force) De Havilland (Twin Otter) aircraft and Rich Bracy's Cessna 180B arrives with perishable food and luggage and Dr. Devon Graham.

The first Tropical Fish Collection Study expedition activities commence and for the next six days were meet with great success for their efforts to collect the famous Discus fish, now packed in great white coolers. They depart for Iquitos. The second group, under the direction of a my good friend Jay Salinger of Ft. Lauderdale and a veteran of many previous fishing expeditions with me, arrive with his rowdy group of friends at San Martin de Soledad. Upon taking all aboard we depart for the village of Huapapa where, upon arrival in the late evening, we dock for a night getting everything ready for the next morning's fishing. The next morning and into the afternoon we fish the local lakes, with mediocre results however. We all decide to move away from Huapapa and next day to go all the way up to above San Martin and fish the black waters of the *Reserva Nacional El Chambiral*.

The same evening, as crew and passengers are visiting with Huapapa folks, I was on the top deck of Tucunare when a young man comes up wanting to buy some flashlight batteries. As I was getting his batteries, he enters my cabin and in a low voice, speaking perfect English says "this village is a very dangerous place for you and your Americans. The Huapapa villagers are cooperating and working with Colombian Communist Forces, the so called, FARC (*Fuercas Armadas Revolucionarias de Colombia*) across the river and further informs me that their recently established outpost on the other side of the river is located at less than a half an hour away by boat. I am already in a state of shock! Once I hand him his batteries he disappears into the night.

Once he is gone I stop and think. FARC guerillas are the last thing in this world I want to see. Straight away I go to find and talk with

Fernando Rios who I finally found and demanded we immediately speak with Don Carlos, the Cacique of Huapapa. In a hasty meeting with the chief we demand the truth of the FARC base across the river. He admits it is true and further volunteers that a small force of FARC guerillas have arrived some five days ago, and has been in contact with him and members of his village. Some real bad news! However, he informs me that we should not worry as their commander, is his friend, and as long as we stay on the Peruvian side of the border we are safe, and since our riverboat is under the Peruvian flag we have nothing to fear. We depart and return aboard where our fishermen and the locals continue drinking beer into the night. I am full of dark thoughts. Fernando suggests we say nothing to our passengers. We are scheduled to receive perishable food supplies on Bracy's flight tomorrow and he should be arriving in Huapapa in the late morning.

We decide to leave tomorrow late evening, and sail up river to put some real distance between us and our FARC friends. Maybe tomorrow I will tell our fishermen about our situation. We will see. It is a beautiful morning at day break and our fishermen have now gone into the jungle to catch fish. We are in SSB (single side band) radio communication with Iquitos. I am afraid to say anything about a developing situation. We are told that Rich Bracy departed at 7:15 AM and should be here soon after 9:00 am. It's eleven and still no Bracy! I call his home and was informed that due to bad weather, he had to return to Iquitos. We will try to leave at about noon but I am getting real nervous! At 2:00 pm a very strong storm hits our area and its visibility zero-minus with strong winds and large waves on the river. Forget about our incoming flight today! I am calling just about everybody I know on our SSB radio.

It is Sunday afternoon and no one is answering their telephones. Fernando Rios is asking me for a permission to go with Huapapa's Cacique to the Colombian side of the river to buy fresh fruit, yucca and plantain for the crew. I say "OK—go." The storm lessens and the weather had cleared. Fernando returns in late afternoon and informs me proudly that besides buying fruit and vegetables, he was taken by his now friend the Cacique, to the FARC encampment to drink beer with "Comendante" and was told by him to inform Don Albert not to worry about his Americans. My God! This guy already knows my name and he further instructs Fernando to inform me that he is going to pay us a visit to talks with me, the last thing in the world I want to happen. Quickly I gather our just returned fishermen and brief them of our very critical situation. Funny, my passengers are very calm and collected and asking me if I have any arms aboard. I say no and just at this moment, as I am looking at the river, I notice a small motor boat pulling away from Colombia and realize it is heading straight for Tucunare. As it nears I can recognize uniformed men armed with AK-47 weapons.

This gives me a chance to holler to my Americans "here they come" and jump down the stairway to the bow area of the boat as they come alongside. I say "Buenas Dias . . . y . . . . Bien venido abordo" and quickly count my uninvited guests. There are five of them, and the first man, dressed in an olive green uniform and is armed with an AK-47 and a side arm, comes aboard, then the other four. Of the five, all are armed and identically dressed like the first soldier. Of the five I notice that two are women.

I invite the whole group up to the top deck. The man wearing a black beret with a large "Che Guevara" metal button attached to it, presents himself to me as *"Comendante Tiberio de Fuercas Armadas Revolucionarios de Colombia"*. I reply in Spanish *"Albert Slugocki Capitan Fluvial Patron De Motonave Tucunare, a su servicios."* And I ask him to take a seat at the top deck's dining table. As he seats in front of me across the table, I notice two of his party are standing behind me at the boat's railing with their weapons at ready. As custom requires, I offer coffee to my visitor, which he accepts, and so, as we drink our coffee, he tells me not to worry about my American passengers and that he respects the laws of Peru.

At this point I actually think myself as being Peruvian, but I am nervous, and don't really think too clearly. At some point in this one-way conversation he assures me that they came in Peace, and that they just arrived in this area to organize and to take charge of this area of operations. *(Sector Sud de Colombia)* All this follows a lecture on revolutionary goals for his country. He seem relaxed so I excuse myself and called for steward Emerson to serve me a strong Cuba Libre, (maybe the last drink on this earth) which Emerson, an expert on the subject of Cuba Libres, my preferred drink, serves it quickly. I notice his hand was trembling. Emerson then asks Comendante would he liked to have a drink. He answers in the negative and now he preaches to me about the glory and wonders of communist Cuba. At this time I offer a short tour of our riverboat, which he accepts. While passing thru our kitchen, we notice the young women soldier, and our cook Danilo, in a deep discussion regarding preparation of "Carne Asado."

We pass through the lower deck's passenger accommodations with all eight of our passengers showing off their tackle boxes with different colored and shaped fishing lures, to two FARC soldiers of which one is the "number two" woman soldier. She asks the Comendante Tiberio if she could have the pictures taken with the "Americanos" to this he says no. I am still looking to something to erupt—but thankfully nothing happens. At 6:45 pm the whole group departs but not for the far shore of Colombia, but to the village of Huapapa, where they are warmly received. About an hour later they board their small boat and once more come aboard just to say good night.

Our passengers are now very much relaxed making jokes about the whole incident, until Jay Salinger makes a strong point quoting a recently released movie in which a small group of American tourists were kidnapped by the same FARC outfit of communist guerillas in the border area of Ecuador and they are all murdered. After that everyone quietly went to bed. The next morning, before daylight, we left Huapapa for a five hour trip to El Chambiral Forest Reserve where we caught a lot of Peacock bass. After a few days of fishing, it was time to return to San Martin and wait for the FAP Twin Otter aircraft to take them back to Iquitos. The whole group insisted that I go back with them and for me not to take a chance of traveling thru FARC controlled waters. All this was confirmed by my crew, who wanted me to return to Iquitos, safely aboard the FAP flight and not to take a chance of being taken by FARC.

They also brought up a possible scenario of FARC's possible boarding Tucunare, letting the crew go, but taking me hostage, stealing its fuel and stores, including a motorized skiff and then sinking the Tucunare. All of this sounded very convincing and make good sense, but I balked and refused to do so. The next day I came to say good bye. The FAP Twin Otter aircraft was a beautiful picture as it gracefully landed on the Putumayo River. Just prior to departure I gave Jay Salinger my watch, wallet, all personal documents including my US Army retirement ID card and a personal note for my wife Margaret. Keeping only my passport and enough money to get us through a return voyage to Iquitos. I asked of all the passengers to say nothing of the boarding by the FARC.

Off they went that Saturday February 17, 2001. I decided to stay but the crew was not happy with my choice, so fuck them too. We are now transferring fuel barrels from shore to aboard and getting ready to be underway "pronto." We departed San Martin at about 2:00 pm and began traveling down river passing the villages of Tres Esquinas, Huapapa, and Rio Yaguas after which we will be in "Indian Country" for two or more hours. All went OK until we reached the area where the FARC were supposed to have their newly established camp. Here we had a great moment of total panic! Someone from the Colombian side of the river signaled us to come to shore. The rules of these rivers are that if there is an emergency and someone needs help, or are looking for a ride, just stop. The persons on shore should wave a white towel or shirt or a piece of clothing over their heads as a signal to a passing boat to come to shore.

There were three of us on the bridge; the crew member Segundo at the helm, River Pilot as the navigator and myself. It was the pilot that had seen a solitary person waving a white piece of cloth over his head and loudly exclaimed they are calling us to shore and commanded the helmsmen to put the engine control at slow and head for the Colombian shore. There was a moment of hesitation by the helmsmen as he looked at me. I immediately counter-ordered the Pilot's command by grabbing the wheel and putting the controls on full while turning away from shore and put the Tucunare back into mid-river channel.

I did this because the person was, in fact, a member of FARC wanting us to come to shore on the Colombian side of the border. I would not obey their command even if it meant to be fired upon. Our pilot, violently objecting my action, began hollering, "they will fire, they will fire, and you are endangering the lives of our crew!" By then Segundo grabbed the binoculars to have a second look. Then addressing the Pilot said "you stupid bastard, the man is just swatting at mosquitoes," and, passing binoculars to me said "Don Albert please take a look". I confirmed Segundo's observation.

This is what tension does to people. The whole drama of this incident evaporated. I then ordered the Pilot off the bridge, and went to my cabin, took several deep breaths and hollered for Emerson our Steward to fix me a double strong Cuba Libre. By late evening we were safe and secure in Tarapaca. Again we meet with a Giant Black man. Again with questions such as; "What have you to report? Have you seen anything"? My answer to all of his questions was "I have nothing to report," and I went to bed. The next day, with the first light, we pulled away from Tarapaca, Colombia and at after about half an hour we arrived at Ipiranga, Brazil's Port of Entry.

All is well with no problems with the Brazilians. Mum is the word. We say nothing to the Peruvian Authorities either. Still I am worried, not so much about my host country, the Republic of Peru, but worried about problems coming from the American Embassy in Lima. Nothing happens until one year later someone gave me a copy of one of the largest newspapers in Lima, Peru, the "El Comercio." Right there in a left top column was a short article titled "The Death of Comendante Tiberio." The context of the article was that as a Commanding Officer of Sector South, FARC, he was killed in ambush by the Colombian Government's Army.

CHAPTER 25

Shamans, Curanderos & Ayahuasca

As you travel over a long period of time in this part of the world, you are certain to, sooner or later, come in contact with these special folks who practice the age-old form of native medicines. How this healing art is acquired is to this day unknown. One thing for sure, this knowledge is being passed on from one generation to next by the so called local village *Shamans* or *Curanderos*. You find these special people living among many of the river shore dwellers and interior jungle villages throughout both the Peruvian and Brazilian Amazonia.

Those who practice this form of medicine art, live together with the rest of the village people, but yet they are apart from others. They are respected and very much feared by their own people. In these remote jungle areas where there are no doctors, the local people are completely dependent upon their medical skills to cure them from whatever ails them. Should their cures fail, they blame evil spirits.

These special people are selected by an elderly Shaman at an early age and become an apprentice to him, and are introduced to the basic arts of healing by taking away all the mysteries surrounding the art. The Shaman is nothing more than a person well versed in the practice of herbal medicine.

Their pharmacy being the vast surrounding jungle, full of medicinal plants and creatures like frogs and insects and like poison ants that can heal a human. This closely guarded knowledge of the jungle's plants in the form of leaves, tree bark, various roots and vines, made into potions and poultices. Insect parts, are used by Shamans in treatments for commonly encountered ills. All this plus many poisonous berries, which a consumption of would normally cause illness or even death, could be used as medicine if administered in right proportions as a cure.

Fluids and secretions extracted from extremely poisonous brightly colored frogs could either kill, or cure, if administered inappropriately. The world renowned poison named *curare* is nothing more than a cocktail prepared from the above ingredients. All of the above forms of medicines represent basic tenets of their medicine formulas and are applicable to treatments of humans. In addition to the above basics, the Shamans also indulge in the darker sides of their trade. When the treatments did not work, they would reach out into the use of a very potent hallucinating native drug called *Ayahuasca*, which is a tomato like, wild growing jungle vine fruit. The preparation of this drug requires a higher ranking Shaman or Curandero who is called Ayahuascero.

This person is experienced in the preparation of this drug. They would use the leaves and stems of this vine, mix it with cane alcohol and other ingredients not known to me, to produce a liquid concoction, which would be drank slowly by the Ayahuascero. Almost immediately after swallowing this potion the Shaman would appear to fall into some sort of a trance. In most cases it caused him to vomit and became convulsive in behavior, rolling his eyes, and having rapid, uncontrolled movement of arms and legs, incoherent speech, salivating and then, after a short while, become quiet and fall into a deep coma, not moving but breathing normally.

They, the Shamans (Ayahuasceros) would refer to this quiet time as to travelling outside the real life, floating somewhere in space and communicating with good and evil spirits of the afterworld. While under the influence of this drug, they would communicate with good and evil spirits, and seek guidance as to what treatment would be right for his patient in order to cure him or her. After a couple of hours and upon return from his journey, the Shaman appeared normal in behavior and ready to prescribe a proper treatment for the patient. In one of those treatments that I personally observed, the Shaman announced to the patient that he had found an evil spirit dwelling within this person's mind. But he had the power to cure her, and would say "do not worry" and commence singing softly a child's lullaby, taking a drink from a bottle containing sugar cane liquor, and spitting it at her face. For a short while he would light a thick Jungle Tobacco cigar and blow tobacco smoke onto her face, at her head, and around the area of her heart, all the while praying and invoking good spirits to return to her mind and body. In the aftermath of this treatment, he would give his patient a gift of *Pusanga,* a amulet usually consisting of a small medicinal bottle filled with unknown liquid and colored seeds mixed in. This would then protect her from any further illness.

I have witnessed several instances of this type of cures in my life. Going a long way back in time, I think the year was 1967, when I served in the central mountain region of Viet Nam as Team Sergeant of a US Army Special Forces in the remote mountain Camp called Dak Pek, I witnessed an unusual event, which was the treatment of a woman with an undetermined severe abdominal pain. Since a very bad weather precluded her evacuation by air to closest medical facility, our Special Forces Medic was at his wits end, unable to determine the cause of her great discomfort. It was then requested by our Indigenous Guerilla Forces Commander that we would call upon the local Jee Tribal *Sorcerer* or *Shaman* to attend to her. I wanted to see this.

A small statured, half naked old man soon appeared outside the camp's dispensary and he asked for the woman to be brought out and had her placed on top of a blanket. Next he built small fire and when it was burning nicely he produced some green leaf branches and placed them on fire. All this produced a nasty, smelly smoke, which engulfed our woman patient and all of us who sat in close proximity around a semi-circle close to her. She began to cry and cough from smoke inhalation. The next thing that I observed as the Shaman continued chanting and at the same time, without an incision, reached with his right hand into her stomach and pulled out a hand—full of small black, flat, round, wet looking stones from her stomach and threw them on fire. The stones burned with great brightness. Was I hypnotized? I will never know. All of us had seen and witnessed this event. The sick woman was cured and in a short while got up and walked away with her husband.

In another time, years later and worlds away in the depths of the Amazon jungle, while travelling aboard our riverboat "Tucunare," I was visiting one of our Project Amazonas Biological Research Stations located on a small Amazon tributary named Apayacu. Having finished with our activities in late afternoon we commenced our return journey to Iquitos. As we passed the small village of Sabalilio, just a short distance downstream, we made a brief stop at the shore house of a village chief named Innocencio. We found him very much upset while his wife was lying on their house floor mat quietly crying and obviously in great pain. One could see a small towel between her legs soaked in blood.

We immediately offered to take him and wife aboard and take both of them to a small medical facility at the larger river village of Yanashi, where there was a small medical facility. He agreed and off we went at full speed traveling on a moonless night for Yanashi, taking great care to navigate this small snake like river at night, manning both our brightly lit bridge and bow searchlights. We travelled like this for about two hours, a rather dangerous thing to do. As we came close to the Amazon River, and as were just about to pass the last village of Yanayacu, Innocencio ran up to the bridge and asked us to stop and come to shore. As soon as we came to, he jumped off and disappeared.

Shortly he came back accompanied by two men, declared he did not want to take his wife to the medical facility at Yanashi, telling us that the local Shaman agreed to cure his wife. As we strongly protested and begged him not to do this, he disregarded our pleas and, with two other men's help, carried his bleeding wife ashore and disappeared. A couple weeks later, as we travelled down river and when passing the mouth of Apayacu, I decided to turn in and check with Francisco Oliveira the local store keeper. There, to our great surprise, we meet with Innocencio and his smiling wife in their canoa (canoe), purchasing some small items from Francisco and getting ready to go home. It was an eight hour trip paddling upstream to Sabalilio. When asked about her health, a curt reply was "The Shaman at Yanaycu village cured her."

Another Incident, a long time ago, comes to my mind. It happened on one of those days and nights I would rather forget. It made me wish I was still in those cargo carrying days and not involved with eco-tourism and with all the personnel responsibilities for life and limb of passengers. This particular voyage was with a very strange group of some ten people, all members of New York State Mycological Society (The Mushroom People). Sometime in the middle of the ten day voyage, I was asked by the group leader, no other than Gerry and his lovely wife Christiane, "Would it be possible for his folks to participate in, or at least witness, the so called Ayahuasca Ceremony"? El Brasico, my personal friend and a well-known Ayahuascero Shaman, was presiding. I immediately denied this request.

This, followed by an official notice by me, as a Captain, to all concerned, I could not be responsible for this rather dangerous undertaking by passengers on my vessel and be responsible for their wellbeing, while aboard. My little group of nuts, however, persisted in their request, and I finally gave up. Summoning El Brasico, I told him to go ahead with it, but not aboard my vessel. He would have it on shore in one of the riverside villages. And so they had their crazy time at some riverside village and were completely blown away with Ayahuasca. They staggered back aboard sober and we continued with our expedition. Then some days later as we were on our way returning to Iquitos and our passengers were still making afternoon mushroom forays in the jungle, Gerry asked me again could we stop somewhere and have a follow up Ayahuasca binge. Again I said definitely no, and even told El Brasico to get lost and go back to his village. As we were some twenty hours away from Iquitos, I now needed all the time possible on our journey in order to arrive and clear Port Captain's facilities before 3:00 pm the next day. So much for that.

Captain Albert Slugocki aboard the river boat M/N Delfin.

And so as my passengers were foraging for their mushrooms I decided to visit the nearby village before sailing. Upon my return aboard Margarita I found all my passengers under the influence of Ayahuasca. It appeared Gerry was able to bribe El Brasico to stay and make it available to all concerned, and although it all started on shore somehow managed to end up aboard. It was no use to get pissed! My entire group certainly were out of their minds, doing some real gross things. After serious consideration I decided to sail anyway. The entire crew, with exception of our river pilot who must steer the ship, began watching and taking care of our spaced out passengers.

As we got underway, and with darkness coming, we found ourselves in a very bad situation and in danger of travelling at night on the Amazon in a full flood. Our Pilot, by himself and dealing with navigation on a river full of floating debris and fallen trees, was working the wheel, and ships lights. The rest of us kept our drugged passengers out of harm's way and from falling and, worst of all, from falling overboard at night in complete darkness. Their drug induced antics continued primarily in the upper part of the vessel, an open air dining mess deck. Two of them were having sexual intercourse right there on top of the mess table while another couple was crying and babbling. A man fell backwards, hit his head on the deck floor and now had a serious injury with his head split open neatly from front to rear.

The worst happening of all, a woman climbed on the stern deck railing and attempted to jump into the river. At the last moment our cook Doña Maria caught her and dragged her down onto the deck. This hell continued for some hours. We managed somehow to forcibly place all of them into cabins and locked the doors. The man with the busted head had to be attended to immediately, which we did by shaving the hair from his head, washing the wound with betadine solution and sewing him up. As morning came they were all back to their senses, clean and dressed, just like nothing really happen last night and were now sitting at the mess table awaiting their breakfast. The stories abounded about what can happen while under the influence of Ayahuasca. Some say one can lose his or her mind, die, or be permanently mentally impaired. Fair warning to all.

The use of Ayahuasca is not only common in the Peruvian Amazonia by local Shamans, but it is well known in the entire Amazon Region including Brazil, where it is known as *DaiMe*, which, in Portuguese, simply means *Give Me*. In Colombia and Ecuador it shares its name with Peru and it is well known by local Indian tribal peoples in the areas adjacent to the Amazon region's heavily forested areas of Amazon tributaries, Putumayo and Caquetá rivers. This highly hallucinogenic tea concoction is made of only stems and leaf matter of a tomato—like jungle vine, prepared for human ingestion by boiling. I am told by Peruvian Shamans that the roots of this plant are a deadly poison. This psychoactive natural drug has been used by the local people as anesthesia.

CHAPTER 26

Conversations with the River Dolphins

This is one of the many legends about the River Dolphins. One of my many frequent voyages took me to Yanayacu, a Yagua tribal village located on a small Amazon tributary named Apayacu, some seventy river miles away from Iquitos. We anchored at a confluence of another small black water stream bearing the same name as the village. On almost all occasions upon my arrival I was greeted by the village elders and many of the village's children, who would come to welcome our arrival. Included was the local shaman by the name of Diego, but commonly called "Brasico" due to his Brazilian ancestry. Brasico would pay his visit in early evening and would regale us with his stories and legends of this land. This time he told me a strange story about river dolphins that would frequent one particular place, which was a small river area located at the confluence of Apayacu river and the Yanayacu, a small black water jungle stream.

According to Brasico this was a special and sacred area to all river dolphins. At the time of a full moon, since time immemorial and during the time of the so called "Madrugada", in the last few hours just before dawn, and with good visibility still offered by moonlight, the dolphins would gather at this place and talk and visit with each other in their own language. People of these small jungle villages actually believe that dolphins are their distant relatives and can talk.

Their conversations could actually be heard by some of the chosen people from this village. All of this of course made me very curious about this strange event and so it happened that at the appropriate time, we were at this sacred place and securely anchored very near the point of confluence. The full moon emerged and shone brightly upon the river's surface. I was saying to myself that "tonight we will see these talking dolphins." I went to bed in my cabin but tossed and turned, unable to sleep and I kept looking at my watch.

It was three o'clock in the morning and the moon was shining brightly. I quietly went down the stairway to the cargo deck area, some three feet above the waterline, where I lay down quietly on the deck with my head protruding over the river surface water. Lying down there in complete silence with all the jungle sounds now gone, a complete stillness prevailed.

While there I noticed the water surface moved and the next thing I saw was the head of a dolphin. It appeared with its long nose clearly out of water, followed by a very auditable sounds like "deep exhaling." The dolphin, apparently taking a deep breath, disappeared. This was an announcement of things to come. Very shortly thereafter, several dolphins surfaced and came very close to me. Now I heard their great cacophony of strange breathing like sounds. This was happening just a few feet from my head. Were the sounds really like someone speaking in a strange garbled language or was it all my imagination?

Obviously these creatures were communicating with each other. Then there was silence, then again a few of the dolphins surfaced, repeating their sounds. At this time I attempted to mimic their sounds with my voice but was meet with complete silence. Little had I known that I was not alone, for some distance away and behind me stood Arsenio, a member of my crew, who, in silence, witnessed the whole thing.

Morning came and shortly thereafter it became known to all concerned, that Don Albert possessed a secret power to communicate with the dolphins as he was seen and heard talking with them. No matter that perhaps the place and time had something to do with the dolphins eating habits at the confluence of the two bodies of water, that this was a usual feeding place. Their "talking" was nothing more than their normal breathing sounds and from the dawn of time, was their proper feeding time. The local Yagua Indians, along with their Shaman, firmly believed I could talk with dolphins. The news spread all through the Amazon and I was given many strange looks by my Indian friends.

CHAPTER 27

The Legend of the Dolphin Bride

The Amazon River and its jungle forest, since time immemorial, has been a place of many legends and mysterious and unexplained happenings. Most to them have always been storied legends that deal with major rivers, black water jungle streams, lakes and the deep impenetrable jungles of the Amazon River rainforest, its forest people, commonly referred as *Cabocles* in Brazil, or the *Riberenos* of Peru, were and always are a superstitious bunch.

The life of these people has always been affected by the lows and highs of this river that gives and takes, is the life of its shore dwellers and forever governs their life rhythm. In my many years of river travels I have heard many stories of real and imaginary events and listened to many legends of years past, retold many times by the these river people, who lived or still live in these small isolated shore communities of this river—sea like waters. My favorite legend, is a story of a beautiful young woman from the small river trading port of *Foz de Ipiranga, Brazil*. She was born and lived in this small river town all of her life. Her family were members of a local *Prominente* family of Don Antonio Almeida Melo and she was the oldest of their three children. Her name is Ana Luiza.

It came about during the annual fiesta honoring a local Saint Protector *Nossa Senhora do Rosario e Benedito*. At this time the little town was in the last days of preparation for this special holiday, its waterfront street was swept clean, houses were white washed, and the only brick house, being the house of Ana Luiza's parents, was, for this occasion, brightly painted in blue and yellow, the national colors of Brazil. There was much to do. The local drunks were locked away and local fishermen cleaned and painted their fishing boats. In the two days before fiesta, a great many people began arriving in their boats from surrounding countryside.

The local ladies busied themselves with preparation of a great holiday meal, the *Calderada de Tucunare* and in hastily built backyard ovens the baking of *Tambaque* fish was taking place. The smell of freshly roasted *Farinha* was in the air and then the Festa began with a church service, followed by a procession of the village Holy Patron. The *"Nossa Senhora do Rosario"* statue was carried high on the shoulders of local elders as it passed thru the village and returned to its place of honor in a small local church. Then a local parish priest blessed the villager's food. After this everyone retired to eat their feast, not to mention the great amount of local alcohol (*Cachaca-sugarcane liquor*) that was consumed. Thus the villagers, having their fill, turned to a great afternoon pastime of slumber, which lasted for several hours. As they all rested, including the village dogs, they dreamt of the coming of the evening's festivities.

With the last light of day, the people started to come to the small village plaza located at the edge of the river. The place was well decorated with pleated palm frond arches with many jungle flowers laced into it. A small stage at river's edge was built and now occupied by a band, which came all the way from *Sao Paulo da Olivenca*, for this occasion. Sometime later, as darkness fell, the festival commenced. I might mention that unofficially and apart from the religious aspects of this special day this was also the time when all the local and other young men who came from other villages, to have an opportunity to meet, dance, and flirt with local girls. Many future marriages and or pregnancies resulted from attendance of this event. Ana Luiza came dressed in her finest and her natural beauty attracted all the young men present. She danced to just about every tune the band would play. As night progressed she became aware of a very a handsome stranger, elegantly dressed all in white, with his black shiny hair well groomed.

Many a local young women were taken in by this handsome man, and local men were visibly envious and resentful of him. Amongst all the people present, none really knew where he came from. Last night, aboard the Manaus/Tabatinga riverboat, some speculated about him while others just didn't know. But tonight he openly disregarded all inviting glances and his eyes became fixed on Ana Luiza. She became overwhelmed by his incredible good looks. In time he invited her to dance and she accepted readily. As they danced, lost in each other arms, she admired his smooth *café com leite* colored skin and his large, deeply set, green eyes. He spoke softly of love and life. She felt enchanted by this person. A love at first sight she thought. Is it possible?

She questioned herself for it must be since she had never felt this way before. As the night continued she would dance only with him. Finally, as the dawn approached and the dance crowd thinned, they left the dance floor to enjoy themselves with an early morning breeze. They walked along the river holding hands. In a little while he suggested they could take a short ride in his canoe to admire the beauty of the river.

She hesitated for a moment, but feeling so enchanted by this man, she accepted. His canoa (canoe) was beautifully carved from a *Black Itauba* trunk, ample in size, and with her settled comfortably the canoa quietly slid into the river's waters, with the man seated slightly behind her and wielding a beautifully carved heart shaped paddle. As they distanced themselves from shore the canoe suddenly turned over. As they fell into water she remembers being kissed. The kiss sealed her mouth to his and at that last moment a strange thing happen, she was now breathing some strange and wonderful tasting air. In the euphoria of his kiss she opened her eyes and looked at her lover who now changed into Dolphin and was taking her now, as his bride, into the depths of his water world.

Project Amazonas

CHAPTER 28

The Good Work

In my early days on the river, even at a time when I was primarily engaged in the commercial/cargo business, either by chance or just circumstance, I became involved in helping local Indian folks. It just became natural when spending nights tied up safely next to a local riverside village. Curious to see who were these overnight visitors, the villagers were would come to the river's edge. The village children always first, sitting or standing on a riverbank timidly staring at what was happening aboard, and then were followed by others. All sorts of questions were shouted, like did we have anything to trade or sell.

While traveling up river, to Iquitos from border areas of Brazil and Colombia, someone was always looking for passage to Iquitos. But in most cases, folks would ask for medicines. Since in almost all these river villages there always is somebody sick with imaginary or very real medical problem and in need of medical attention. The most prevalent were folks sick with malaria, stomach problems, untreated wounds and always kids with worm infestations.

Somehow, these people knew we would help. There was also something about our riverboat, although initially a cargo vessel, painted white and of neat appearance, the very well maintained "Margarita," always attracted extra attention.

Quite frankly, reflecting into those times, I would say this is why these river people expected to get help from us, especially since the word had spread across the Peruvian Amazonia and all of its tributaries that Don Alberto's "Margarita" would help. At times, while on the river and underway, we would be hailed to, by local people in their canoes, asking for medical attention. As for myself, I tried to help, but keeping aboard only a limited inventory of emergency medical supplies and medicines, much of the time we would come-up short. Slowly, as the time went by, the long-ago and half—forgotten medical emergency skills learned while serving with US Special Forces in many *God Forsaken World Places* kicked—in. At the same time we began to acquire, an ever growing medical kit aboard. And that's how it all got started. Shortly after, when we entered into Eco-Tourist ventures carrying international passengers, we really needed a well-equipped medical kit, to take care of our travelers.

Of course I always continued to take care of these remote village dwellers as much as I could, to include at times, an emergency evacuation of more serious injuries to Iquitos hospitals on "my dime." This was done by use of our outboard equipped skiffs. Helping these poor people proved to be the right thing to do, as with time, people got to know me. My crew and I became their benefactors and friends. Having established a good relationship, they in turn would permit us the use of their black water jungle lakes (Cocha's) and streams for sport fishing, plus other eco tourist expeditions. They became very valuable to us, as jungle guides, being remunerated by for their services and brought forth a temporary means of employment and much needed cash to purchase basic life's necessities.

As good luck would have it and almost by chance, I was away from the river visiting my family in Florida when a thought came to mind. Perhaps my former comrades at arms from our days in the service and who were still around Fort Bragg, NC would help me to scrounge some malaria medicines from military sources. And so I called upon my old service friend Master Sergeant (ret) Mike Hollingsworth, and found out that although retired, he was in fact working as a civilian at the Special Warfare Medical School in Fort Bragg, NC as the Chief Trauma Instructor.

Just the kind of medical specialty I had in mind. Broken bones, bullet wounds and machete cuts, snake bites, and all of that. Initially and full of hope at this discovery I was only going to ask him for some medicines. When I told him about my part time life on the Amazon, he not only would help me with meds but two or three days later he volunteered to help me in person, providing I would cover his travel expenses. And so two old friends were to be together again, in a quite different circumstances to be sure, but united by faith in doing good work. A partnership of cooperation developed between us. Mike, "The Medic Extraordinaire", although partially crippled from the his war wounds would come to Peru three or four times a year, always with a duffle bag loaded with medical goodies. He would take care of the native jungle folks while I was busy with eco travelers.

It all came to an abrupt and sad ending when he passed away on October 13, 1998 while at his home. Little did I know that I would never see my friend again. It was a sunny Autumn day and Mike was sitting on his veranda. He made a comment to his wife "God, it's getting dark outside" those were his last words and at that moment he died. We will always miss him, for he was a good and kind man, and very much a part of our humanitarian good work.

We also carried aboard with us these same basic necessities, like salt, sugar, rice, flashlights batteries, fishing lines and hooks, sewing needles, matches, candles, plus other items. This way our guides could receive cash for their daily work, or purchase at our cost, items from our aboard canteen. I personally became very attached to these river and jungle dwelling tribal people. The Yagua Tribal Council of the small jungle village of Yanyacu, located on the Amazon tributary river of Apayacu, officially elected me as a *Morado* (resident) and member of the Yagua Tribe. All these lovely people, who since time immemorial, have lived on the shore banks of this great river, its channels, and deep within remote jungle tributaries, embraced me as one of them.

They represent the last vestiges of tribal peoples in Peruvian Amazonia, some having lost their tribal association and roots, especially those living on the banks of the Amazon, who now simply call themselves *Roberenos* that simply means People of The River. Others who live in the interior of its black water jungle tributaries still try to cling to their tribal roots, customs and language. They are, for the most part, members of the Yagua People. Other tribal folks found in the remote regions of Peruvian Amazonia, are the Witoto, Boras, and Achual. All these jungle people of mixed blood are referred to as Nativos, which sometimes translates as a derogatory racial term. Folks from small river towns, including the capitol city of Iquitos are called Mestizo

The Amazon River dominates all. The dwellers of its forever changing banks of this great River-Sea are always affected by these rivers seasons, its high and low waters, its times of great storms and forever changing navigation channels. Islands are formed at its mid-stream every year, only to disappear a few years later together with new villages and sometime with its people. For this untamed river has no master. The village people, the *Riberenos,* who live on its forever changing shore live within the rhythm of its currents, highs and of its waters. During the low water times they plant rice, corn and other vegetables on its sandy lagunas, and fish in the receding pools of water.

With the greatest of luck they may have a good harvest, for should the unexpected high water coming, all will be swept away including, maybe, their family. The coming of the high water, life on the river changes almost immediately. The Amazon swells its waters and now flows fast and furious. One begins to see large trunks of trees, some still with green leaves on its branches, a tremendous amount of litter floats on its surface making it a great menace to navigation. Its waters rising above the river banks spread into the jungle. In some areas the high water enters at some 5 to 10 miles in land creating a half drowned world of jungle and river.

The dry land becomes scarce. Living becomes very difficult for local people. As the jungle becomes inundated, the fish, one of the major sources of food, enter jungle inundated areas, where they find a great abundance of food, eliminating the possibility of fishing. Such is the proverbial way of life for these river people. Life as you can see is really tough. But in some ways it is better than moving from this environment to which they are accustomed. And so goes the life in this beautiful, but harsh place, governed by the world's largest river-sea and its rainforest jungle. And so went my years of living a full life among all these elements. Life aboard the river can really be nerve wracking, and at times reaching the impossible. Running a riverboat without charts and navigational aids, depending on one diesel driven engine for days and nights to far destinations, at times an incompetent crew drunk or sober, totally dependent on your wits when in danger and all without communication with the outside world. Being responsible for the lives of others is really tough on you.

The rewards were few. Then there were always good days, beautiful sunny days, helping others, living a life to its fullest. Sitting on the bridge watching the river, day dreaming, and feeling the pulse of this magnificent river running under your boat's keel. Abilities to help others less fortunate. Knowing the wonderful people of the Amazon jungle rain forest. There came a time when many of my friends and former clients of past expeditions came to have one more experience of just traveling the river with me. It was a good voyage. The exact date now escapes me but it was in the springtime very early in the 1990's.

The water was still high with some of the downstream areas still a bit flooded. Our voyage had taken us all the way to the tri-border area of Brazil, Colombia and Peru, which would represent some twenty four hours down river time and thirty four hours return voyage to the Port of Iquitos, our home port in Peru.

We managed to stay at Santa Rosa Port on the Peruvian side of the border and made daily forays to Leticia, Colombia and Tabatinga Brazil. Good times were had by all. We did not do too much cooking aboard and ate at local restaurants, either in Tabatinga or Leticia. The evenings were spent in Tabatinga night clubs. Everybody was having a good time. We pulled away from Santa Rosa Island on our return trip up river. As we were traveling we passed many small river villages still flooded. Our small group was busy putting candy into brightly colored balloons, blowing them up and throwing them to the village children. All this to the great delight of these small kids racing up from shore in their little canoes. As we sailed on, a couple of the village folks signaled us from shore with a "white flag," a common practice to get the attention of a passing vessel as to an emergency existing in the village. Each time we went to shore. I attended to several children suffering from severe diarrhea.

Having witnessed a couple of my unscheduled stops to take care of the local people, my friends came upon an idea that perhaps, with their help we could organize a small humanitarian, not for profit, organization in the USA. Therefore, in August of the same year, Project Amazonas became a reality.

Project Amazonas, Inc. was organized as a nonprofit corporation, dedicated to the preservation of the Peruvian Amazon Rain Forest, as well as being the provisioned of medical care and a sustainable development opportunity for the people living in remote river areas of the Peruvian Amazon. All of these folks never had the opportunity to obtain modern medical care and even fewer employment chances. And yet they were generous, friendly, happy and optimistic people. It was because of a personal affection I developed for these people that the whole thing came about.

The logo of the Project Amazonas
—a not-for-profit organization

My friends and acquaintances personally funded the initial establishment of two Biological Research Field Stations on one of the tributaries of the Amazon, on Rio Orosa and, since 1994, have consistently ensured that the operational costs are met. I might add that no officer or members of the project's Board of Directors, nor I, have ever received any remuneration for our contributions, time, or expertise and our involvement has always been purely humanitarian. In addition to financial contributions the members of our Board of Directors have dedicated thousands of hours without recompense. At this time our activities involve the development of three fully functional biological research field stations that are open to researchers, graduate students, high school and teacher groups, etc. and the development programs for villages in our areas of operations and, dearest to all our hearts, medical care programs.

The Project Amazonas has now been in operation for 15 years. As of today the Project has solicited and arranged for transportation, distribution of medicines and medical supplies, all of which have been donated to clinics and hospitals, throughout the Peruvian Amazon. Because of our and my concern for these people, who by our standards have virtually nothing, there are now remote communities in the Peruvian Amazon that have an assured access to ongoing medical care, have increased employment opportunities and have tools and knowledge to develop their own local resources. We now have implemented and successfully developed a Medical Expedition Project, working together with The Peruvian Government's Regional Health Department in Iquitos, an integral part of the Ministry of Health, Republic of Peru and have launched a very successful project of Medical Expeditions. This project is being sponsored by and financed by us, but working together as a team with the Peruvian health authorities.

We, as a private NGO (non-governmental organization) are responsible for the provision of a riverboat, motorized skiffs, its crew, fuels, lubricants, food and medical supplies purchased at a great discount from Peru's national pharmacy. Our host country, Peru, provides, medical doctors, nurses, medical technicians and village health workers. Our medical expedition's staff travels aboard our riverboat, the M/V Nenita, which was recently acquired and outfitted to our special needs and the river vessel is constructed entirely of native hardwoods.

A three-decker, powered by a new 150 horsepower marine engine, in a 76 gross ton vessel, equipped with passenger accommodations for 16 persons in 8 double occupancy cabins and all the comforts of home, serves us well in our travel to distant, isolated areas of the Peruvian Amazonia to attend the to the medical needs of far off villagers. Due to our limited resources, we presently are able to launch only two or three medical expeditions each year. In the conduct of each expedition we manage to offer medical attention to approximately eleven hundred patients. In the year 2008 we managed to exceed that number with four, seven day journeys, treating some six thousand patients. The bottom line, as always is the availability of funds.

Project Amazonas's extended family consists of over 1700 volunteers, professors, doctors, ecologists, biologists, students and nurses, and even a healthy sampling of housewives and accountants. What they all have in common is that they have come to love the Amazon just like all of us, through working with Project Amazonas.

As of this writing (2013) we now operate three field research stations located on over 27,000 acres of rainforest. These sites are maintained by families from local communities and used by student groups, researchers and other who want to immerse themselves in the jungle. These stations embody a sustainable infrastructure that preserves and protects the rain forest, educates outsiders and promotes positive and sustainable growth. We are pleased to be able to act as a host and facilitator for a great number of researchers and project groups during the year 2012. For me, the conservation highlight of this year will be the development of a recently purchased (May, 2010) plot of jungle land on the Mazan River at Santa Cruz Reserve.

As a pretty much an all-volunteer organization, we know the value of volunteer talents and energy. We were blessed with a great number of dedicated volunteers in 2010 through 2012. They spent two weeks to three months working at our field stations in surrounding areas. Their projects and activities were very varied—from health education activities to trail mapping. The volunteers have covered their own travel and living expenses while in the Amazon Region of Peru. Not only did they generously donate their time, but their financial resources as well. The high point for Project Amazonas was the notice we recently received from the National Geographic Fund that the grant proposal we submitted back in 2009, had been approved. The grant will be used to promote cultural and language retention among the Yagua Indians in the area where we serve, with Yagua themselves taking the lead in video-documenting their language and customs.

CHAPTER 29

A Farewell to the River

It has been some six plus years since I said goodbye to the Amazon River, its forests, friends and its people and went home to Florida. All of this was for the good, as it was time. Over the past twenty-two years I had seen a lot, lived through good, as well as tough times on the Amazon River. My life on the river left me with many fond memories, to be sure, all treasured in my heart. My long absences from home and my long wandering life is now well behind me. In the end, my wandering spirit caused me very serious legal problems, which brought much suffering to my immediate family and more than anyone, to my wife Margaret.

Fortune wise there was not much of a gain at all. I left all material things, including my riverboat and a few other things, in the good hands of my longtime friend and business partner Devon Graham, PhD. A person very much like me, who cares for the River, its tropical rain forests and above all, its people. A perfectly suited person to replace me as steward and leader to take on and to build upon, our humanitarian organization, *The Project Amazonas, Inc.* An organization initially founded and mutually conceived by a small bunch of well-meaning folks. An organization that, to this day, is fully operational, well managed, with very good prospects of doing better in the immediate future.

It was now 2009 and after being away from my beloved river for some time, there came a call with a degree of urgency. It was to be one of my last active in-country involvements. I was asked to search for a suitable riverboat to replace the M/V "Tucunare" which had been designed and built together with Sr. Fernando Rios-Tulumba, the

Project Amazonas in-country Chief of Operations, myself, plus local master carpenters and our faithful crew members. The "Tucunare" was launched into service in 2000. This river boat now found itself no longer fit for further service. Time and continuous use contributed to her almost total deterioration. As those who sail these waters, the Peruvian wooden hulls, even those built with best local Amazon hardwood, reach a maximum life of ten years.

There are many factors involved in its rather short life span. The extreme tropical weather, wear and tear from its dangerous currents, continuous bucking against the river's flotsam, forest debris, half submerged logs and tree trunks continuously beating against its hull. including its damaged keel at amidships. I must mention, however, the art of boat building in Peruvian Amazonia by its local shipwright carpenters, especially hull construction skills, somehow fail in their design and workmanship. Here in Peru you do not find the excellence and superior craftsmanship of Peru's neighbor, Brazil. The wooden boats built in Brazil of "Itauba Prieta" (Black Mahogany) is a tree rarely found in Peru. Brazil's master shipwrights produce beautifully designed, strong hulls with a life span of twenty to thirty years.

My first Amazon riverboat *"Cidade de Natal"* and then the *"Margarita"* were constructed in Santarem, Brazil. They were well constructed and beautiful. Fernando and I were on the lookout for a local boat for sale that would be the Tucunare's replacement. After a few days of intense searching, nothing could be found. We decided to take the ten hour speedboat trip to the tri-border area of Peru, Colombia and Brazil, to see what can be found in this very busy frontier river port. We were hoping to find something for sale first in Brazil, as at present the wooden hulled Brazilian boats were rapidly being replaced by steel hulled vessels. We found nothing for sale in this Brazilian frontier area and we were told to go as far as Manaus, but due to lack of sufficient funds could not make the trip.

We tried the border town of Leticia, Colombia and we did find a suitable Brazilian made riverboat in good shape, but ran into a situation where the boat owners were two brothers who could not make up their minds as to price. We left empty handed and headed back to Iquitos. A couple of days later, Fernando and I were drinking our coffee at local café on Plaza de Armas where we both commiserated on our bad luck. Just then a fellow known to both of us, came to join us and, after a short conversation, told us that he had heard from one of his friends that a fellow from Lima made an attempt locally to enter into tourist business. He had recently commissioned the constructed of a riverboat to suit his needs, by *Astillero Rodriguez Co.* Mr. Rodriguez was well known as a good and reputable boat builder. The owner, for whatever reason, went broke and returned to Lima.

Our acquaintance suggested we take a look and check it out. Sure enough we did find a brand new wooden-hulled river boat named *Nenita* whose Lima, Peru owner, a very anxious and financially stressed man was desperately trying to sell. It's a long story, but M/V Nenita today is the Projects riverboat. Now came the sad part of shoring, and breaking up Tucunare. I did not want to participate. With my mission accomplished, I left for home. As for right now I have no plans to return, as all is well with the Project. In retrospective, and in the winter of my life, looking back into my previously very turbulent life style. the river and its jungle had incredible redemptive qualities for me. It is here that I found peace and tranquility in its jungle forests. Perhaps they were the qualities I always have been longing for and finally, found—a perfect calm. Yes, the quiet, solitude and time I have spent in this self-imposed isolation helped me rid myself of my demons and nightmares of my past. I miss the ship's diesel engine heartbeat somewhere below the decks telling me all is well. I learned to read the river, its currents and ever changing channels as there are no navigation charts. I miss sitting in the small fishing skiff on picture perfect black water jungle lakes or at day break and under way, while sitting in the wheelhouse pilot's chair, enjoying a cup of Brazilian coffee and taking in the river's early morning splendor. Yes, finally, I found peace in my heart, and I owe it all to the river.

AN ODE TO MY MOTHER
Regrets

I came to look for you in shame and with
feelings of despair—You did nothing to hurt
me, ever. And all time has gone by, and tears
washed nothing away—All is still inside of me.
I found you in the cold ground almost lost
in a poorly marked grave—The smell of coal
burning in the air—a bleak burial place
without trees—and without cry of ravens.
Your faded photographs of good times
when we were family. Now standing mute
forever in time, a witness of events long gone by
to this date, I try to recall your face—I cannot
no matter how hard I try—Your image is
lost before my eyes.
I still think of you, and love you. Too late to
say it now, looking at the frozen ground and
in darkness where you lie. Your love
rejected by me–from your grave asking me
Why?

About the Author

The life of Albert is documented by this book and by records of the U.S. Army. A young boy when WWII broke out, Albert saw the ravages of war in Poland and he quickly learned the value of life and the tragedies that man pronounces on his fellow man. Albert's history starts in Poland and takes him through the war, reparation and the vagabond life—mostly of a military nature even as a teenager. His adventures start in Poland, his escape to France, a brief tour in the French Foreign Legion and finally—a taste of freedom in America. After a short time in the U.S.A. he joined the American army and distinguished himself in Korea and later, Vietnam. His army record gained the attention of the C.I.A. and he was recruited for several adventures. After Vietnam and one more Purple Heart, he joined the U.S. Marshal service and left with unpleasant memories. His adventures up and down the Amazon River are right out of Hollywood. He loves the Amazon and the people who live and depend on the river. His charitable efforts will continue on while Albert is finally able to enjoy a life of leisure in Florida with his wife "Margie".

CPSIA information can be obtained at www.ICGtesting.com
Printed in the USA
LVOW08*1322161013